Emergency Preparedness for
Business Professionals

Emergency Preparedness for Business Professionals

How to Mitigate and Respond to Attacks Against Your Organization

Bradley A. Wayland

Certified Project Management Professional Member,
International Association of Professional Security Consultants
President and Owner, Sentry Security Consultants, LLC

AMSTERDAM • BOSTON • HEIDELBERG • LONDON • NEW YORK
OXFORD • PARIS • SAN DIEGO • SAN FRANCISCO • SINGAPORE
SYDNEY • TOKYO
Butterworth-Heinemann is an imprint of Elsevier

Butterworth-Heinemann is an imprint of Elsevier
The Boulevard, Langford Lane, Kidlington, Oxford OX5 1GB, UK
225 Wyman Street, Waltham, MA 02451, USA

Notices
Knowledge and best practice in this field are constantly changing. As new research and
experience broaden our understanding, changes in research methods, professional practices,
or medical treatment may become necessary.

Practitioners and researchers must always rely on their own experience and knowledge in
evaluating and using any information, methods, compounds, or experiments described herein.
In using such information or methods they should be mindful of their own safety and the
safety of others, including parties for whom they have a professional responsibility.

To the fullest extent of the law, neither the Publisher nor the authors, contributors, or editors,
assume any injury and/or damage to persons or property as a matter of products liability,
negligence or otherwise, or from any use or operation of any methods, products, instructions,
or ideas contained in the material herein.

ISBN: 978-0-12-802384-6

British Library Cataloguing in Publication Data
A catalogue record for this book is available from the British Library

Library of Congress Cataloging-in-Publication Data
A catalog record for this book is available from the Library of Congress

For Information on all Butterworth-Heinemann publications
visit our website at http://store.elsevier.com/

  Working together
to grow libraries in
developing countries

www.elsevier.com • www.bookaid.org

Contents

Introduction

Developing and directing an organization's response during an emergency situation is one of the most demanding responsibilities any executive would ever hope to successfully accomplish; however, despite the challenges, this task is rarely planned for, practiced, or emphasized until an actual event occurs. Although emergency planning has always been part of most safety and security plans, there are several factors that make this planning more and more important. More and more businesses are victims of incidents; whether these events are workplace-related or driven by a natural disaster, there is an increasing number of security incidents happening to companies today as opposed to 20 or 30 years ago. Additionally, the types of incidents that can have an impact on an organization are ever-changing. All types of industries can fall victim to embezzlement, workplace violence, vandalism, and even terrorism. All of these factors should provide the impetus and need for you to ensure your own organization ensures they have adequate planning with regard to these possible emergency situations.

This book is designed to assist you in making adequate plans and procedures to have in place for your own emergency response program. I hope to provide any executive manager—even with little or no security training or in-house expertise—with the tools and processes that will ensure your organization is reasonably prepared to respond to various emergency situations. With this planning, your business should be able to respond to and recover from situations that could significantly affect, or potentially shut down, your business without this preparation.

Overview of the Areas to Be Covered

To assist you in planning and developing an emergency response program for your organization, we will look at the following areas over the course of this book to provide the basic level of information that will enable you to plan and prepare for any type of emergency situation.

First we provide an overview of several emergency incidents along with their outcomes to a business and its facility. This overview is meant to provide an idea of what types of emergency situations can occur and how they can affect an organization and its business operations. As we look at the types of incidents, we also cover the standardized response actions that have been found to work best against each specific type of event. With the information in this chapter, along with the areas we cover in the Introduction, this information shall provide the background, recommended guidelines, and accepted actions that security experts recommend when responding to several typical types of emergency situations so that we can begin to explore proactive measures to stop or deter emergencies before they occur.

Next, we begin to lay the foundation for the many areas that encompass emergency response as we cover a methodology to help develop an organization's plans and procedures. To start this process, we initially look at the four planning factors within emergency response—mitigation, preparedness, response, and recovery. These planning factors are the primary considerations that an organization should ensure are included in the development of its specific emergency response plan so that it has a comprehensive program. These planning factors cover proactive measures that work to deter and minimize the damage from an emergency situation, but also the necessary actions to take in reaction to an incident to enable the rapid recovery of an organization to full business capacity. These include tailoring emergency response procedures to the specific details that are particular to an individual industry and company makeup, but they also include measures that should be taken prior to the occurrence of an incident. These planning factors also provide information necessary to prepare a company's individual emergency response plans and procedures and what items should be included in these documents. Planning factors also include the establishment and maintenance of relationships with local law enforcement and emergency management agencies and what external organizations should be considered as you develop your own plans. Last, the planning factors cover how to respond to an actual emergency in the event that mitigation does not prevent an occurrence, along with the actions that assist in recovery of the business. We will look at all of these planning factors in detail over the next several chapters.

After we have provided an overview of the basic planning factors involved in emergency response, we then go into detail within each of the areas. Of these four emergency planning factors—mitigation, preparedness, response, and recovery—many argue that the first planning factor we look at, mitigation, can perhaps be the most important in relation to a viable emergency response program. If an organization can effectively apply mitigation within its emergency response program, it can possibly stop many of the potential emergencies that could disrupt its operations before they even occur. This planning factor is an evolving process that continuously looks at the potential risks and disruptions against your own organization and then identifies actions to prevent or minimize the possible incident from occurring through management of these risks to better focus an organization's emergency response capability. To properly mitigate against these potential incidents, it is critical for an organization to identify and assess the possible risks that could occur. Once this has been done, the probability of each risk's occurrence must be prioritized along with its effects on business operations to ensure that resources are deployed and concentrated against the scenarios that have a higher probability of happening. The risks along with their probability of occurrence are unique to each organization and will be based on its type of industry, its location, the facility in which it operates, its employees, and the its business culture. Once these risks have been identified and prioritized, mitigations can begin to be developed to protect against these specific risks and vulnerabilities. Mitigation will typically include security measures and initiatives, procedures, training, and equipment, all of which will make it more difficult for a particular type of emergency incident to affect your organization. The next planning factor that we look at involves the preparation that must occur for an organization to be ready to minimize any potential damage to its business and personnel in the event of an emergency incident. This preparation primarily includes the implementation of security measures and procedures to ensure your organization is ready to react to an emergency incident to mitigate damage and injury. After looking at preparation we next cover the necessary response an organization should take in the event of an emergency incident. Response refers to the actions, processes, and procedures that an organization should accomplish once an emergency has begun. These response actions will ensure that the organization can defeat any threats, along with their effects against the business capacity of the company, as they might occur and also protect the organization's personnel and resources from further damage. The last emergency planning factor, and the last chapter in which we discuss these specific planning factors, involves recovery after the occurrence of an emergency incident. Recovery includes the necessary actions that assist with the reestablishment of a business back to its full functionality prior to the onset of the emergency. The discussion of these four emergency planning factors— mitigation, preparedness, response, and recovery—over the course of these chapters will assist you in including each of these areas within your own company's emergency response planning and, as a result, you will greatly enhance your own organization's ability not only to rapidly recover from an incident but potentially to stop many types of emergencies from ever affecting your internal business operations.

After our discussion on emergency response planning factors, we discuss how to organize your business to better prepare and react to an actual incident. One of the best methods to assist in this planning and preparation is the formation of a Crisis Management Team. This group of personnel will greatly assist your business in the creation and development of an organizational emergency response program. As with any task that is not directly involved in your day-to-day business operations, it can be easy to overlook or even forgo these responsibilities; however, the results of not adequately planning for an emergency can be catastrophic and cause significant adverse effects on your company. To better enable your business to plan and prepare for your emergency response, the formation of a specifically designated team that addresses the responsibilities and duties within this important area not only can provide a method to delegate many of the tasks involved in emergency response but also can ensure that more personnel within the entire organization can fully understand the roles and responsibilities that go along with these efforts prior to the actual occurrence of an emergency. This chapter will assist your business in forming a Crisis Management Team by showing what functional areas should be included, how to form and train such a team, and what duties they should have prior to the onset of any emergency, in addition to the deployment and coordination efforts that the team members should utilize throughout an actual emergency to synergize their efforts.

The next two chapters after we have discussed the Crisis Management Team will look at training methods for your company's personnel as they relate to an emergency response program. These chapters look at ways to include emergency response training within your current organizational training program and how to conduct and incorporate exercises and simulations into your training program. Our discussion on training covers various types of formal and informal emergency response training methods and how to incorporate this training into your everyday operations. Once we have looked at the formalized training methods, we then cover information that will enable you to conduct exercises to help reinforce this training among your employees. We have segregated our discussion on training from the processes necessary to conduct exercises in order to properly discuss the many details that are required to plan, prepare, and conduct emergency response simulations and exercises for an organization. This training and the exercises that go along with any valid training program will help to better prepare your employees and organization to properly react in the event of an actual incident.

Once we have covered the various items that form the foundation of an organization's emergency response program—planning factors, the Crisis Management Team, and training—the next topic we look at involves a discussion of the specific types of emergency incidents that businesses could experience and that can pose concerns for many organizations and their associated critical resources. These emergencies include the following:

- Criminal acts, which include workplace violence incidents such as active shooter events, unauthorized visitors, and hostage situations; we also cover terrorism
- Financial loss, which includes embezzlement, fraud, and theft
- Natural disasters such as floods, tornadoes, hurricanes, and earthquakes
- Fire/arson
- Major equipment breakdowns
- Sabotage from both internal and external sources
- Travel security
- Loss of key personnel
- Labor disputes

As we look at each of these types of emergency events, we also discuss the appropriate and accepted responses to each type of incident.

Finally, after our discussion regarding the basics that should be incorporated into an emergency response program and the standardized responses, you should have a good idea of what is necessary to mitigate and react to an emergency situation. With this background, we then look at several actual case studies of different emergency response situations. With your newfound knowledge, along with our overview of lessons learned and areas for improvement based on these real-world incidents, it is hoped you will be able to avoid some of the pitfalls other organizations experienced in their response to an actual event. In addition, not only should these case studies help to emphasize many of the concepts we have covered regarding emergency response, but how to avoid these pitfalls can be incorporated into your organization's emergency response training to assist you in your own program as you educate your personnel and provide lessons learned in preparing to respond to emergencies.

In the last chapter is a discussion on the legislation related to emergency response. This section looks at legislation applicable to emergency response, to help managers understand concerns and compliance issues, including requirements established by the Occupational Safety and Health Association along with the National Incident Management System developed through the Federal Emergency Management Agency (FEMA).

Why Should Your Organization Plan for Emergency Response?

As we cover the various areas involved in an emergency response program, it becomes obvious that preparing and planning for your own organization's program can be a significant amount of work. Based on the amount of effort required, many managers will simply not bother with accomplishing the work, and instead they will roll the dice and either knowingly take the chance that their company will not experience an emergency or stick their head in the sand against this type of situation. Another rationale that executives will use to forgo the work required to develop an emergency response program is that many believe that their expertise and experience will ensure they will react appropriately in the event of an actual emergency—how hard can it be to react to an incident when one is very familiar with his or her organization and its operation? The problem with these excuses—because that is truly what these rationalizations are—is that this type of inaction can have catastrophic consequences on the company. Look at some of the organizations that failed in their response to a significant emergency, including the Jefferson County School District and the Colorado police departments that responded to the Columbine High School shooting, or FEMA and the federal government as a whole during Hurricane Katrina. Not only did these organizations fail to respond appropriately to the respective emergency situation, but it was apparent that several of these agencies had not even conducted adequate planning for similar types of incidents. These failures resulted in a significant loss in public opinion with regard to their ability to accomplish their normal duties, but also deeply affected their organizations in negative ways for several years afterward. All of this was due to their inability to adequately respond to their respective situations.

Although these organizations still remain in existence after their emergency, this is only because they were public entities and not allowed to fail; however, because of the problems in their response to these two emergencies, all of them experienced severe hits to their operation and public perception. The effects of a similar failure in response to an incident with a for-profit business that has not conducted proper planning for emergency response would probably be catastrophic and likely to destroy the business. Added to the negative effect to public perception is the significant costs created by any disruption in your organization's business capability, and this is precisely why your organization should plan for emergencies. In response to the excuses not to accomplish this preparation, the first rationale—that of rolling the dice and taking the chance that their company will not experience an emergency—is the same as simply sticking one's head in the sand; someone hopes that the problem will go away because they don't want to take on the task because of the effort involved. This excuse is moot, however, because this effort can be divided through the use of delegation among various personnel—personnel that are members of a Crisis Management Team, as we have mentioned. Another method to alleviate much of the work is for your organization to take on small portions of the overall task in the development of an emergency response program through the prioritization of potential risks and vulnerabilities. Not only do these smaller tasks become much easier to accomplish—tasks that when combined will form a coherent emergency response program—but your organization will work to address the most significant risks and incidents that could cause significant disruption to your company. The second excuse, that many personnel believe their expertise and experience will ensure they can react appropriately during an actual emergency, may be even more difficult to fathom because many executives forget that professions that routinely deal with emergency situations—the military, police, and fire departments—continually train to respond to these events. Although these professions are intimately familiar with working various emergency situations, they do not stand on their experience and they still spend a significant amount of their time training and practicing to ensure they can respond and react to various incidents that may occur, and they will typically have the most robust emergency response programs. With this in mind, it is extraordinarily naïve to think that an executive who is trained in other types of business operations but has little experience in overseeing the response during an actual emergency—a situation that by the way will test anyone's skills owing to the high stress and dire consequences—will be able to react appropriately to an actual emergency incident. For these various reasons, it is imperative that all organizations work to develop a comprehensive emergency response program in a thorough manner. Furthermore, the additional advantages an organization gains by being prepared to respond to emergencies prior to their actual occurrence include cost savings related to their business operations and the added positive public perception that can result from proper planning and response to an emergency; it now becomes a necessity for any company to have an emergency response program that ensures its continued business capability in the event of an actual occurrence.

In the long run, emergency response planning and preparation will save organizations money. Any type of emergency incident will cost any company money—through losses in productivity, key personnel, or equipment. These losses will result either in a company's inability to conduct operations or in a loss of efficiency as it attempts to accomplish its business operations. With proper planning and ensuring that it has addressed the four emergency response planning factors—mitigation, preparedness, response, and recovery—the organization will be more prepared and able to resume its full operational capability much more rapidly than a company that has failed to develop an emergency response program, which results in lower costs to a company's bottom line.

In addition to the decreased costs from an actual incident, an organization that properly prepares for an emergency incident will also benefit from the positive perceptions among the community and the public that come along with the organization's appropriate response to an emergency. As we discussed earlier, the flip side to this public perception factor is that an organization that fails to properly plan and react to an emergency will receive significant negative publicity and public reaction—these negative perceptions can have an extremely severe impact on an organization's future success. If the public sees that an organization has failed to take any action prior to the onset of an actual emergency or that its response to an actual incident appears disorganized, this can translate to the public's overall perception of that company. Right or wrong, an organization that does not properly plan for emergencies will receive a significant amount of negative publicity due to the problems or mistakes in its reaction and response, which will probably result in a loss of business owing to the belief within the community that this lack of emergency response planning is indicative of other aspects and business practices regarding that particular company.

Based on the several reasons we have looked at, the lessened costs and positive public perception that come from proper planning for emergency response, an organization is negligent if it fails to ensure it has appropriate plans and procedures, along with a program that ensures its personnel are prepared and trained to react to typical emergency situations that could be experienced by any organization.

Risk Assessment and Emergency Response Planning

As we have previously mentioned, a significant consideration that will assist in the development of an emergency response program is the risk assessment process. This process not only will ensure that the emergency response plans you develop will fit your specific organizational needs, but also will help you prioritize what types of incidents should be focused on as you begin to develop your emergency response program. Unless you have an individual that can dedicate her or his entire workload to the development of an organizational emergency response plan, this prioritization process will help you implement this program in small steps over a period of time. Through the use of a risk assessment process, you will be able to identify what incidents are the most likely to occur and to have the most severe consequences for your company and you can better determine in what order specific emergencies should be addressed to guide you in what steps to take as you move along in the development of your program.

We first cover the basics of the risk assessment process and how to develop a Risk Assessment Matrix for your organization that will eventually lead to this prioritization. Once a risk assessment has been accomplished for your company, we will then look at how this assessment can be used in the development of your organization's emergency response program.

Risk Assessment

Because developing a risk assessment for your organization is a very good starting point when you are looking to develop an organizational emergency response program or make any revisions to your current plans, we will walk through the methodology to accomplish this analysis. As we discussed, a risk assessment helps to identify all the potential threats and vulnerabilities that could occur to your business and facility and enables you to prioritize which threats and vulnerabilities are most critical, and this will ultimately enable you to determine what security measures to immediately focus on with the limited time and resources available to you. Because nobody ever has enough time to accomplish all that is necessary in a given business day—particularly if you are trying to develop an emergency response program in addition to working on your other duties—this prioritization can help you identify what emergencies should be addressed immediately and what areas can be addressed at a later time as you further develop your program. In addition to providing you with this prioritization, this risk assessment will also provide you with a great deal of information regarding your business that not only can be used in the development of your organizational emergency response program but also may bring up many concerns that could lead to disruptions to your business capability. As we have also discussed, this prioritization will further help you divide the various tasks involved in the development of an overall emergency response program into smaller tasks, so that you are not overwhelmed by trying to develop an entire program all at once. Additionally, this prioritization will provide you with better information on how best to spend the limited money and resources you have allocated for the safety and security program.

There are several different methods to accomplish a risk assessment, including a Hazard and Operability Analysis, or HAZOP; Fault Tree Analysis; or Risk Assessment Matrix. The HAZOP is a bottom-up method to identify potential hazards in a system and help identify operability problems that can create an event.[1] Fault Tree Analysis examines the system from the top down and investigates potential faults to identify possible causes.[2] A Risk Assessment Matrix is also a bottom-up method; however, it differs from a HAZOP in that it looks at potential threats and prioritizes these based upon their probability and the severity of their impact on a specific organization or facility. With respect to emergency response and security concerns, the best method to use is the Risk Assessment Matrix. This is based on the fact that many of the other risk assessment methods are designed to provide information after an incident has occurred. Although this works for minor manufacturing errors, since the goal with these is to ensure the event is not repeated, emergency incidents can be catastrophic to an organization (such as an active shooter incident or the significant loss of an organization's critical resources owing to some type of disaster), and thus, we cannot afford to be reactive to these types of events. The Risk Assessment Matrix enables you to concentrate your efforts on working to mitigate these incidents before they even occur, so with this in mind, we will show you a step-by-step process to develop a Risk Assessment Matrix over the next several sections.

Step 1—Determining the Probability of Threats and Vulnerabilities

There are a large number of potential threats and vulnerabilities that can occur to businesses operating within the United States. Table 1 shows a fairly comprehensive list of these possible threats to provide you with a starting point to identify all possible threats and vulnerabilities against your particular organization.

This table may not include all the possible emergencies that could occur to your organization and there may be other incidents that could occur based upon the area your organization is located and operates in. With this in mind, it is a good idea to coordinate with your local authorities (law enforcement, FEMA, and the regional health department) to ensure this list is complete and contains all the possible emergencies and disruptions that could occur.

Once you have identified all the potential threats and vulnerabilities that could occur to your organization, the next step in developing your organization's Risk Assessment Matrix is to determine the probability of occurrence for each of these

Table 1 **Potential Threats and Vulnerabilities to Businesses**

Absenteeism	Explosions	Major Accidents	Structural Collapse
Active shooter	Fire	Malicious, willful, or negligent personal conduct	Terrorist threats/ threats of violence
Alcoholism	Forgery	Medical emergencies	Theft and burglary
Biological/chemical threats	Fraud	Misrepresentation	Traffic accidents
Bombs, bomb threats, suspicious packages	Gambling	Natural disasters	Unauthorized visitor
Car theft	Gang activity	Pilferage	Vandalism
Computer crimes	Homicide	Protest activity	Vehicle-borne explosives
Disgruntled employees	Hostage situation	Records manipulation	Violent/uncoopera- tive visitor
Disruption or downtime to information systems	Illegal drugs (selling or possession)	Sexual harassment	Workplace violence
Embezzlement	Improper maintenance	Staff narcotics and drug use	

incidents. Much of the probability depends upon the location your business operates in. For example, if you operate in a large metropolitan area that experiences high crime rates the probability of theft, burglary, and other felony crime will be much higher than if your business is located in a rural area far from any major population center. Although identifying an exact probability for each type of incident may sound daunting, it is not necessary to accomplish an exhaustive research project to do this. Instead, the process of determining the probability of each incident can be fairly subjective based on the crime rates and societal factors within your specific region of operations. Thus, identifying each probability can simply be a matter of designating a number between 1 and 10 (1 being that the incident is improbable and 10 being that the incident could frequently occur). This identification of each individual risk's probability can be accomplished by coordination with local law enforcement, having one individual within your organization develop the numbers (to maintain consistency in the subjective nature of these probabilities), surveying several employees within your organization on their assessment of various probabilities, or a combination of these methods. Once you have determined the probability of occurrence for each potential threat and vulnerability, you will have a completed list for your organization. To better illustrate the overall process of developing the Risk Assessment Matrix, we will use a make-believe business (XYZ Corporation) throughout this section. In Table 2, we have identified the probabilities of the various threats and vulnerabilities that could potentially occur against XYZ Corporation.

Table 2 **Example Worksheet of Probabilities of Threats and Vulnerabilities for XYZ Corporation**

Potential Threat/Vulnerability	Probability
Absenteeism	9
Active shooter	1
Alcoholism	6
Biological/chemical threats	3
Bombs, bomb threats, suspicious packages	3
Car theft	4
Computer crimes	5
Disgruntled employees	2
Disruption or downtime to information systems	3
Embezzlement	2
Explosions	1
Fire	1
Forgery	3
Fraud	3
Gambling	6
Gang activity	3
Homicide	1
Hostage situation	1
Illegal drugs (selling or possession)	3
Improper maintenance	6
Major accidents	5
Malicious, willful, or negligent personal conduct	4
Medical emergencies	8
Misrepresentation	5
Natural disasters	5
Pilferage	4
Protest activity	2
Records manipulation	4
Sexual harassment	5
Staff narcotics and drug use	3
Structural collapse	2
Terrorist threats/threats of violence	2
Theft and burglary	4
Traffic accidents	7
Unauthorized visitor	8
Vandalism	4
Vehicle-borne explosives	2
Violent/uncooperative visitor	5
Workplace violence	6

Now that we have determined the probabilities of the various threats and vulnerabilities, the next step is to determine the possible severity of each incident to the organization should it occur.

Step 2—Determining the Severity of Threats and Vulnerabilities

This step is similar to the determination of probability in that it is subjective, and to accomplish it you simply need to designate a number between 1 and 10 based on the severity should that particular incident actually occur. The scale is based on 1 being the designation for an incident that would cause negligible results within your organization and 10 for an incident that would result in catastrophic consequences on your business—on the order of ruining your company. It should be noted that although none of the potential threats and vulnerabilities are desired, their outcome regarding the long-term health of your business and organization is what the basis of the severity number should focus on. For example, the severity of chronic absenteeism from one employee is going to be much less than the severity of a hostage situation that occurs within your facility. This determination of severity should also ensure consistency between the various threats and vulnerabilities possible, without consideration of their respective probability of occurrence. To maintain this consistency, it is a good idea that, once you have completed these ratings, you review your overall numbers and ensure all risks with the same number designation have the same severity for your particular organization.

Again, we provide an example using our mythical company, XYZ Corporation, to illustrate the determination of these severity ratings in Table 3. Here, we provide our subjective numbers for the severity of each of the potential threats and vulnerabilities that could occur.

Step 3—Combining Probability and Severity of Threats and Vulnerabilities

The next step in the process to develop an organizational Risk Assessment Matrix is to consolidate the information using the number designations for the various probabilities and severities you determined for your specific organization into one table. This process is very straightforward in that you simply place all the values into one table and multiply the probability and severity for each of the possible threats and vulnerabilities and document the product. Table 4 shows how this is accomplished for XYZ Corporation using our example numbers.

The last column within the table shows these products, which again were obtained by multiplying each respective incident's probability and severity. This number will help rank each threat and vulnerability based on the potential to damage your particular organization. Using our example numbers, the highest ranked incident or threat is absenteeism and the lowest is protest activity. These products of the probability and severity are the overall results that are used to produce the finalized organizational Risk Assessment Matrix, which will ultimately provide you with a method to display all of the potential risks and how they could affect your own organization.

Step 4—Development of the Risk Assessment Matrix

The final step is to consolidate all this information into an easy-to-understand format. Although the rank order in Table 4 is what will be used to determine the priorities to be addressed through mitigation measures within the safety and security

Table 3 **Example Worksheet of Designated Severities for XYZ Corporation**

Potential Threat/Vulnerability	Severity
Absenteeism	6
Active shooter	10
Alcoholism	4
Biological/chemical threats	8
Bombs, bomb threats, suspicious packages	8
Car theft	2
Computer crimes	6
Disgruntled employees	4
Disruption or downtime to information systems	7
Embezzlement	8
Explosions	9
Fire	10
Forgery	6
Fraud	6
Gambling	4
Gang activity	3
Homicide	10
Hostage situation	10
Illegal drugs (selling or possession)	6
Improper maintenance	4
Major accidents	5
Malicious, willful, or negligent personal conduct	2
Medical emergencies	2
Misrepresentation	2
Natural disasters	8
Pilferage	5
Protest activity	1
Records manipulation	4
Sexual harassment	6
Staff narcotics and drug use	6
Structural collapse	8
Terrorist threats/threats of violence	7
Theft and burglary	6
Traffic accidents	2
Unauthorized visitor	2
Vandalism	2
Vehicle-borne explosives	10
Violent/uncooperative visitor	4
Workplace violence	6

Table 4 **Example Worksheet of Combined Probabilities and Severities**

Potential Threat/Vulnerability	Probability	Severity	Product
Absenteeism	9	6	54
Natural disasters	5	8	40
Workplace violence	6	6	36
Computer crimes	5	6	30
Sexual harassment	5	6	30
Major accidents	5	5	25
Alcoholism	6	4	24
Gambling	6	4	24
Improper maintenance	6	4	24
Theft and burglary	4	6	24
Active shooter	1	10	10
Biological/chemical threats	3	8	24
Bombs, bomb threats, suspicious packages	3	8	24
Disruption or downtime to information systems	3	7	21
Violent/uncooperative visitor	5	4	20
Pilferage	4	5	20
Vehicle-borne explosives	2	10	20
Forgery	3	6	18
Fraud	3	6	18
Illegal drugs (selling or possession)	3	6	18
Staff narcotics and drug use	3	6	18
Medical emergencies	8	2	16
Unauthorized visitor	8	2	16
Records manipulation	4	4	16
Embezzlement	2	8	16
Structural collapse	2	8	16
Traffic accidents	7	2	14
Terrorist threats/threats of violence	2	7	14
Misrepresentation	5	2	10
Fire	1	10	10
Homicide	1	10	10
Hostage situation	1	10	10
Gang activity	3	3	9
Explosions	1	9	9
Car theft	4	2	8
Malicious, willful, or negligent personal conduct	4	2	8
Vandalism	4	2	8
Disgruntled employees	2	4	8
Protest activity	2	1	2

program, it may be necessary to provide this information in a format more suitable for presentation. This format can better highlight the significant threats and vulnerabilities that pose the greatest risks to your organization, which can be done through the use of a Risk Assessment Matrix. This matrix shows all the potential threats and vulnerabilities based on their combined probabilities versus severities. A Risk Assessment Matrix is typically color coded to help identify the higher risks more easily and also as an improved method to show the information. The threats and vulnerabilities with the highest potential for risk are shown in red and are located in the upper left-hand corner of the matrix. As one moves toward the lower right-hand corner of the matrix, the threats and vulnerabilities have a lower potential to damage the organization based on the probability and/or severity, and the color moves from red to green to better identify the emergency incidents having the lowest risk for that particular organization. Figure 1 shows a generic Risk Assessment Matrix to illustrate this explanation.

To complete the Risk Assessment Matrix using the example data we calculated for XYZ Corporation, it is best to start with the highest and lowest values and then fill in the matrix as you work between both extremes. In our example, the highest risk is absenteeism and the lowest is protest activity, so these items will be placed into the upper left-hand and lower right-hand corner, respectively. We then work back and forth between our remaining high and low risks, trying to match appropriate number values for each incident's product, probability, and severity until the matrix is complete. The final Risk Assessment Matrix using our example values is shown in Figure 2.

Please note that the placement of many of the potential threats and vulnerabilities within the matrix may not align perfectly with the actual number designation for each respective probability and severity. This is not a significant issue because the placement of each item in relation to the other potential risks is more important than trying to place each incident's probability and severity against a specific number. As a result, the placement of many risks will probably be somewhat subjective—particularly when filling in incidents that have similar number values; however, the important aspect to remember is how you and your senior leadership perceive each individual item's location within the matrix and how they relate to neighboring events. As you accomplish your own organization's Risk Assessment Matrix, you will probably find that it may take several attempts until you are satisfied that the location of each incident matches your perceptions in comparison with the overall risks of all the incidents that were developed through the combination of both the probabilities and the severities.

Using the Risk Assessment Matrix to Develop an Emergency Response Plan

Now that you have a Risk Assessment Matrix tailored for your own organization, you have a prioritized list of what threats and vulnerabilities pose the biggest danger to your business operations. As you develop your emergency response plans, it is best to

		Probability				
		Frequent	Probable	Possible	Remote	Improbable
Severity	**Catastrophic**	Potential Threat / Vulnerability	Potential Threat / Vulnerability	Potential Threat / Vulnerability	Potential Threat / Vulnerability	Potential Threat / Vulnerability
	Serious	Potential Threat / Vulnerability	Potential Threat / Vulnerability	Potential Threat / Vulnerability	Potential Threat / Vulnerability	Potential Threat / Vulnerability
	Moderate	Potential Threat / Vulnerability	Potential Threat / Vulnerability	Potential Threat / Vulnerability	Potential Threat / Vulnerability	Potential Threat / Vulnerability
	Marginal	Potential Threat / Vulnerability	Potential Threat / Vulnerability	Potential Threat / Vulnerability	Potential Threat / Vulnerability	Potential Threat / Vulnerability
	Negligible	Potential Threat / Vulnerability	Potential Threat / Vulnerability	Potential Threat / Vulnerability	Potential Threat / Vulnerability	Potential Threat / Vulnerability

Extreme Risk Incidents

High Risk Incidents

Moderate Risk Incidents

Low Risk Incidents

Figure 1 Risk Assessment Matrix.

Probability

Severity	Frequent	Probable	Possible	Remote	Improbable
Catastrophic	Absenteeism	Natural Disaster	Major Accident	Biological / Chemical Threat · Bomb Threat	Vehicle-Borne Explosive · Structural Collapse
Serious	Worksite Violence	Computer Crimes · Sexual Harassment	Theft / Burglary	Downtime / Disruption to Information Systems	Embezzlement
Moderate	Alcoholism	Gambling · Improper Maintenance	Fraud · Forgery · Illegal Drugs	Terrorist Threat	Active Shooter · Fire · Homicide · Hostage Situation
Marginal	Pilferage	Violent Visitor	Gang Activity	Explosion	Disgruntled Employees
Negligible	Medical Emergency · Unauthorized Visitor	Traffic Accident	Misrepresentation	Car Theft · Malicious Personal Conduct · Vandalism	Protest Activity

Extreme Risk Incidents

High Risk Incidents

Moderate Risk Incidents

Low Risk Incidents

Figure 2 XYZ Corporation's Risk Assessment Matrix.

use this prioritization and simply address the emergency incidents that pose the most significant threat to your organization during the initial development of your plan. It will also be useful to group similar types of incidents and address these as you develop your plans based on the type of response for certain emergencies. In other words, the response actions for similar incidents will be the same or related to one another, so as you develop specific procedures to address one of these emergencies, these procedures will probably be very much the same for other similar situations. For example, the response to many types of disasters will necessitate an evacuation of some type, and as such these response actions can be used for other emergencies, thus saving you time as you develop your emergency response plans.

Summary

Before we begin our work to develop emergency response plans for your organization, it is necessary to accomplish some preparatory work to better guide our effort. These guidelines included a brief discussion on what we will look at over the course of this book. One of the special areas we emphasized was a brief introduction to the four emergency response planning factors—mitigation, preparedness, response, and recovery—as these areas will guide much of the process to develop an overall emergency response program for your organization. We also discussed some rationale for an organization to take the time to develop an emergency response plan. The primary reasons for taking the effort include the savings an organization experiences when an actual incident affects its business and the positive public perception resulting from an effective response to an emergency. The alternative—failing to effectively respond to an actual incident—can not only severely degrade an organization's ability to continue its business operations but also deter customers and the public from working with an organization in the future. This is due to the failure to effectively respond to an emergency situation, creating negative perceptions with the public and potential customers regarding all other business operations within that organization. Last, we covered the methodology to develop an organizational Risk Assessment Matrix. Because the amount of work necessary to develop and implement an overall emergency response program can be substantial, it is necessary to prioritize this effort into smaller tasks to allow an organization to accomplish this work. A Risk Assessment Matrix provides this prioritized list of all potential threats and vulnerabilities that an organization could experience so that senior management can begin to mitigate against the most severe types of emergencies as they begin this process.

As we proceed through this book, we provide tools and instruction to assist a business executive in developing a complete and thorough emergency response program to eventually address all the potential threats that could disrupt your business. This program will not only provide your organization with the readiness to respond and recover from an incident, but can potentially deter many of the emergencies your organization could experience.

End Notes

1. Product Quality Research Institute, Hazard & Operability Analysis (HAZOP). Manufacturing Technology Committee – Risk Management Working Group (n.d.). Retrieved from web on February 17, 2014, www.oshrisk.org.
2. Jane Marshall, PhD. *An Introduction to Fault Tree Analysis (FTA)*. Presentation 2011. Retrieved from the web on February 17, 2014, www2.warwick.ac.uk.

Emergency Incidents

In this first chapter, we will cover some of the basic background information with regard to emergency response—specifically, we will look at the various types of emergency incidents, their potential outcomes, and their effects on a business's operations. We will also briefly cover some of the accepted responses that are considered appropriate in the general planning for many of these potential events. Please note that we will discuss response actions only in general terms within this chapter, as we will look at the specific response actions that should be taken for each individual type of emergency in Chapter 8. In that chapter, we cover individual actions necessary to respond to specific emergencies in much greater detail, whereas the purpose of this chapter is simply to provide a basic idea of the various types of responses, along with other methods that can assist an organization in recovering more rapidly from an incident that has occurred.

Types of Emergency Incidents

There are several types of emergencies that can affect your organization, and the response to these various types of incidents will differ based on the nature of that particular emergency along with the damage or disruption that each incident can create to an organization and its personnel. Emergencies can be categorized into three main types: natural disasters, human-caused incidents, and business-related incidents. We will look at each of these categories of emergency and discuss actions that have been shown to minimize damage for that specific type of incident.

Natural Disasters

Severe weather and other geological incidents account for emergencies included within the natural disasters. These incidents include:

- Tornadoes
- Hurricanes
- Earthquakes
- Flooding
- Snowstorms

The responses of an organization to natural disasters are similar, as all of these disasters will typically affect your organization in much the same way. These severe weather incidents will normally result in damage or destruction to your facility and may also cause injuries to your employees. In addition to damage and the potential for injury to individuals, many of these natural disasters can also result in interruptions to utility service, and this effect should also be considered when looking at your emergency response plans. Such aftereffects can sometimes be overlooked when developing procedures to respond to these types of emergencies. Another consideration of these types of disasters is that your organization will normally not be the sole organization affected—these types of incidents can create similar issues for all organizations operating within the area affected by the specific severe weather. This can have both positive and negative aspects. The positive aspects include the likelihood that it will be easier to qualify for and obtain emergency relief funding from the local, state, or federal government, because there is going to be a greater number of organizations affected by the incident, and there will be a greater understanding and willingness to overlook a business's initial reduction in its ability to meet customer needs immediately after a natural disaster as a result of the reduction in business operations. Some of the negative aspects of the greater scope of a severe weather incident is that many relief and rescue agencies may be overwhelmed. Add to this the probability that companies providing construction and renovation services may also be overwhelmed–this could result in a longer period of time for your particular organization to receive the aid it requires to fully recover from the emergency.

Regardless of these aspects (both positive and negative), it is necessary to establish procedures to ensure your organization can adequately respond to these types of emergencies. Response to severe weather incidents should include the following actions. The first action is to notify your organization's staff of the severe weather alert and advise them of actions to be taken (e.g., release, evacuation, shelter in place, etc.). If the appropriate senior manager decides to have all personnel remain in the facility and take cover—typically termed shelter in place within most emergency response plans—personnel should move to basements or hardened shelter if available. Shelter-in-place responses for severe weather incidents should NOT use large rooms, such as warehouses or manufacturing areas, as shelter because these areas are going to be more susceptible to structural damage, a major threat to personal injury during most severe weather incidents. At the conclusion of the emergency, as with any type of disaster, supervisors should account for the personnel within their teams and report any missing personnel to a designated point of contact within your organization in order to track accountability.

If your company is located in a region where earthquakes can occur, there are some additional and specific response actions that should be taken for this type of natural emergency. Once the shaking starts, personnel should be instructed to immediately drop, cover, and hold their knees to the chest until the earthquake stops. If indoors, personnel should remain indoors. They should move away from windows, shelves, heavy objects, or furniture that may fall and take cover under desks, tables, counters, and open doorways. If people find themselves in hallways, stairways, or other areas where cover is unavailable, they should move to an interior wall. Personnel should also be instructed to turn away from windows and remain alongside the wall, as the greatest danger from earthquakes is injury from glass or other falling debris. If personnel are outside at the onset of an earthquake, they should remain outside and move away from items that could cause damage by falling such as walls, power poles, trees, wire fences, and rolling rocks. During the earthquake, any individuals who are outside should lie down or crouch low to the ground—even in a small depression or ditch if possible. Other considerations for procedures in the event of an earthquake are injuries that can be caused by damage to utilities and other powered equipment. To ensure this possibility is minimized, maintenance staff should conduct checks of utilities, electrical systems, and appliances and shut off main valves at the onset of an earthquake, if this is possible to accomplish in a safe manner. As with every type of emergency, once the earthquake is over supervisors shall account for their teams and report any missing personnel through your organization's designated point of contact to track accountability. Another item to consider with earthquakes is the need to ensure that maintenance staff conduct checks to determine if any hazardous material has spilled or leaked as a result of the earthquake. If they find any evidence, the staff should follow the appropriate procedures, including isolation of the area, sealing off the location, and accomplishing the proper notification to appropriate agencies of the spill.

A last consideration for response to any type of severe weather is to ensure your organization coordinates and works with governmental agencies to determine if any emergency relief funding is available and, if so, to perform the necessary actions to obtain this funding, since these monies can assist your business to resume normal operations.

Human-Caused Incidents

The other primary type of emergency incident is human-caused events, which are primarily terrorism and criminal acts, both of which can significantly affect your organization and its business capability. A significant difference between natural and human-caused incidents is that human-caused events have the potential to be mitigated and possibly even prevented by aggressive security and mitigation measures, whereas there is less ability to prevent a natural disaster from occurring. This is because many potential perpetrators will conduct reconnaissance against a possible target as they consider action, and if an organization or its facility looks too difficult to ensure success, they may choose to look elsewhere. Unfortunately, there is no such choice in the event of a natural disaster. We cover many of the measures that can help in minimizing the potential of an emergency incident in Chapter 3, when we discuss mitigation in much greater detail.

Terrorism

Terrorism is one type of human-caused incident and it includes hostile acts against your organization by one individual or an organized group. We look at specific incidents that encompass these types of situations in Chapter 8, when we discuss active shooter scenarios, hostage situations, violent or uncooperative visitors, and vehicle-borne explosives. As stated, we also look at various measures that can mitigate your organization's risk against these types of incidents when we cover the topic of mitigation in Chapter 3. Many of these mitigation factors include physical security measures such as a viable access control system that provides for limited entry points into your facility, such as entry guards or receptionists, and duress alarms for these entry controllers to notify others of an incident. These measures can hinder or even deter a hostile intruder from entering your facility. Other physical security measures that can mitigate against several types of terrorist incidents include placement of barriers that can disable vehicles from getting close to, or even entering, your facility, as these measures can greatly minimize the threat from vehicle-borne explosives. Using these physical security measures, along with others we discuss, can make your facility a much more difficult target and potentially deter a terrorist from acting against your facility.

In the event that an actual terrorist incident occurs, there are a great many variables to consider when determining what specific response action should be taken. In general terms, evacuation is the best alternative; however, the safety of each individual must be taken into account. Obviously, in the case of an active shooter scenario, people should not try to evacuate if it might bring people in direct contact with the shooters, but in the event that personnel can leave the building safely, it is best to conduct an evacuation. We look at each individual type of terrorism incident in Chapter 8 and cover the proper response procedures for that respective emergency.

Criminal Acts

Criminal acts differ from terrorism in that they will normally be less destructive and in many cases will avoid injuries to your employees, as the primary motivator behind this type of incident is monetary gain rather than creating headlines. Because the focus of this type of emergency is financial, there are a variety of mitigation measures that can assist against these situations. One of the best measures to combat criminal acts is to ensure the organization has adequate inventory and accounting systems so that any missing funds or equipment can be quickly identified, which will assist in deterring theft. Another mitigation measure against this type of incident is to provide a system of checks and balances to ensure no one individual has the ability to track and obtain funds within an organization. In the event that your company experiences an act of this type, the best course of action is to ensure the organization has a well-established process to conduct investigations to identify any perpetrators who have committed the crime.

We look at various criminal acts that your emergency response planning should take into account, along with considerations to minimize their impact, in much greater detail when we cover specific procedures against these types of incidents in Chapter 8.

Business-Related Incidents

Business-related incidents are the final category of emergencies we will look at, and this type of event results from the nature of your organization's business, its function, and the employee base within the company. For example, if your company's business operation requires the handling of hazardous materials you will need to plan for response in the advent of a chemical spill or safety issue related to the handling of these materials. If your organization has a large unionized workforce, your company may see certain types of situations that a small business with few employees would not normally experience. Last, if your organization has a cafeteria that serves food or your business is responsible for food production or delivery, you will need to address any food-borne emergencies that could occur. Any of these considerations in your type of business will have risks that may be associated with these unique characteristics that other companies may not need worry about.

Hazardous Materials

If your company works with hazardous materials or dangerous chemicals, you will need to ensure not only that all regulations and requirements are met, but also that you have plans in place in the event that an accident occurs. In the event of such an emergency, the primary threat during any type of hazardous material incident is toxic fumes associated with the spill; therefore, plans must be developed to ensure everyone is safe through evacuation, decontamination, and sealing off the affected area. One of the primary response actions to any type of hazardous material incident is to seal off the area, which is typically accomplished in conjunction with a determination to shelter in place. Based on this response, your plans should address methods to secure all windows, doors, and vents to minimize further contamination. Additional considerations that should be included in emergency response plans include notification of appropriate agencies, determining if evacuation is appropriate, and ensuring your maintenance staff can obtain information regarding the specific type of hazardous material in order to provide this information to first responders.

Threats to Larger Organizations

Emergencies that can affect larger organizations more so than small businesses with few employees include protest activities and health concerns among a larger employee population. Protest activities are normally associated with unionized labor; however, it is possible for any organization to be subject to protestors from either inside or outside the organization. In the case in which this type of activity is preannounced and the time and place of the protest are known, your organization should coordinate with local law enforcement personnel a few days prior to the event to ensure they are aware of the protest and on alert to any repercussions from such an event. During an actual protest, the following actions are recommended. Employees who will continue to work during the protest activity should be advised to minimize contact with any protestors and they should continue with their normal activities. In the event the protest becomes violent, your organization's response procedures should ensure your staff immediately secures the facility and notifies law enforcement to respond to the situation.

In addition to protest activities, large employee populations can also be affected by health epidemics. Typically, any determination of a potential medical health epidemic is accomplished by the appropriate local health organization. With this in mind, your business should ensure you have plans to notify the local health organization of any potential health issues and also that you have appropriate response actions in the event that your business receives such a notification to minimize the further spread of any illness or disease.

Food-Borne Threats

If your organization has a cafeteria, serves food in some manner, or deals with food distribution or manufacture, your emergency response planning should account for a food-borne incident such as food poisoning. Whereas the best mitigation measure against this type of incident is to ensure your food-handling staff actively enforces proper food storage and handling practices (including hygiene and cleanliness standards), your procedures must also ensure that all food preparation and food deliveries are accomplished in a controlled and uniform procedure across all aspects of your operation. Response to a possible food-borne incident includes notification of any local health services agencies and consideration of closing any affected facilities or manufacturing processes.

Standard Response Actions to Emergency Incidents

Although there may be a variety of types of emergency incidents that an organization can experience, there are only a few general response actions that most employees need to be aware of. This can greatly simplify the training and ability of your organization to effectively respond to an emergency incident. These response actions are typically going to be limited to only two options that your employees should practice: evacuation and shelter in place.

One response to any type of emergency incident is the evacuation of affected personnel. Evacuation is a relatively simple operation; however, there are some considerations for an organization to take to reduce any potential risk to individuals as they move out of the facility. Planning can minimize the risks associated with an evacuation and ensure these considerations are accounted for by allowing for the following.

- Decision to evacuate: Making the decision on whether to evacuate will be based on the availability of timely and relevant information. If the decision to evacuate is made too early and the hazard recedes, the evacuated population will have been exposed to unnecessary risk and inconvenience. Conversely, if the decision is made too late, the affected community may be forced to evacuate under high-risk conditions or shelter in place and accept the risks associated with the ongoing incident. Additionally, a method to communicate this evacuation decision must be available and must ensure that all employees can be notified of the evacuation.
- Authority to evacuate: Evacuation planning must establish the legal basis to direct this action and cover any conditions that may apply. This consideration applies more to area-wide evacuation decisions than to one building, but in these types of cases, in some localities there is no authority to force personnel to evacuate, so factors such as this must be taken into account during the planning process.
- Awareness and education: Awareness and education among your employees are critical to the successful implementation of an evacuation plan. This plan should provide responsibility for raising community awareness and education prior to an actual hazard. An effective community education program should help establish awareness of hazards that may lead to an evacuation, discuss preexisting and hazard-related conditions that would support a decision to evacuate or shelter in place, and emphasize the importance of warning and informational

messages regarding potential threats. This consideration is critical if your organization handles hazardous materials that could affect an area outside your immediate facility.

- Self-evacuation: Experience has shown that in the face of impending hazards, many personnel will self-evacuate—that is to say, they will make their own decision to evacuate using their own means of transport prior to any decision made by their own organization. Evacuation planning must ensure this contingency is addressed and a method to account for these personnel is available to ensure your organization is aware of the safety of all employees in the event of an emergency.
- Media: Communication with the media requires a skilled liaison and a system for the authorized release of current information. Planning should include the identification of a point of contact responsible for handling this information dissemination along with a media strategy in place prior to the activation of any evacuation plans.

There may be situations, depending on the nature and circumstances of the emergency, when it is best to have your employees remain where they are. This response action helps to avoid some of the uncertainty associated with evacuations and is termed shelter in place. Several considerations should be accounted for in planning and executing this shelter-in-place response. One consideration is based on the length of time that your organization would be required to shelter within the facility. It is important that your organization plans for water and food supplies to be either available or procured in the event that sheltering lasts for a long period of time. It is also vital that your plans provide a method to coordinate with local authorities to determine when it is safe to leave the building, in the event that shelter in place is in response to an external situation. Another consideration for the shelter-in-place option is the circumstances that called for this response and what effect they have on the process and the methods necessary to ensure the safety of all personnel. If shelter in place is used to create a barrier between personnel and some type of external contamination, sealing the rooms against this contamination is necessary to ensure the areas where personnel are located are protected to the maximum extent possible. This option may also require additional equipment to assist with sealing these areas off, such as specially designed ventilation systems for companies that routinely work with hazardous materials or simply ensuring that rooms have plastic sheeting and duct tape to provide some ability to seal off work areas from external contamination. Other methods of sheltering personnel may be necessary during hostile actions to create safe and secure locations that separate employees from threatening individuals, as in the case of some active shooter scenarios. In these instances, simply using items already located in work spaces (such as furniture, paper or posters that can be placed over windows to limit visibility into rooms, and door locks) can be used to assist with sheltering in place. By planning for these considerations and procuring any additional materials prior to an actual incident, your organization will be much better prepared to successfully accomplish a shelter-in-place response when necessary.

We look at more specific response actions involved with both evacuation and shelter in place as we discuss these responses in more detail as they apply to individual emergency incidents in Chapter 8. However, if your employees are aware of these two types of response actions—evacuation and shelter in place—they will be much better prepared and able to minimize any damage or injury that may occur within your organization. Additionally, limiting the types of response actions that the majority of your employees must remember and be aware of will make it much simpler for them to have the necessary knowledge of what they should do in the event of an emergency. For these reasons, ensuring your personnel are aware of these response actions and that they have practiced evacuation and shelter-in-place procedures will greatly enhance your business's ability to properly respond to an emergency.

Planning for Emergency Incidents

Through awareness of the various types of emergency incidents that can affect your organization, you can greatly assist in planning responses to minimize potential damage and mitigate injury to your personnel. When coupled with the two standardized and simple responses that enable your employees to better remember what they should do in the event of an emergency—specifically either evacuation or shelter in place—these plans will greatly enhance your organization's ability to respond and recover from potential incidents that may occur.

Emergency Response Planning Factors

Emergency response planning factors are the primary considerations an organization must account for when developing its plans and procedures to address potential incidents. These planning factors include mitigation measures that should be taken prior to the occurrence of an incident, preparation of an organization's emergency response plans and procedures, how the business will respond in the event of an actual emergency, and how to recover the company's business operations after an incident occurs. Each of these planning factors covers the necessary tasks to prepare procedures and obtain resources to ensure the organization can properly implement any plans that have been developed. These planning factors will provide an easy-to-follow guide for an organization's emergency response program, and we will cover each of these four areas in the necessary detail over the subsequent chapters. Before we cover each of these planning factors we look at them in general terms here to provide you with an overview of each item and enable you to focus your attention on any one chapter covering an area that may require immediate attention.

Emergency Response Planning Factors

As stated, emergency response planning factors are considerations that every organization should take into account when developing its own emergency response procedures. These planning factors are designed to accomplish several objectives: provide a safe environment for staff, visitors, and community members; provide guidance for an organization's employees to effectively prepare for, respond to, mitigate, and recover from emergencies or disasters; and reduce the potential for damage, injury, and loss of life in the event of an emergency. With this in mind, the four factors that any comprehensive emergency response plan should consider are as follows:

- Mitigations: the measures taken prior to any type of emergency incident to either deter the occurrence or lessen the impact of an event.
- Preparedness: the training that will prepare your organization's staff to implement effective response and recovery requirements.
- Response: the actions that should be taken to address events as they arise over the course of an emergency.
- Recovery: after an emergency has occurred, recovery includes the necessary actions and avenues to take to receive aid and assistance enabling the organization to return to full, pre-event operational capability.

Mitigations include a variety of security measures that are implemented with the intent to minimize risk against significant emergencies and reduce the threat of damage to your organization. To ensure the greatest effectiveness, mitigation measures should be in place prior to the initiation of any emergency and are composed of security measures, personnel to enhance security, and any plans and procedures implemented within your company. Measures that provide this mitigation will typically involve resources and equipment that provide added security to protect your organization's critical resources—these types of security measures may include fencing, alarms, and safes. These physical measures are intended to ensure detection of an unauthorized access or to provide deterrence against various emergency incidents. Use of guards or other personnel to enhance security of your facility is another measure that works to mitigate potential emergencies. Last, plans and procedures that your organization has implemented and disseminated in relation to your safety and security program provide a basis for your employees to assist in deterring, detecting, and responding to possible incidents. These mitigation measures are a critical part of an organization's emergency response program because they have the potential to stop several different types of emergency incidents before they even occur.

The next emergency response planning factor is preparedness. This area typically comprises the guidelines, plans, and procedures that have been implemented within your organization. These documents must be clear and easily understood to ensure that employees understand their roles and responsibilities in the event of an actual emergency. Preparedness is accomplished not only through the development of these documents but also through emphasis of your organization's safety and security program, training and awareness programs, and any exercises your organization may conduct to assist with employee emergency response awareness and training.

Response to an emergency incident deals with the actual procedures and subsequent actions your employees should follow in the event that a specific emergency incident occurs. We have already discussed that most incidents require one of two standard responses—evacuation or shelter in place; however, your employees should be familiar with their necessary actions for either of these responses and how to react should they be called upon to implement either of these. Although it is best to limit the response to these two overarching actions for most of your personnel, there are differences in every particular type of emergency that key players within your organization must be aware of. There are specific actions that will enable the key individuals to tailor the response actions for all the organization's employees based on a particular type of emergency and the changing conditions that are bound to occur during the actual event. Another consideration that must be accounted for in the response is the necessity to communicate effectively across the organization, both at the initiation of the event, to notify employees what actions they should take, and during the course of the emergency, to ensure personnel know what to do as the incident progresses. The ability to interact with other agencies is another item that should be accounted for during any emergency response. This can include coordination with first responders, local law enforcement, rescue personnel, and fire officials to assist them in their response to the incident. This interaction should also include the methods your organization plans to conduct as you communicate with the media, because any emergency will probably involve questions and concerns from the local community. A final consideration is the ability to ensure you can account for all personnel within your organization and identify any individuals who are injured or missing as rapidly as possible. This may include not only employees but also any visitors to your facility when the emergency occurred. All these items are critical to ensure your organization can respond appropriately to an emergency incident.

The last emergency planning factor, recovery, is designed to assist with the ability of your organization to overcome the effects of an emergency incident. Recovery operations are meant to repair any damage, augment any disruptions or losses that may have occurred in the supply of materials from either external or internal sources, provide for any individuals that were lost as a result of the incident, and ultimately ensure your organization regains its full business operational capability. One of the key considerations with any recovery operation is the opportunity that presents itself within the organization to identify and implement process improvements based upon losses or disruptions. In many cases, these opportunities may have been apparent prior to the incident itself; however, they could not be implemented because of resistance to change. In other cases, a specific disruption to your organization that resulted solely because of the emergency may require the creation of a new process that ultimately results in a more efficient and effective operation. These opportunities should not be overlooked as an organization recovers from an actual event.

Over the next few chapters, we will discuss each of these four emergency response planning factors in greater detail, to ensure your plans account for each area and to provide for a more robust and effective emergency response program.

Mitigation

3

This is the longest chapter within this book and for good reason. The ability to properly implement measures that help with mitigation—one of the four emergency response planning factors—can significantly reduce the impact of an actual incident occurring within an organization. In fact, the proper implementation of security measures within the three main areas that should compose any viable security program, physical security, information security, and personnel security, will minimize the impact of an emergency. When coupled with an organization that is able to enhance security awareness and provide well-written emergency response plans and procedures, it is possible to conceivably stop many types of human-caused and business-related incidents from occurring altogether, through deterrence or the ability to detect incidents before they can cause irreparable damage or disrupt business operations. To ensure that an emergency response program can actually minimize or even prevent potential incidents from occurring, proactive actions must be taken, long before any emergency occurs, through the proper implementation of mitigation measures.

To start synergizing your organization's efforts in the most effective and efficient manner possible with regard to these mitigation measures, it is best to first look at the threats that pose the greatest risks to your company's critical resources. These critical resources are the essential resources, assets, equipment, and methods and processes that are necessary to ensure your business is fully operational and can help your company meet your key organizational goals and objectives. Because every organization has limited resources to use in regard to choosing and implementing mitigation measures, it is best to initially concentrate on protecting only these critical resources and identifying the highest probable threats against these items. This not only ensures the highest threats are dealt with initially but also provides a long-term plan to integrate many of the different mitigation measures into an overall security program. This is particularly important because many of these mitigation measures can take time to implement or install and should be approached through a long-term implementation effort. By prioritizing your efforts against the most likely threats to these critical resources and then following up with other mitigation measures designed to protect other resources and company assets, you will better ensure you protect your key organization and business interests as quickly as possible. Once this is achieved, it will become easier to implement additional mitigation measures against other threats and vulnerabilities.

To properly mitigate against these potential incidents in the proper order, it is critical for an organization to identify and assess the possible risks that could occur, to ensure resources are concentrated against the scenarios that have a higher probability of occurrence. This was accomplished when you developed your organization's Risk Assessment Matrix as was discussed in the Introduction section of this book. With this Risk Assessment Matrix, you will have identified the risks and vulnerabilities particular to your organization. As we discussed earlier, these risks are unique to each organization and are based upon the type of industry, its location, the facility it operates in, its employees, and the culture of its business. This analysis and assessment of threats shows the areas that pose the most significant risks to your organization and provides a listing of the various threats in their relative priority that your organization could face.

With a completed Risk Assessment Matrix for your organization, you will also be able to focus your limited time and effort planning mitigation measures and emergency response actions against the most likely emergencies that provide the best bang for your buck. For example, if your business is located on a plot of elevated ground in Phoenix, Arizona, it would be a waste of time and effort to develop emergency response procedures against flooding—especially during your initial planning. Although this is an obvious example of working to combat probable threats and vulnerabilities, it should provide you with the mindset to better focus your efforts on the most realistic and significant threats to your organization. It is amazing how many organizations fail to do this and instead they will work to mitigate against emergencies that are well down their prioritized list of potential risks and vulnerabilities; instead these organizations will spend their limited time and resources fighting against threats that have recently occurred within the local area or even the country owing to a knee-jerk reaction created by a similar event elsewhere. A good example of this occurred shortly after 9/11 based upon the threat of similar attacks by aircraft. In the aftermath of this tragic event, many organizations spent a great deal of time and money working to combat against the threat of an aircraft crashing into their building or location. In many cases, however, the probability of this emergency was so remote that they would have been much better served if they had dedicated this time and their resources to mitigating against other more likely incidents. Although it may be a good consideration to incorporate procedures that combat these less likely threats against your business over time, the prioritization contained within your Risk Assessment Matrix will ensure you work smarter—particularly during the outset of your emergency response program development. This is why it is so important to develop this prioritized list of risks and follow this guide when developing your own organizational emergency procedures. Once these risks have been identified, mitigations can include security measures and initiatives, procedures, training, and equipment that make it more difficult for an intruder to gain access to your facility or for a perpetrator to commit potential actions or attacks. Because many of the mitigation measures we will look at over the course of this chapter involve equipment or resources that add to your company's and facility's security, this prioritization will provide you with an idea of what security measures should be addressed first.

As we begin to look at various mitigation measures against the prioritized threats and vulnerabilities your organization is faced with, we first discuss some basic security principles. This discussion provides background on how various security measures work together to provide better protection against potential emergencies. Once we have looked at these security principles, we will then look at various methods that help mitigate against potential threats that can lead to emergency incidents. These mitigation measures include enhanced security awareness within your organization;

security measures within the three security program areas, physical security, information security, and personnel security; roles and responsibilities of personnel involved in emergency response within your organization; and emergency response plans and procedures.

Security Principles

The primary goal of a comprehensive security program is to protect your organization's critical resources—those people, items, information, and equipment that are vital to the operation of your business. This program should develop methods to ensure employees consistently practice any procedures and processes through documented plans in addition to the acquisition and installation of any necessary equipment to improve your organization's security measures. To properly maintain your organization's security program, it is important to ensure proper procedures and equipment are used in conjunction with one another and to identify the best solutions to mitigate against any possible threats. These procedures and equipment should work in concert with one another to ultimately meet the goal of deterring any potential intruders or terrorists from acting against you and your critical assets before they attempt any type of action and to do so in the most cost-effective and efficient manner.

The ability to accomplish this is to deter against any potential criminal acts or attacks prior to their actual occurrence through the implementation and practice of security plans and procedures along with safety and security measures put into place to protect the critical resources within your organization. The goal of implementing these safety and security initiatives is to provide the appearance that any potential act, or even an attack, will be too difficult to successfully accomplish and thus the intruder will deem the risks too great to even attempt any planned action against your organization. Based upon this perception of an extremely secure location, the potential perpetrator will decide to look elsewhere rather than your own business or facility. It is important to note that no location can be absolutely impervious to all types of attacks. If an intruder or terrorist truly wants to attack a specific location, either because of personal grievances he or she may have against the target or because of the symbolism or high-profile nature of the location, this willingness and motivation will prompt the attacker to work that much harder to identify ways around the existing security measures and still attempt the attack. Numerous examples have shown that an attack against a specific location can be accomplished if the attackers are motivated and willing to throw their own safety away. Columbine High School, the site of the notorious school shootings in 1999, is one example, because this location was the only target for Dylan Klebold and Eric Harris based on their intention to harm their fellow students at the same school they attended, and no amount of security at the school would have been likely to deter the attackers from their attempt. Another example can be found in the infamous 9/11 attacks, as Al Qaeda was determined to attack several specific high-profile buildings within the United States. They were successful in eventually destroying or damaging their primary targets, the World Trade Center and the Pentagon; and although the intended target of the fourth plane that crashed in Pennsylvania was never confirmed (possible targets included the White House, the U.S. Capitol, the Camp David presidential retreat in Maryland, or one of several nuclear power plants along the eastern seaboard),[1] these terrorists succeeded in attacking and destroying facilities that were thought to be invulnerable based on the security measures in place, their sheer size, and their location. In these incidents, and many others like them, the perpetrators' intention to attack a specific facility because of notoriety or personal issues resulted in the perpetrators finding ways around the security measures that were in place for these locations. Unfortunately, there is no perfect or impenetrable security system that can be put into place—no matter the cost or inconvenience—to protect a location against a motivated intruder or terrorist. If they have decided upon an attack against a specific location, it is likely that they will be able to find a weakness to exploit in their planned attack. Fortunately, the likelihood of an attacker specifically targeting your particular business organization is small, and proper safety and security procedures and mitigation measures can significantly mitigate the potential for any unwanted action. The bottom line is that, regardless of a motivated criminal who is intent on acting against a specific location, it is still good practice to provide a significant deterrence against any security incident. This not only will stop most, if not all, of the potential actions against your location by many random perpetrators but can also minimize damage or injury in the event your company is attacked.

To develop an effective and cost-efficient organizational safety and security program that will help to deter any possible action against your organization, the first and primary task is to consider and become familiar with the security principles that are necessary to ensure such a program is effective and efficient—this should be accomplished even prior to writing procedures or purchasing security equipment because these principles will guide you in making the correct decisions as these appropriate plans and procedures are developed, with the purchase of particular security equipment items, and in the integration of all these areas into an overall safety and security program that positively affects the protection of your organization's critical resources.

The safety and security principles that assist in this and that we will look at include:

- Preparatory actions by perpetrators and terrorists prior to incidents or emergency situations
- Primary fundamentals of security
- Balancing the needs of safety and security with business efficiency and effectiveness

Preparatory Actions to Emergency Incidents

The first security principle we cover looks at specific actions an attacker will take prior to creating an incident. Like any military unit, a terrorist or criminal will conduct some type of planning and preparation prior to the actual event. Knowing what types of actions are included in these preparations can provide you with the awareness of what activities should constitute concern for your organization and this knowledge will also assist you in planning and developing effective security plans and measures that you should implement within your organization. These actions include reconnaissance prior to any type of attack and conducting an assessment of various security procedures.

Reconnaissance

Any potential perpetrator will accomplish some type of reconnaissance prior to any attempted action. The purpose of this reconnaissance is to obtain as much information as possible regarding the targeted facility and its surrounding terrain; security measures that are in place, along with the capabilities of the personnel responsible for protecting the location; and the surrounding people and structures that could affect any type of attack. All of this information helps the perpetrators better know the layout of the facility and determine any obstacles they must overcome, which in turn will allow them to further refine their plans so that they can provide a greater degree of success when they conduct their operation or attack. Depending upon the size of the target facility and levels of security surrounding the resources targeted by the perpetrators, this reconnaissance can take a few minutes, a few months, or even years. Prior to the 9/11 attacks, Al Qaeda conducted reconnaissance for several years, beginning in 2009. This reconnaissance included in-depth studies on airport security, both outside and inside the United States, along with identification of specific flights that met the planned targets and objectives for their attack.[2]

In the vast majority of instances in which a potential attacker conducts reconnaissance, the perpetrator can be identified by certain suspicious actions. These actions can include taking pictures, making sketches, or taking notes in and around the location he or she is targeting. At this point in time, the perpetrator can be very vulnerable and potentially caught or stopped as long as this suspicious activity is identified and reported. If the perpetrator is aware that he or she has been seen and wants to avoid being caught at this early stage of planning, it is very likely that he or she will forgo the attack against that particular location. To increase the chances that suspicious activity is noticed and reported, it is vital to involve all your employees and promote a high level of security awareness throughout your organization. This security awareness is one of the greatest (and also one of the cheapest and easiest) ways to augment your organization's security program. This is because the total number of employees will always outnumber the number of personnel directly tasked with security, so if you are able to ensure all these personnel have a heightened awareness to identify suspicious activity—and more importantly to report it—your organization will make it very difficult for any potential criminal or terrorist to conduct reconnaissance and other preparatory actions. This could ultimately cause the perpetrator to move to another target or abandon his or her plans altogether.

Assess the Effectiveness of Security

The other action conducted by potential perpetrators prior to any attack is to attempt to assess the effectiveness and response of the security measures in place. To accomplish this, the criminals or terrorists will normally attempt to gain information on two specific areas: any assigned security personnel and security measures that are in place at the facility they are targeting. The assessment of any dedicated security personnel will normally include determining an accurate count of the number of guards, their methods and procedures, and the time it takes to for these personnel to respond to an incident. The perpetrators may also attempt to determine the response time of any additional security personnel who might assist any onsite guard force such as local law enforcement personnel. All of this information will provide the potential criminals with a timeline so they know how long they have to accomplish their desired objective prior to the arrival of additional security or law enforcement personnel. The last major piece of information perpetrators will typically need to know prior to their attack is what security equipment and procedural measures are in place. This will enable them to know what obstacles will have to be negotiated to gain access to the target. If the individuals can obtain specific information on what types of alarm systems, security cameras, door locks, or entry systems are in place, they will be able to prepare and obtain equipment to ensure they can overcome these security measures. This information will enable them to enter the location and reach their objective in less time and, in turn, this quicker entry will make it more difficult to stop the perpetrators.

With the knowledge of what information a potential perpetrator may wish to gain prior to any type of incident or attack, it becomes possible for anyone, including your security guards and even your employees, familiar with the types of activities conducted prior to a criminal incident or attack can be aware of these activities, recognize them, and report them. As we discussed in the previous discussion on reconnaissance, promoting security awareness among your employees can greatly deter a criminal or terrorist from gaining this information without being detected and this awareness can deter many types of emergencies and incidents taken against your organization.

Security Fundamentals

Now that we have looked at what actions a potential perpetrator will normally take prior to conducting an attack against a facility or business, we will discuss the fundamentals of security that should be considered when looking at possible mitigation measures. These fundamentals include:

- Identification of critical resources
- Defense in depth
- Notification
- Response
- Simplicity
- Securing the weakest link
- Use of choke points
- Unpredictability
- Separation of duties

We look at each of these security fundamentals in turn over the next several sections.

Identification of Critical Resources

Identification of critical resources is not only the first security fundamental we will cover, it is also one of the initial tasks you should undertake when beginning to develop your security program. Although we have mentioned this term previously, let us define what is meant when we are discussing critical resources before we move on to our discussion of this security fundamental.

A critical resource is any essential resource, asset, piece of equipment, or method or process that is necessary to ensure your business capability is fully operational and can meet your key organizational goals and objectives.

This means that the loss of a critical resource would probably result in the failure of your business—either in the short term or based on a more permanent loss in productivity. An error many organizations make is to designate too many items as critical resources. This will lead to spending far too much time and money on protecting items that may not be necessarily critical to your business or spending too much time and money to overprotect an item that could be replaced without any appreciable loss to your business's activities. It needs to be noted that when we are discussing these types of critical resources, this term differs from critical paths or bottlenecks that may exist within your organization's processes. Whereas these items are still important to your company's business effectiveness, they deal more with operational efficiencies, rather than with an item's importance within the overall business operations, and their ability to actually ensure that operations can be conducted rather than simply being slowed down. With this definition in mind, a critical resource will typically be a specific piece of information, a required piece of equipment, or a key individual who cannot be easily replaced.

To assist in identifying these critical resources, your Risk Assessment Matrix is a valuable tool. Once you have identified your organization's critical resources, your safety and security program should ensure that mitigation measures are built around these items before you work to protect other resources.

Defense in Depth

Once you have identified your organization's critical resources it is necessary that security and other mitigation measures you put in place to protect these items are layered around these items—this is normally termed "defense in depth." To accomplish this, you should use several different security measures in order to form redundant systems so as not to rely on one sole protection device to protect an individual critical resource. To provide the most effective security umbrella, it is also necessary that these security measures do not use the same protective capability. For example, if you have a room with a safe containing critical resources, having only cameras both inside and outside the room would not be the most effective solution to provide protection and security for the items within the safe. Instead, using fewer security cameras but augmenting the area with a contact alarm on the safe and other types of alarms within the room (perhaps motion detection or beams to detect individuals moving through the area) will provide a better defense in depth and result in a much safer and more secure environment.

A good rule of thumb when designing security and protective systems that incorporate defense in depth is to provide a minimum of three security layers around your critical resources. Depending on the criticality of the resource and the potential costs due to its loss or damage, it may be prudent to place even more layers of security around the asset; however, the number of layers will ultimately depend upon the money you are able to allocate to security based upon cost analyses weighing loss and damage versus

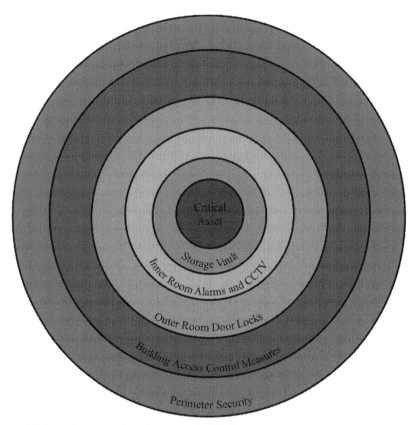

Figure 3.1 Layering protection of assets and critical resources.

costs of the security and mitigation measures. Regardless of how many layers you are able to employ, providing redundant security measures around your critical resources will ensure defense in depth and result in mitigating potential threats. Figure 3.1 highlights this process: protecting the asset in layers through defense in depth.

Notification

The next security fundamental that should be considered within any safety and security program is the need for some type of notification method. Even if an organization has the best security system in the world with the most sensitive alarms available, all these mitigation measures will be useless without some method to notify personnel of any attempts to gain unauthorized access. Alarm systems are the most common method to provide this notification. These types of systems provide notification by detecting changes in the environment around the object or by detecting breaks in some type of pathway (e.g., electrical, infrared, etc.) surrounding an area.

Another notification method, although one that can be overlooked by many organizations because of its simplicity, is through the maintenance of up-to-date inventories and logs that track not only your critical resources but all of your organization's high-dollar equipment. There are several reasons to keep and maintain these inventories and logs. First, a significant amount of equipment theft and loss occurs from an organization's own employees. A 2013 study of U.S. retail businesses showed that apprehensions of employees for theft had increased by 5.5% since 2011.[3] In many cases, the likelihood that these acts can occur will significantly increase when there is no notification method in place to deter employees or other perpetrators—something that is done by having logs and inventories of these items. Second, by maintaining up-to-date inventories, your organization can quickly identify exactly what items were stolen and you can be sure you are aware of any theft of or access to not only critical resources, but also other high-dollar assets. Finally, the available information from an accurate inventory will assist law enforcement in their investigation of any theft and provide you with an accurate accounting of any missing items for insurance claims and replacement.

Another method to assist with notification of unauthorized access to critical resources can be accomplished with security personnel. If your organization utilizes onsite security guards, one of their primary functions is to identify and notify supervisors of any unauthorized attempts to access your critical resources. Although this can be a very effective method, it can also be costly depending upon the size of your company. Contracting or hiring your own security guard force will be an expensive proposition—especially for smaller businesses—and although they provide a much higher level of security to your facility and resources, you should look at the long-term costs associated with this solution and weigh these against the risks to determine if this is an appropriate method for your organization.

A last method to assist with notification and augment alarm systems is to promote security awareness among all your employees so they can report any unauthorized attempts to access your critical resources or provide information on any loss or theft of company equipment. We have already emphasized the need to gain a high level of security awareness among your employees as it can help with so many different areas within your safety and security program. The best method to achieve this heightened security awareness is through initial and recurring training of your employees. We will discuss some detailed methods for this training in Chapter 9 to assist in promoting this awareness. This training, and the resulting security awareness among your organization's employees, will greatly improve the notification of any unauthorized attempts to access your critical resources, as each individual employee is much more familiar with her or his own work area than any other individual, and she or he will be much more likely to determine if any unauthorized access has occurred.

Response

The next security fundamental to discuss is response, which goes hand in hand with notification. This fundamental differs from response as it relates to emergency response, in that it describes the need to have at least one individual, and if possible a group of trained individuals or even security personnel, able to respond to an incident once notification of a security concern has been received. This is an important security fundamental—especially if the perpetrators have conducted reconnaissance of the location with the intent to assess the response of any security personnel. If a potential perpetrator is aware that there is no response force once notification of any attempt to access the location has occurred, there will be no deterrent and it is very likely he or she will proceed with the planned action. Thus, this security fundamental goes hand in hand with the notification of your security systems and it is vital that some type of response occurs once an alarm notification is received.

Simplicity

Everyone has heard the saying "Keep it simple, stupid." This adage works well for most everything, including security programs, and applies to both the types of equipment you are using and your organization's safety and security procedures. Keeping things simple is a significant determination in the complexity and technology of the security equipment you are considering within your security system. When deciding what type of security equipment to incorporate, you should look at the following:

- Track record and reliability of the security equipment
- Dependence of the security equipment upon humans
- Ability to integrate newer and more advanced security equipment into an existing system
- Higher cost of more complex and more advanced security equipment technologies

In regard to security equipment, it is normally better to look at purchasing and using good equipment that has been used for a while and has established a reliable track record rather than using brand new equipment that incorporates the latest technologies. Security equipment that has been in operation for a while will have a proven record and will probably have worked out any problems or kinks in its systems, whereas equipment that incorporates state-of-the-art technological advances has probably not been able to work out many of the bugs that can occur with newer equipment. Additionally, many newer technologies may have significant difficulties integrating with older equipment. This could create significant problems because most security systems should work together to provide a comprehensive and easy-to-understand notification system.

The other primary area to consider as you work to keep things as simple as possible is your security processes and procedures that must be followed by your employees. Let's face facts—most organizations are too busy working their day-to-day business operations to allocate a significant amount of time to their security program. The time that it can take to train your employees on each and every one of their security procedures and conduct exercises to ensure they are understood to the degree necessary can be staggering if you allow it to be. Based on most, if not all, real-world emergencies, after-action reports from these actual incidents have highlighted the need to train your employees on the organization's emergency response procedures. To make the most effective use of time in this training, it is important to keep your safety and security procedures as simple and basic as possible. We have already discussed some methods to make these emergency response procedures simple, by limiting response to two primary methods—evacuation or shelter-in-place operations. By minimizing the number of things your employees must accomplish in the event of an actual emergency, you will make it much easier to ensure they are knowledgeable of the necessary actions and prepared to react to the actual incident.

Securing the Weakest Link

When evaluating your organization's security and mitigation measures, it is always a good idea to identify and strengthen the weakest links in your organization's overall security system. This fundamental is particularly necessary if any of these weak links in your security system can lead directly to access to a critical resource within your organization. Determining the weak links can be accomplished through objective assessment of equipment and procedures within the security program. Once the weak links within your security system have been identified, it is possible to ensure these areas are strengthened through either equipment or procedures. Many organizations will look at solving these issues first with the purchase of additional security equipment to provide greater protection to these problem areas; however, it should be noted that many times there may be no-cost options that can resolve these issues. These no-cost options can normally be accomplished by revising or augmenting existing procedures within a safety and security program. By identifying the weak links and providing corrective action, working to correct these concerns will greatly enhance your security program.

Use of Choke Points

Choke points are another security fundamental that, once identified, will assist in a more effective development of your organization's security program. Choke points can actually be areas you wish to develop as they relate to safety and security programs because these areas help to funnel and narrow access into your facility for both personnel and packages that enter your business. Narrowing, or funneling, traffic through these locations has a couple of purposes. First, it helps to better identify locations where security and mitigation measures are needed and should be focused. These measures can include entry and access control procedures that can check personnel and packages prior to entering the facility. Second, by creating and identifying choke points you may be able to limit the number of security equipment items required because they will be implemented primarily at these funnels. The use of choke points can actually shut down some other entry points, and if this is done, you will have limited the need to provide security and mitigation measures at additional locations.

Unpredictability

Being unpredictable can greatly enhance security. We have all seen movies in which an intruder wants to gain access into a restricted area and, to do so, he or she is able to time a security guard's patrol route down to the minute…although this level of predictability rarely happens in real life, any security guard that uses the exact same route movements and patrol zones day after day can make it very easy for a potential perpetrator to time his or her entry when there is little chance of detection.

During my security training in the military, I was taught about the significant impact of unpredictability. In an interview conducted with a Viet Cong general after the conclusion of the United States' participation in the Vietnam War, the importance of this security fundamental was truly emphasized. The general was part of a panel discussion with several senior American military officers from all the different U.S. uniformed services–Army, Marines, Navy, and Air Force. When asked what forces had posed the greatest problems to the Viet Cong, most of the U.S. officers thought it was obviously their service that had achieved this distinction and been the most difficult to overcome for the enemy. The Army officer thought it would have been his normal soldiers and, if not, definitely the Army Special Forces personnel, that would be singled out by the general. The Marine officer felt his marines would be singled out by the Viet Cong general because of their esprit de corps and training. Even the Naval officer felt his sailors would be singled out in significant part based on the accomplishments of the SEALs. Surprisingly though, the Viet Cong general stated that the most difficult troops they had to contend with were U.S. Air Force Security Forces personnel, who were primarily tasked to guard air bases in Vietnam. When asked why he had named this group, the general stated that it was because of their unpredictability. These forces never defended the base in the same way on any given day. One day, they would be posted in only a few locations with small numbers of defenders. On other days, they would have large numbers of personnel located at every security post along the perimeter of the base. Still other days, the Air Force Security Forces troops would be moving about the base perimeter in vehicles and foot patrols that were not fixed to any specific locations. Although this unpredictability may not have always been planned (it may have depended on the size of the party the night before or how many troops had a pass to go off-base the day before), the Viet Cong general stated that these unpredictable actions made it extremely difficult for his forces to locate the exact number of defenders and neutralize them. Unpredictability can greatly assist in an organization's security program and make it more difficult for a potential perpetrator to gain access to a location without detection.

Separation of Duties

The last security fundamental we will look at is separation of duties. This concept is much like a check-and-balance system because it avoids the possibility of one individual being fully responsible for different functions within an organization, which, when these tasks are combined, may result in an undetected security violation. Separation of duties is all about validation; in fact, there is an old Russian proverb (which was also used by President Ronald Reagan) that sums up the concept: "Trust, but verify."[4] An additional consideration in separation of duties is to provide redundancies in a safety and security program. Understanding the meaning behind the Russian saying and providing for redundancies are very important when it comes to understanding the principle of separation of duties.

When separation of duties is first introduced into organizations there can be some significant discomfort—sometimes this discomfort can come from trusted employees and other times from employees who have not had to undergo any type of check-and-balance process to review their actions; however, there are several reasons to implement this concept. First, having separation of duties can resolve issues in instances occurring without any ill motives. In all areas of work, any individual can make a simple error or accomplish his or her task incorrectly with the best of intentions; and it is unlikely that even the most conscientious of workers will catch their own errors. By implementing a check-and-balance system to separate these duties, a second individual who is verifying the task will provide the organization with assurance that the processes are being done accurately and correctly. The second reason is to ensure employees are not taking advantage of their authority and responsibilities. An example would be having only one employee responsible for both maintenance and accounting of all funds within the organization. In this case, the one employee would be easily able to embezzle funds from the company because there is no other individual who checks, or is even aware, of the status of the funds. By dividing tasks involved in obtaining, tracking, and spending money it becomes more difficult for the organization to lose funds and makes it easier to identify concerns.

Summary of Security Principles

We have looked at various factors that should be considered in the development of an organizational security program, which in turn leads to an emergency response program. These factors include knowledge of preparation accomplished by perpetrators prior to an actual incident or emergency and security fundamentals. Now that we have provided a foundation of security and its guiding principles we look at how to better balance security with business efficiency and effectiveness. After this discussion, we will cover an area that can greatly assist any organization in regard to their security program: that of enhancing security awareness within the company. We then look at specific mitigation measures within each of the three areas within security—physical, information, and personnel—as we continue our discussion on mitigation.

Balancing Security Measures with Business Efficiencies

Now that we have looked at several of the security fundamentals, we will discuss the need to balance security and mitigation measures with convenience and efficient business operations and considerations on how to achieve this balance. Security by its very nature is inconvenient; thus, to ensure your employees and senior managers will support security measures and initiatives to better protect your organization, it is necessary to balance the inconvenience inherent in most of these security procedures necessary to help mitigate against possible emergency incidents with both the operational needs of your organization and the tolerance of your employees to put up with the inevitable inconveniences that are going to occur as many of these security measures are implemented. Although it may seem easy to simply put security and mitigation measures in place, it is best to consider this balance so that you are able to provide a safe and secure environment for your employees while ensuring you do not make it too difficult to accomplish day-to-day tasks and potentially squash personal initiative at the expense of these security measures.

As we discuss this principle of balancing security along with a company's culture, we look at three areas that must be taken into account. These three areas include the

Figure 3.2 The Security versus Business
Operations Triangle.

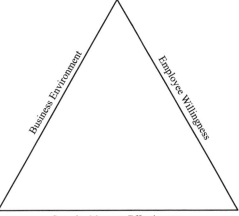

Security Measure Effectiveness

necessary effectiveness of security measures, your organization's business environment, and employee willingness to put up with inconveniences from security measures.
These three areas form a triangle that helps you to visualize the necessary balance
between these concerns as you begin to attempt to balance security and mitigation
measures for your organization along with the need to accomplish standard business
operations and produce the right mix for your particular organization (Figure 3.2).

As we begin to explore this triangle and the balance between the three areas, one of
the first items of note is that it is not necessary that the three sides of this triangle are
equal. Instead, the length of each side—which corresponds to the relative importance
an organization places on each area—will vary greatly from organization to organization because each area's individual weight and importance is based on the specific
needs of that particular company, the relative criticality of the resources they work
with, and the culture of the company and employees within its business and operating
environment. Although the goal of each company's Security versus Business Operation Triangle is to attempt to keep each side relatively equal, it is inevitable that each
organization will have a different philosophy and as such each area's weight will provide you with an idea of the respective length of its side. This overview of the Security
versus Business Operation Triangle will greatly assist you in determining how best to
develop your own organization's security and emergency response program by defining the importance of each of these areas and how they relate to one another. With this
brief overview of the balancing act between business efficiency and the inconvenience
of security and mitigation measures, we will now look at factors that affect the relationships between these three areas and follow with an explanation of each of the three
areas of this triangle to provide you with a better understanding of this concept.

Factors Affecting the Security versus Business Operation Triangle

The first factor to consider as you begin to formulate this balance is what level of
emphasis the organization's senior management places on safety and security. This

is a critical factor, as the level of emphasis and involvement in safety and security from your organization's senior management will directly influence another factor—the overall culture of the organization—and tie in to two of the areas that form the triangle (your business environment and employee willingness in relation to security). It is vital that senior management within your organization be honest and truthful about how much importance is placed upon safety and security because it can have an impact on so many other areas within the company. For example, if a high level of security is desired or necessary within your organization, this will lead to more stringent security practices and in turn to a higher level of inconvenience. Thus, this factor not only shows the level of risk senior management is willing to take but also has an impact on the amount of inconvenience caused by these additional security measures that your employees must work around to accomplish their normal duties. This higher level of inconvenience can lead to workers' complaints and additional explanations by management to employees of the reasoning behind many of the security procedures that are implemented, so if the high level of emphasis on safety and security by senior management is simply lip service, it will become apparent, and many areas—in addition to your safety and security program—will suffer. It is important to note that most employees will go along with the implementation of more stringent security processes as they get used to these procedures; however, senior management must truly believe in their decision regarding the level of importance of safety and security and be behind this decision to ensure continued support.

The next factor to consider when determining the level of emphasis of each of the three areas contained within the triangle is the cost and importance of your organization's critical resources. If your critical resources are so vital that any attempt against them would be catastrophic (nuclear weapons or components would be a perfect example of this), then the level of security you will need to implement will be much different from that of a business that manufactures low-cost and common items. The company that works with nuclear components will be required to place a huge emphasis on the effectiveness of the security measures that are put into place based on the catastrophic consequences of *any* action against the business and its critical resources. With this example, the other areas that form the triangle—business environment and employee willingness to work around inconvenience—become secondary owing to the criticality of the business's critical resources.

The last factor that should be considered when determining the level of importance and how to balance each area within the triangle is the culture within your organization. As we discussed earlier, emphasis by senior management on safety and security can influence this factor; however, this emphasis can influence the organizational culture only in incremental degrees over time. Normally, a corporate culture that is extremely open and casual will not readily embrace strict security measures as much as an organization that is more autocratic. For example, if the current organizational culture is extremely uncluttered and easygoing (Google is a company that comes to mind as an example with this type of company culture), it will be very difficult to immediately implement a large number of security measures that create a great deal of inconvenience to the employees. If it is determined that an open and casual organization needs to implement more controls and more stringent security measures, not only will the culture of the company need to be considered but also, it should be noted, these initiatives should be introduced over time to ease employees into the newer and more strict procedures.

Individual Areas within the Security versus Business Operation Triangle

Now that we have discussed several factors that affect the relationships between the three areas that form the Security versus Business Operations Triangle—senior management emphasis on safety and security, the organization's critical resources, and organizational culture—we will look at each of these specific areas in more detail to better enable you to determine how to balance these three areas within the triangle within your particular organization.

Effectiveness of the Security Measures Portion of the Triangle

Effectiveness of the security or mitigation measures describes the level of detection that the security system protecting a specific item should achieve. As we have mentioned previously, this level of detection will depend upon the criticality of the resources you are securing and what repercussions would occur to your business or reputation if any loss or damages to these items were suffered. For example, the repercussions based on the loss of the weekly coffee fund are going to be dramatically different from the repercussions due to any security breach that would occur with any type of biological or chemical material. These repercussions lead to very different levels of detection necessary to protect either item along with the effectiveness of the security measures that are necessary to protect either item. In the case of the coffee fund, it may be determined that the loss of this item is not a critical issue and that the ability to detect the loss is fairly small—perhaps a security effectiveness rate of approximately 50%; however, because of the sensitive nature of biological or chemical materials, the level of detection may need to exceed 99%. These rates of security effectiveness will have repercussions on the type of security measure needed to protect that item and the amount of redundancy in the various types of security systems.

The significant differences in the sensitivity of the items result in vastly different levels of detection necessary to protect the two items in our example, which in turn affect the other areas within the Security versus Business Operations Triangle. In the case in which a very high level of detection is necessary to protect extremely sensitive or critical resources, the amount of emphasis on this one portion of the triangle will result in less consideration of the other two sides in the triangle—the business environment and employee willingness areas. For this reason, the effectiveness of the security measures area forms the base of the triangle, because this area will normally be the one area your organization has the least flexibility to change. As we had earlier discussed, the overall triangle denotes the relationships between the three areas and it is unlikely that it will be a perfectly equilateral triangle, because one area can dictate the impact and importance of the other areas.

Business Environment Portion of the Triangle

The type of business and the resulting company culture within your organization will also have an impact on the amount and level of security you are able to provide within your organization. As is the case with all three areas that form the Security versus Business Operations Triangle, this area will affect how much you can accomplish with the other areas. For example, if your business depends on external customers and you allow them to freely visit and have access to your facility, the level of security and access you will need to establish will be different from that of a manufacturing business that does not require any outsider access and sells only to suppliers located off-site. Another way to illustrate this point is to use retail business as an example. A retail store will not be able to implement significant security and mitigation measures put into place simply to enter the facility, because these could make it difficult for customers to gain access into the building and make it likely that they would simply take their business elsewhere.

With the need to balance each of the three areas, it should be obvious that any security and mitigation measures that are implemented should not take away from your ability to accomplish your primary business function. Whether your business requires that external customers have free access to your facility or if you must tailor security measures to ensure your business operations are not hindered, you will need to look at what accommodations must be made between this area and the other two areas of the triangle, to ensure the least amount of impact on your customers as you implement appropriate security measures that work around these considerations.

Employee Willingness Portion of the Triangle

The willingness of your employees to work around inconvenience is the last side of the Security versus Business Operations Triangle. As mentioned earlier, the more security is present, the greater the inconvenience to various tasks. To impose stringent security and mitigation measures, it is necessary that employees be willing to work around these measures and your organization must keep tabs on the pulse of your workforce to ensure your employees are satisfied with the working conditions. As we have discussed earlier, there are several factors that can influence this willingness of employees. First, by placing a high level of emphasis on safety and security by senior management, it is likely this will lead to an increase in the amount of inconvenience employees are willing to endure. Second, the culture of your organization will have a direct impact on the amount of inconvenience employees are willing to work around— an open and free organization will have a different level of support with regard to safety and security initiatives and greater inconvenience, compared to an organization that follows a strict hierarchy and is autocratic in nature.

One of the primary factors in relation to this particular area when looking to implement changes in your organization's safety and security posture is the impact upon your existing employees, as these are the personnel who will need to be sold on any modifications. Should it be determined that more stringent protection measures are necessary, there are several options you can use to ensure success when discussing this with your employees. One option is to provide several methods of communication to notify employees of any upcoming changes in safety and security well before they are to occur.

These communications should discuss not only the changes in security procedures that will be taking place but also why these changes are occurring (e.g., correcting current deficiencies in the organization's safety and security program, mitigating risks or vulnerabilities in the organization, saving money, etc.). Another option is to conduct group meetings with employees to personally discuss the changes and answer any questions or concerns. These forums can provide employees the opportunity to obtain information on the changes and hear from management on the reasons the more stringent security and mitigation measures are being considered. A final option to provide employees with information regarding any changes in the organization's security posture is by simply walking around the various offices within your organization and talking with individuals or small groups to alleviate concerns and answer questions. Commonly termed "management by walking around," this option will provide senior leadership with an untarnished view of any changes. Any of these options will help employees better understand these changes in your safety and security program and result in greater success.

Once changes have been made and more stringent security and mitigation measures have been put into place, over time these changes will begin to become the standard within the organization. This will make it easier for both long-term employees and new hires. Fortunately, new employees who come onboard after any modifications to your safety and security program will rapidly adapt to the new procedures and security environment; however, it will still be necessary to spend effort through communication with older employees as you continue to work to implement any additional safety and security initiatives. Ultimately, in time all employees will learn to work within the new processes and procedures but it is important that senior management continue to show their support for the greater security.

Security Awareness

Security awareness is one of the greatest (and also one of the cheapest and easiest) ways to augment and improve your organization's security program. Whether you have an actual security guard force or a few staff personnel tasked to work safety and security issues as an additional duty, the total number of employees within your company will always outnumber the personnel directly tasked with security duties and responsibilities. Add to this the fact that individual employees are much more familiar with their own work areas—more so than any other person—and they will be much more likely to determine if any unauthorized action has occurred.

There are several areas in which a viable security awareness program among your organization's employees can assist to minimize or even mitigate potential emergency incidents from occurring. One example in which enhanced security awareness among your employees can help to deter certain unauthorized actions is theft by another employee. It is much more likely that a co-worker, rather than a supervisor or manager, not only will notice theft, but may even be in the immediate area when an employee attempts to steal company resources. If you can heighten the awareness among your entire workforce to identify suspicious activity—and more importantly, to report it–your organization will make it very difficult for any potential criminal or perpetrator to accomplish many of the activities that can harm or disrupt your business activities. As we discussed earlier, this will make it difficult for a perpetrator to plan and prepare for an incident, which could ultimately cause him or her to move on to another target or abandon his or her plans altogether.

One of the best methods to enhance security awareness within your organization is the emphasis of safety and security by senior management. Employees notice when their supervisors simply provide lip service to certain areas and it is no different with security and protective measures. Despite this, many leaders will simply ignore issues that do not directly affect the organization's business operations; however, it is vital that supervisors discusses their commitment to safety and security. One simple method to accomplish this emphasis is through occasional communications from leadership within your organization regarding various safety or security issues. Another method is through the attitude of your organization's senior management in relation to safety and security issues. If employees see that their supervisors are concerned about security and willing to spend some time and resources, it is much more likely that this attitude will permeate down to all levels.

Another method that promotes security awareness is employee training. If your personnel are trained, both during their initial hiring and periodically over the course of their employment, this will ensure they are much more likely to be able to identify and report any activity that could interfere with safety and security and ultimately mitigate or stop a potential emergency incident. To ensure your training program includes security awareness, it is necessary to provide three different opportunities to train your personnel in any current training program within your organization.

First, an initial safety and security training course should be included as part of your initial employee indoctrination or in-processing program. This is likely to be the most important training that you will conduct within your organization because it sets the foundation and establishes your organization's commitment to safety and security and ensures your employees understand the various aspects of your company's program. This can be easily accomplished in an hour or two by your organization's primary security point of contact through a professional presentation during the standard company in-processing and indoctrination. A formal classroom presentation sets the tone for your organization and promotes the concept that safety and security is an important part of doing business within your company.

Second, recurring safety and security training should be conducted for all employees within your organization. This training should be conducted on a periodic basis—once or twice a year should be the frequency goal—and can include any number of issues pertinent to your organization's safety and security program. Topics that you may consider for this recurring training can include emphasis on items that were covered during the initial indoctrination training, concentration on specific response actions for a particular type of emergency or incident based on management concerns, and actions against potential threats that may specifically exist against your company or are possible in the region where you conduct business, or it can simply involve a discussion and analysis of recent security incidents that were in the news. This last subject—incorporating recent incidents and events—has the advantage of making one of these recurring training sessions more interesting and having a greater impact on individuals, which will be more likely to achieve a buy-in among your employees in relation to your organization's security and emergency response program.

The last training method that helps promote greater security awareness is the conduct of exercises and simulations to practice the organizational emergency response plans and procedures. These exercises not only reinforce classroom training, they also provide employees an opportunity to learn their roles and responsibilities in the event of an actual emergency—which is ultimately the primary objective for any safety and security training. Any plan that exists only in a binder on the shelf, or on a hard drive or server, is not one that will be successfully put into practice when the need arises. Exercises and simulations require a little more time and planning than other training methods; however, they provide several significant benefits to any organization's safety and security program. One benefit is that a good exercise provides the most accurate assessment of the current safety and security plan's response actions to a particular incident, with the exception of an actual emergency. A well-run exercise provides the most realistic evaluation of your organization's response and, as such, will highlight any significant areas for improvement so that an organization can correct its plan prior to an actual emergency. Another benefit is to identify any training deficiencies or confusion regarding your employees' actions during their response to an emergency. An exercise will make it easy to identify whether most personnel understand their particular roles and responsibilities in the event of an incident. If there are any issues or if employees are unsure what should be accomplished during the response to the incident, the emergency response plan should be looked at to ascertain whether it contains clear directions and, if not, management may need to correct this deficiency and consider additional training so that employees better understand what actions they need to take. Exercises also provide a more valuable and realistic training, which is more likely to be internalized by the employees who participate than any training from a classroom presentation that they might receive. Another benefit exercises provide is the ability to determine if there are any equipment or procedural shortfalls required in meeting the organization's planned response to an emergency. For example, if communication was not addressed in the response plans to a natural disaster, an exercise may highlight the need to obtain portable radios or walkie-talkies to ensure your business can communicate during the event.

We will look at training and the process of conducting an emergency response exercise in Chapters 9 and 10 in much greater detail; however, these areas are critical to helping your organization establish and promote security awareness among your workforce. By incorporating a robust security awareness program, through senior leadership emphasis and training, you will have already begun the process of mitigating against a variety of possible emergency incidents.

Security and Mitigation Measures

Security and mitigation measures are the actual procedures and equipment that contribute to your organization's ability to minimize and deter any potential emergencies. These measures involve actions within the three primary areas that are necessary in any comprehensive organizational safety and security program. These three areas—physical security, information security, and personnel security—all contribute to an organization's ability to provide protection and security within various elements of your business. Security and mitigation measures that have been incorporated within these three areas will deter or even prevent emergencies from occurring within your business. Over the next several sections, we look at specific measures within physical security, information security, and personnel security that help in this mitigation.

Physical Security Measures

Physical security is one of the three primary areas that compose an overall security program and arguably is the most significant area. Physical security measures focus on equipment, including fencing and physical barriers around the perimeter of property or structures, door and window locks, lighting, access controls for entry into and exit from a facility, alarm systems, closed-circuit television, and safes and vaults. In addition to these actual equipment items, the other important item within these physical security measures includes processes and procedures that provide guidance for your employees in relation to threats against your organization's critical resources—guidance that can help to ultimately heighten security awareness within the organization.

As we look at the various physical security measures over the next several sections, we will move through them, working our way from the exterior of a facility's property, moving inward toward the interior of the building, and ultimately looking at security measures that are designed to protect an organization's critical resources. With this in mind, we begin with physical security measures placed at the perimeter of the property.

Perimeter Security Measures

Perimeter security measures are designed not only to hinder access to the facility and any surrounding property but also to help define your facility's physical limits. These limits can include areas that are necessary for the activity of the organization, such as warehouses, storage and loading areas; multiple facilities; parking structures; and any common areas within the compound. It is important to remember that perimeter security measures are not meant to stop all access onto your property; however, this type of mitigation measure has several other uses and advantages that we will discuss.

Perimeter security measures not only help to delineate the property, but also provide a means to funnel people and vehicles toward primary pathways and entrances into your facility—attempting to accomplish one of the security fundamentals we discussed earlier: establishing the use of choke points. As mentioned earlier, these choke points are extremely useful in that they limit the number of locations that allow access to the facility and thus they can help minimize security costs by limiting the areas that require observation devices along the exterior of the facility to these primary entry and exit points. There are also several types of perimeter barriers that can stop a vehicle from approaching the facility, which protects against a vehicle-borne explosive threat (as was used in the Oklahoma City bombing). Last, most perimeter security measures, such as fences and walls, provide the opportunity to clearly identify the property through the use of warning signs or notifications announcing that the enclosed area is private property. Although signage will probably not stop a motivated intruder from gaining access to your location, a clear delineation and notification along your property boundaries can deter some individuals and make it easier to stop others who may suddenly wish to create problems simply because they wish to pass through the area. These boundaries also clearly highlight individuals who attempt to access the facility without authorization—it is much more difficult for an alleged perpetrator to justify why she or he cut through a fence as opposed to entering a facility that had no perimeter security measures to protect its property. Finally, signage and clear delineation of your facility boundary with some type of perimeter barrier will also help to cover your organization from liability issues.

Whereas there are several different types of perimeter security measures that can be used to take advantage of these benefits, a major factor to consider when you are looking at what specific type of measure works for your facility is the type of impression you wish to convey to the public and your potential customers. Although it is also important to consider the threats based upon your facility's location and your local area, your business's culture and the outward appearance will have a significant impact on your choice of perimeter security measure. This consideration is a good example of the need to balance between various aspects of the Security versus Business Operations Triangle, which we covered earlier. There are many options to consider along your perimeter, including natural or naturalistic barriers, such as berms, ditches, water features, and stone walls, that can be used or artificial barriers such as fencing or constructed walls. Whereas these perimeter security measures delineate your property boundary and help deter entry, they can provide vastly different impressions to the public while still meeting the need to provide some type of obstacle onto your property—an attractive pond provides the same result as a fence topped with razor wire—but these options portray vastly different personas. It is up to each company and its unique personality and culture to determine what solution works best for its business and the type of impression it wishes to convey to the public and potential customers. We look at each of these types of perimeter security and mitigation measures over the next several sections.

Natural Barriers

Natural or naturalistic barriers consist of topographical features that normally provide an attractive landscape feature but still ensure that access is limited to your facility's boundary (Figure 3.3). These barriers can include terrain (such as berms or ditches), vegetation, obstacles (such as rocks, stones, walls, etc.), and water features.

The obvious advantage to natural barriers is that when they are properly designed and placed, they can provide a striking and aesthetic appearance to your facility while still maintaining a significant deterrence against unauthorized entry. Unfortunately, natural barriers will typically be more expensive than artificial barriers unless you are able to incorporate some of these natural barriers during the initial construction of

Figure 3.3 Natural and naturalistic barriers.

your company's facility or if the topography surrounding your building already has many of these features in place.

Certain types of plants or vegetation can provide a lower-cost alternative to terrain barriers, providing security to your property and facility while still portraying a gentle impression to the public. Like many other types of perimeter barriers, vegetation can be used to funnel people, and even vehicles, depending upon the type of plant, toward primary entrances and areas that are under observation of either cameras or personnel. When using vegetation to prevent or hinder access onto your property or facility, you should consider thorny and hardy types of plants, which will deter people from trying to move through these areas. Of course, another major consideration in using vegetation is that it may take several years for these plants to form an effective barrier after they have been planted, so you would probably require another type of perimeter security measure in the interim. A last consideration is the upkeep required for many plants—it can take a significant amount of work to maintain plants as an attractive and useful feature. If you are considering using plants as a barrier, it would be recommended to work with a landscape designer or a local nursery in your area to get advice on what type of vegetation would work best in your environment and region.

Another natural barrier to consider is a water feature. These provide a superb barrier against either people or vehicles and, as with other perimeter barriers, they will also funnel traffic to areas that are under observation by cameras or security personnel. Additionally, there are a variety of water features that can be used to provide attractive barriers or pathways for your facility, such as waterfalls, ponds, and running streams. Unfortunately, there are several disadvantages to these types of natural barriers: water features have very high initial costs for installation; they require a good deal of time and effort to perform daily maintenance, cleaning, and upkeep; and there are periodic costs needed to properly maintain water features and keep them in working order. Even with these disadvantages, many companies still utilize these types of natural barriers because of their attractive features—particularly compared with many of the other perimeter security measures.

Artificial Barriers

Like natural barriers, artificial barriers also deny access to your facility's boundary; however, most of these perimeter security measures require some construction to the area (Figure 3.4). Although they are normally not as attractive nor do they blend in with the environment to the extent of natural barriers, they are usually much less expensive and can be added to existing facilities much more easily.

A common perimeter security barrier is fencing. There are many types of fences that you can use should you decide upon this type of perimeter security and mitigation measure and the different types can provide very different impressions to customers and the public. Types of fences can range from very attractive and open (such as wooden fencing), to the other end of the spectrum, demonstrated by the forbidding nature of concertina wire fencing typically used by the military in hostile locations. Although fencing is one of the least expensive perimeter security measures, it has

Figure 3.4 Artificial barriers.

an important limitation in that it will not provide a serious deterrent to a motivated intruder—military security planners have found that most fencing will delay an intruder for only 10s[5]—so your security plan should not depend solely on building a fence around your facility and thinking your building is secure. As discussed earlier, using the security fundamental of defense in depth requires that you incorporate redundancies within your security system. Fencing (or any other perimeter security measure) is not foolproof; however, it does provide several additions to your physical security measures, including providing a clear delineation of your facility's boundaries, controlling pedestrian and vehicle traffic, and providing a means to identify potential intruders when they climb or cut these obstacles.

Constructed walls provide another artificial barrier option and in many cases will offer a more attractive feature than many types of fencing, although this type of barrier will typically be more expensive. Walls will also limit visibility into your facility and grounds, whereas most fencing provides some ability to see beyond a facility's perimeter. This limited visibility can hinder the ability of security personnel and other employees inside the property to see along much of the perimeter. If it is necessary to ensure visibility outside your location owing to the types of threats to your location, this lack of visibility can be resolved by placement of closed circuit television cameras along the wall; however, this will further add to the cost of this perimeter security measure.

Doors and Windows

Doors and windows are part of the inner barriers of a building and are one of the weakest links in the security of the structure because they are much more fragile than the surrounding walls and foundation. To strengthen these weak links, aside from the obvious consideration that all doors and windows should normally be closed and locked, they must also be designed to resist attempts of forcible entry. This included not only the doors and windows themselves, but also the surrounding frames.

Exterior doors to your facility, along with interior doors located at entrances to areas housing critical resources, should to be evaluated with regard to their structural strength and the type of locking mechanism. The doors themselves should be made of heavy and solid material, either solid wood or, ideally, steel. It is also a good practice to have doors that open toward the likely threat direction to preclude an intruder from being able to kick the door inward. In addition to construction of the door itself, the frames, hinges, and locking mechanisms should also be reinforced. Last, hinges on exterior doors, along with doors that provide entry to areas storing critical resources, should never be located along the exterior of the structure (or the area from where a potential intruder would be approaching).

Because windows are easy to break in order to gain access into a facility, they are typically viewed as the least secure point in a building's defenses. As such, potential intruders will typically look to these when attempting to gain entry to your facility. One option to combat this vulnerability is to consider placing bars, grills, or heavy screens across any windows that are less than 18 feet from ground level. Although this is one of the most secure options to protect windows, placing bars along all your exterior windows may not promote an open and inviting environment—particularly if you are in a customer-service business. If this option is undesirable, other options can be used to reinforce these windows to provide protection to these vulnerable points:

- Burglar-resistant glass or safety glass that meets Underwriters Laboratories (UL) standards
- Glazing, using either plastic or acrylic (Plexiglas), which will provide shatter resistance and in some cases bullet resistance
- Wired glass, usually used in fire doors and windows
- Tempered glass, which is four times stronger than annealed glass; when shattered, it will usually break into small fragments to protect against flying glass hazards, which may be a good option if a vehicle-borne explosive threat is a possibility

Lighting Measures

Lighting is another essential element of your physical security and mitigation measures because this item can make detection of potential intruders more likely (Figure 3.5). Furthermore, proper use of lighting can provide a significant psychological deterrent against individuals who are considering actions against your organization. In fact, it is important to note that effective lighting is the single most cost-effective deterrent against crime because it is relatively inexpensive to maintain and when used effectively can reduce the need for security personnel or other measures in some cases. As is the case with many other security measures, redundancy and defense in depth should always be a consideration, and as such, security lighting is one of the many physical

Figure 3.5 Lighting.

security measures that should not be used as a stand-alone system because the purpose is to provide observation to some type of response. As a result, lighting should be augmented with other physical security measures such as cameras or alarms to allow detection of any unauthorized individuals and ensure an appropriate response to assess their intent.

The primary purpose of exterior lighting is to allow observation in and around your facility. This improved observation should enhance the detection of unauthorized personnel by whatever security personnel and/or cameras are available to respond to these incidents. Adequate and necessary exterior security lighting consists of even light along areas bordering your facility's perimeter. Exterior lighting should ideally create glaring light into the eyes of potential intruders while providing lower light in areas where security posts and patrols operate. There is a balance in the amount of lighting; too much lighting can actually become detrimental because it will make it difficult to see into surrounding areas. This results in standard exterior security lighting having less intensity than working lights.

Interior security lighting differs slightly from exterior lights and will normally serve two purposes: to provide additional lighting to improve observation of your organization's critical resources and emergency lighting. Critical resources should be kept under continuous surveillance, by either security personnel or cameras, and the additional use of dedicated security lighting directed onto these resources enables improved observation and provides a level of deterrence against any unauthorized personnel who may be able to get near these assets. Emergency lighting is another security measure that should be considered for interior lighting. This type of lighting operates on an alternative power source so that it provides illumination to enhance safety for all employees during power outages and it provides visibility to security personnel should they need to respond to an incident during a power failure.

Access Control

The security fundamental involving the use of choke points was discussed earlier and access control is the security and mitigation measure that directly ties into this fundamental (Figure 3.6). Access control provides a process to identify the authorization of all individuals attempting to enter the facility through these choke points. If your organization is able to account for and validate the authorization of all people entering and exiting your facility, it is extremely difficult for any individual to surreptitiously gain access not only to your critical resources but into your facility itself. This ability can make access control the single most important measure of any physical security system. An access control system must be able to accomplish several objectives:

- Allow only authorized personnel to enter or exit the facility and provide information on visitors wishing to enter the building
- Control access to sensitive areas inside the facility and ensure this access is granted only to personnel with the appropriate clearance
- Detect and prevent the entry or exit of contraband materials
- Notify and provide information to security personnel for assessment and response as necessary

Figure 3.6 Access control.

An access control system can be as simple as checking an individual's identification against an approved list of authorized employees on a hand-written list or it can be an automated, computerized system that integrates employee identification cards with card readers and information databases to record each and every entry and exit for any individual. Another physical security and mitigation measure that is also included within the realm of access control, but one that is typically overlooked, is a process to maintain facility keys and locks—typically designated a key control system. We will look at these various areas within access control and provide you with guidance on what you need to consider and what types of items you should include when designing your access control system.

Access Control Considerations

As discussed in the security fundamental of choke points, it is important to limit the number of entry points into any facility when working to control access into a particular location. Most facilities have more exterior doors and entryways than is necessary to conduct business and allow access into the facility for all your employees during normal activities. Although all these doorways must allow for exit in the event of an emergency, the number of entry points for day-to-day business should be minimized in order to funnel any people entering the facility through a minimum number of entries—preferably limited to only one central reception point. This area should normally have an individual (either a security guard or a receptionist) who not only can verify the authorization of any individual attempting entry into the building but also can provide a greater degree of customer service and professionalism to guests and visitors. Because a primary obstacle to minimizing the number of entry points is usually related to the convenience of your employees, they can be better sold on the idea based on the advantage to the company in having an individual with a professional demeanor greeting individuals who are entering the building. This is another example of using the balance found in the Security and Business Operations Triangle to limit the number of access points into your organization's facility.

Another consideration to providing proper access control is to ensure there is a system to identify individuals as they enter and exit the facility. To better determine which personnel are authorized within the facility and particularly in certain areas containing critical resources, your organization should provide employee identification cards to all your personnel and require everyone to wear these cards while at work. By issuing and mandating the wearing of identification cards, it will become much easier to identify employees—particularly if your organization is large enough that all your personnel do not know one another. Additionally, these employee identification badges will cause many personnel to question an individual who is not wearing one, so that over time through training along with emphasis by management, employees will gain heightened security awareness and they will begin to assist in access control by identifying personnel within the building who are not wearing the proper identification.

Access Control and Individual Verification

We have alluded to some different methods of access control; however, a major decision you will need to make is how your business will actually control access into your facility. There are two primary methods to accomplish this: having personnel specifically designated to accomplish entry control or the use of an automated access control system. We will look at each of these systems and discuss the advantages and disadvantages of each.

An advantage in having an individual dedicated to checking the authorization of personnel as they enter your facility is the ability to quickly identify personnel who are not authorized to enter the facility. There is another advantage to having an employee dedicated to identifying authorized personnel as they enter the building and that is the higher degree of customer service and professionalism provided to visitors when entering your facility. This advantage provides a significant reason to use some type of receptionist or entry controller, but again the improvement in security within your facility cannot be discounted. The bottom line is that having an individual checking identification of all personnel and validating their need to enter the facility is an extremely effective deterrent against unauthorized entry.

An automated access control system is another option when looking to improve your entry control processes. Automated access control alleviates the need to hire a full-time receptionist or entry controller and instead determines the authorization of an individual through the use of some type of credential issued to employees and authorized visitors. These credentials can include some type of key, token, or transmitter. The most effective credential in this type of system is a photo identification card that can double as your employee ID. This photo identification card is encoded with each employee's personnel information and each exterior entrance to your facility, along with any entry into restricted areas, will have some type of card reader and key-card entry. These card readers can work by a variety of methods, such as a card swipe, card swipe plus a personal identification number, or card swipe combined with the use of biometrics identification (e.g., voiceprint, fingerprint, retinal scan, etc.). This type of automated access control system is arguably the best system because it can provide a record of every entry and exit by an individual at all doors with an installed card reader; however, this can be expensive depending upon the size of your organization, the size of the facility, and the number of entries and exits that should contain a card reader. The type of access control system you choose for your own organization should be accomplished by the type of business you operate and by conducting a cost–benefit analysis between the methods.

Key Control System

A final aspect of access control is the need to have a process to maintain control over keys and locks within the organization and all facilities. This key control system is designed to provide positive control of all building keys and locks. This system should ensure that all keys can be accounted for and that each individual with an issued key can be identified. Last, the system should be able to identify the location of each key and the corresponding door or lock in which each key can be used. With a system in place within an organization, you can significantly enhance your ability to provide access control and improve security and mitigation across the entire company.

Alarm Systems

Alarm systems are another physical security and mitigation measure—these systems are a standard item within any organization's security system and are the primary method of providing notification, another security fundamental (Figure 3.7). The basic operation of any good alarm system is to provide the needed notification of any unauthorized attempt to gain access to a building, room, or specific piece of equipment. This is normally accomplished by detecting changes in the environment around the object or by detecting a break in some type of pathway (e.g., electrical, infrared, etc.). We will look at the various considerations you should look at when determining when to use an alarm system and what type of system will work best in a particular application.

Most people are familiar with alarm systems; however, there are several considerations before you decide to utilize one particular type of system in your overall security program.

- What risk or vulnerability you are protecting against
- Past history of any burglary, unauthorized entry, or vandalism
- Type of sensors needed based on their location and the environment
- Whethertamper-resistant or tamper-indicating devices are necessary for the particular application
- Who will be notified of an alarm and what is the response time to the location
- Cost–benefit analysis

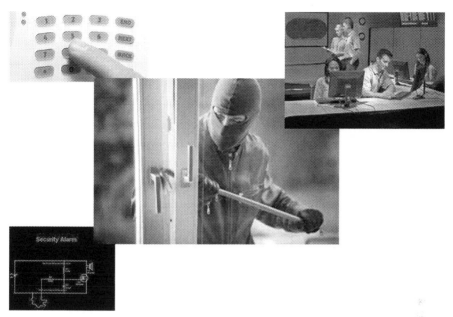

Figure 3.7 Alarm systems.

Alarm systems are primarily used to protect critical resources or at least the areas surrounding these assets; however, like many other security measures, an alarm system is useless unless it is used in conjunction with other systems. For example, if an alarm sounds but does not provide any type of notification to a response force, the usefulness of the alarm is negated. This will typically make an alarm system more expensive than simply the initial installation cost. These types of systems should also account for the ongoing and long-term costs to ensure notification and these costs should be factored in as you consider whether an alarm system will be used.

Closed-Circuit Television

Closed-circuit television, more commonly known by its acronym CCTV, is another security and mitigation measure that can augment any physical security system (Figure 3.8). Like many of the security measures we have already discussed, CCTV cannot be the only item or act as the only protection asset within your system. Additionally, if cameras cannot be kept under continuous observation—ideally by an individual or at a minimum by recording their output—other security measures should be considered instead of CCTV. I have come across many individuals throughout my career who believe that having a camera, even if it is not kept under observation, can provide a deterrent sufficient to alleviate all other security measures. Although the deterrent value of a camera is valid, simply having a camera will not outweigh the actual cost of the installation and maintenance. For example, I have seen many organizations that have had cameras that were not under any observation or, in some cases,

Figure 3.8 CCTV systems.

not even working. Although the deterrent effect may work for a short time, in the vast majority of these instances the personnel within the facility usually know within a few days that the cameras are not working and thus these pieces of equipment are not going to catch anybody. These cameras had minimal deterrent value and as a result, these items did little to deter bad behavior or even criminal activity. Despite these issues, if your organization still wants to use security cameras by themselves to deter unauthorized activity, it is advisable to use fake cameras that provide the façade of CCTV but are not operational. These items are very inexpensive and you do not need to worry about observation; however, as we discussed earlier, the deterrent value will quickly go away as people realize these cameras are fake.

Safes and Vaults

Valuable assets belonging to your company need to be placed in some type of high-security storage area, such as a safe or vault. The primary difference between the two is size—a vault is a larger storage area that is normally a separate room and is part of the building's structure. This enables vaults to be significantly stronger than safes, with thicker walls, floors, ceilings, and doors. Vault doors should be made of a minimum of six inches of steel and the walls, floors, and ceiling should be reinforced concrete at least 12 inches thick—normally twice the thickness of the door. Vaults must usually be located at or below ground level because of their structural strength and significant weight. A primary disadvantage of vaults is the expense in construction. If you have an existing facility that does not have a vault, the construction may be cost prohibitive; however, if you are currently constructing your facility or accomplishing a major renovation, it may be advisable to consider addition of a vault.

A key item of consideration for safes and vaults is what you wish to protect against—burglary or fire—because these compose the two separate categories of protection for safes and vaults. Whereas most secure safes and vaults provide protection against both to some degree, you should ensure that any device you are considering meets UL minimum ratings against your primary concern for your specific company assets. Many burglar-resistant containers may not provide against fire and, conversely, many fire-resistant containers may provide only a minimal deterrent against theft. Typically, the higher the rating in either category, the more expensive and more secure the safe or vault.

Summary of Physical Security Measures

Central to providing a viable security program is the need to employ physical security and mitigation measures in layers around your critical resource or to provide what is commonly termed by security professionals as defense in depth. In the manner of concentric circles moving inward, it is important to work from the perimeter of your property and facility and incrementally strengthen the security measures as you work your way in, as you design the security measures to be installed. Using this concept, you will eventually provide the strongest security measures to protect your organization's designated critical resources.

Starting at the boundary of the property, perimeter security measures provide a barrier that not only helps to distinguish the property boundary or facility but also limits access onto the property. Security measures along the inner barrier to your facility must take into account the doors and windows, as these items are the most susceptible to damage and break-in. In addition to ensuring your organization always locks and secures these openings, it is also important to strengthen these areas with robust frames, solid construction doors, and strengthened windows. Lighting is another important physical security measure. Exterior lighting is meant to assist with observation in and around your facility for security personnel and/or cameras, whereas interior lighting should provide additional lighting to critical resources and meet any emergency lighting requirements. Access control is a critical piece of your physical security system—perhaps the most critical piece. This aspect of the physical security program ensures that only authorized personnel can enter or exit the facility. Access control also controls entry into sensitive areas, it detects and prevents contraband materials, and it alerts security personnel of any potential issues. Some easy methods to improve access control for any organization include limiting the number of entry points into the facility, providing a process that identifies employees and other visitors, and providing personnel who are responsible to monitor entry into and exit from the facility. The next mitigation measure we discussed was alarm systems, which are designed to provide notification of unauthorized entry onto the grounds or into the building or attempts to gain access to your organization's critical resources. Another security and mitigation measure we covered was closed-circuit televisions and their use within a physical security system. Cameras provide observation of areas that are vulnerable to unauthorized entry or access. The last physical measure we reviewed was safes and vaults that are designed to provide additional security and protection for an organization's critical resources.

To ensure an adequate number of layers within your organization's physical security program to provide adequate defense in depth, it is important that you employ equipment and procedures that cover most—if not all—of these areas and that there are secondary systems to augment the initial security and mitigation measure. This not only provides multiple problems for a potential intruder, but it also offers redundant systems to increase your organization's security posture.

Information Security Measures

Information security has become an increasingly prominent aspect of any organization's security program as computers and information systems have become more and more predominant. Prior to the age of computers, information security was limited to ensuring files and hard copies of your sensitive information—normally your employee's personal information—were properly secured. However, now with the vast amount of critical information contained in media other than the older (and in many cases antiquated) hard copies and filing cabinets, these electronic storage means demand that all organizations have an information security program to ensure they have adequate procedures and processes in place to protect information contained within computers, servers, and wireless networks. Add to this shift from paper to computers the explosion in the amount of information that must be protected because of the significant increase in these electronic information storage means. Add to the massive increase in electronic storage of information the interconnectivity among these data in various business environments, and the result is an ever-growing number of threats and vulnerabilities to information. All of these factors have resulted in a need for successful organizations to have a comprehensive information security program.

To develop this comprehensive information security program, an organization must account for the three main pillars that form an effective program, confidentiality, integrity, and availability, termed CIA by many information security professionals. It is important to ensure these areas are applied to the protection of any type of information and data, including any hardware, software, or communications that form the foundation of any information system. The following factors[6] should be considered when looking at each of these three pillars and are often instrumental in the successful implementation of an information security program within any organization:

- Information security documentation
- Approach and framework to implement, maintain, monitor, and improve information security that is consistent with your organizational culture
- Visible support and commitment from all levels of management
- Understanding information security requirements, risk assessment, and risk management
- Effective marketing of information security to all managers and employees to develop security awareness
- Funding of information security management activities
- Establishing an effective information security incident management process
- Implementation of a measurement system used to evaluate the current information security program and suggest improvements

Within these three information security pillars, it is still important to remember the security fundamentals that we discussed earlier and work them into your security and mitigation measures for your information systems. With the uniqueness of electronic data and the systems that support this information, there are some additional information security fundamentals that should also be considered specifically in regard to the protection of information and data[7]:

- Principle of least privilege, which stipulates that an organization should "not give any more privileges than absolutely necessary to do the required job"

- Minimization of your system's information system configuration so that you do not run any software, applications, or services not strictly required to do the entrusted job
- Compartmentalization to limit damage and protect other compartments when software in one area is malfunctioning or compromised
- Incorporation and use of the concept of failing securely, which means that if a security measure or control has failed, that portion of the information system is not placed into an insecure state; for example, when a firewall fails, the system should default to a "deny all" rule rather than a "permit all" rule

We will be looking at all these various factors, the three overarching pillars of information security (confidentiality, integrity, and accountability), the standard security fundamentals, unique information security fundamentals, and the components within an information system (hardware, software, and communications), as we briefly cover what is required for an effective information security program.

Confidentiality

Confidentiality is the first information security pillar we will discuss. Confidentiality is defined as "ensuring information is accessible only to those authorized to have access."[8] To ensure this occurs, it is necessary to provide appropriate security and mitigation measures that protect all confidential and sensitive information. To accomplish this protection, one of the first things every organization must do is make certain every employee who comes into contact with that information understands the added responsibility to maintain its confidentiality. With this inherent responsibility, each person who is provided access should be given several tasks through her or his initial training and indoctrination into the company:

- They must be able to identify and understand that certain information is designated as confidential or sensitive.
- They must understand their responsibility to help protect that information.
- They can communicate their responsibility when accessing the sensitive information.
- They will maintain the information in accordance with any requirements for handling sensitive information.

To assist your employees and provide them the necessary tools to ensure they can meet their responsibilities regarding sensitive and confidential information, there are some general considerations that your organization should develop and disseminate to all personnel who work with this information. These considerations not only provide the means and equipment to protect information, they also ensure your employees have the necessary resources and procedures to accomplish their tasks and responsibilities regarding all confidential and sensitive information, whether it is in hard copy or electronic format. The first consideration is that personnel must ensure that sensitive and confidential information must never be left unsecured and unattended. In addition, any storage containers for this information must be able to be locked and secured when not in use either during or after business hours. The next consideration is that your organization should also develop and provide a process to formally identify who is authorized access to the sensitive information. This process should include a method that designates their ability to access specific information—usually accomplished through some form of identification or credentialing to access the specific information. Additionally, there should be a process to conduct regular training on the employees' responsibilities, which should include:

- Ensuring information is accessed only by authorized individuals
- Updating combination locks and passwords as required by company policy and procedures
- No disclosure or sharing of their own personal authentication credentials, such as user identification, passwords, key-cards, or other forms of electronic authentication with any other individuals should be done
- No use of their own personal authorization to provide sensitive information to other individuals–even those they think may be authorized—should be done
- Reporting requirements and procedures of any violations of the company's information security requirements

These considerations, never leaving confidential information unsecured or unattended, credentialing identification for authorized individuals, and training, should be utilized to secure sensitive information in any format.

Integrity

The next pillar of information security is that of integrity. Integrity involves maintaining consistency, accuracy, and trustworthiness of critical information and data over the entirety of their life cycle. Integrity means that information must be able to remain unchanged throughout transmission, integration with other data, or other instances in which the data are sent. This pillar not only includes information as it is being transmitted but also should include data that are maintained within your company's storage devices, including computers and servers. The concept of data integrity, along with its importance, can be shown through the following hypothetical example. A hospital patient is in treatment and is prescribed a daily medication dosage of 10 mg by his physician. This hospital maintains its information on a computer system, so the doctor enters the correct dosage and medication into that patient's electronic medical record. Unfortunately, the integrity of the hospital's information system is poor and a glitch in the program that transmits the electronic record adds a zero to the dosage amount so that the patient's dosage now reads 100 mg in this electronic record. With the critical nature of medication dosage, this lack of integrity within the hospital's information system could result in fatal consequences for this particular patient. To preclude this incident from occurring within your own information system and ensure data are correctly maintained throughout transmission and storage, data integrity must be a critical component of any information security program.

There are some key security measures that every information system should adhere to in order to provide for the integrity of the system's information and data. These measures include:

- Equipping and maintaining up-to-date hardware
- Utilizing the right software that is maintained and updated with easy-to-use and automated techniques
- Developing the right policies to guide business practices

As you look at ensuring the integrity of your information system, there are certain steps necessary to guarantee that transmitted data cannot be altered by unauthorized individuals, all of which will help to ensure critical information cannot be changed, either in transit or in storage. These steps include requiring that your organization continually procures up-to-date hardware. This will ensure that your employees work on equipment that is able to support the most recent versions of software and hardware upgrades—particularly when dealing with information protection applications. In addition to maintaining up-to-date information systems hardware, it is also important to provide consistent software applications that are properly updated and maintained to protect and operate your entire information system. The last step that ensures the integrity of an information security system is to provide and adhere to proper policies to guide your business practices. As with any area within your safety and security program, data integrity requires that appropriate policies and procedures are well documented and fully understood across your organization. These documents should address the specific responsibilities necessary to ensure integrity—accountability, access rights, and separation of duties—across three different areas: the overall business and its employees, the information technology staff, and internal audits. By working to ensure your hardware and software are up to date, along with providing the proper policies, your organization can ensure the integrity of your information security program.

Availability

Availability, as it relates to information systems, means that the proportion of time your organization's system is in an operational condition and that the data contained within the system are available for use. In other words, availability describes your organization's information system's ability to deliver the correct data and information to the correct person within the bounds of the correct policies for your organization. Security and mitigation measures that must be taken to ensure that your information system maintains this availability, both to your employees and to outside vendors and clients, include:

- Ensuring proper maintenance is accomplished for all hardware
- Providing redundancy within your information systems
- Providing adequate communications bandwidth
- Guarding and protecting against malicious actions

We will look at each of these security measures in detail over the next several paragraphs to provide you with the information necessary to ensure your system meets information availability requirements.

Availability within any information system is best ensured by rigorously maintaining all hardware and by performing repairs immediately when the need arises. Two groups of individuals can assist in maintaining hardware, your specific points of contact within your organization for information systems (an information technology section or computer services) and your employees themselves. Hardware maintenance can be accomplished by either your system administrator or your information technology department by conducting frequent checks of the system that ensure all system components are in proper working order. These personnel are not the sole individuals that can assist with keeping hardware up to date, as employees also have a key role in ensuring information systems are maintained and available. This is the case because individual employees are the personnel using the information systems hardware and software on a daily basis. In the event they see any problems or issues with the information or data they are working with, employees must understand they have the responsibility to notify the appropriate personnel. With checks accomplished by systems administrators and notification by employees when they see any issues, it is much easier to ensure hardware is properly maintained and in operational order.

Redundancy is a must, to ensure the availability of your organization's information system. One method to ensure redundancy is to have multiple pieces of equipment performing the same task. Although this is a relatively foolproof method, it can also be expensive and time-consuming, because it will probably result in the need to procure more equipment than is necessary to do the job. Still, for areas that are truly critical to your overall information system this may be the most viable option to ensure no loss or damage; however, there are other options that can be used to provide for redundancies in information systems. One option is to provide backup of data to ensure redundancy of your information system. This can be accomplished either using your own resources, such as purchase of additional servers or other storage devices, or by working with a vendor that provides information storage services. Failover describes another option that helps provide for redundant information systems. Failover is a backup operational mode in which the functions of a system component (such as a processor, server, network, or database) are assumed by secondary system components when the primary component becomes unavailable through either failure or scheduled downtime. A good example to illustrate failover is an emergency generator system that senses any type of electrical power interruption and then provides continuous power with no break in electricity to the location it protects. Although there are several options that are available to ensure redundancy within your information system, it is up to each organization to determine the criticality of the information and equipment and balance it between the costs of the various options.

Bandwidth is the next security and mitigation measure to ensure the availability of any information system. In information systems and computer networks, bandwidth is often synonymous with the data transfer rate of the overall system. In other words, bandwidth describes the amount of data that can be carried from one point to another in a given time period (usually a second). In general, the more information your organization sends across your network, the higher the bandwidth your information system will require. Providing additional bandwidth within your information systems will normally require more advanced equipment to allow for this increase in data transfer rates.

The last security and mitigation measure that helps to ensure availability within your information system is protection. This includes maintaining current upgrades to your information systems—in relation to both hardware and software. By maintaining up-to-date hardware and software, you will help to ensure your organization's information system can guard against malicious actions such as denial-of-service attacks. A denial-of-service attack is accomplished when a malicious hacker exploits flaws or vulnerabilities in a computer system (often a Web site or Web server) to fool the location into thinking that they are the master system. Once this occurs, the hacker can then obtain confidential information or disrupt your information system. Protection can be accomplished with current software and hardware within your organization's information system.

Summary of Information Security Measures

Information security can be very complex owing to the technology and computerized information systems that are involved; however, implementing a viable information security program one area at a time can make the task a little easier. To ensure your information security program properly mitigates risk, it is best to develop your organization's program by using the three pillars of information security as a guide—confidentiality, integrity, and availability. Keeping each of these three pillars in mind as you implement your information security program through various mitigation measures will enhance the ability of your organization to minimize the risk against various types of emergency incidents that can occur against hardware, software, and networks within your particular business.

Personnel Security and Mitigation Measures

Personnel security is the last major area that should be covered within any organization's security program. Many organizations concentrate their personnel security programs through the protection of individual employees' personal information; however, this is only a minor portion of an organization's personnel security program. A more important aspect of personnel security should ensure that all hiring and retention actions across your organization locate employees who not only pose no risk to the organization but also meet your own company's business and moral interests. This aspect is critical because it can alleviate many problems before they occur. Unfortunately, ensuring that employees meet your organization's interests can be easier said than done—particularly because it can be extremely difficult to determine a person's character traits during a standard hiring interview. Thus, an effective personnel security program that provides an overarching process to determine if a potential employee meets the interests of your company prior to actually working within the organization is what we will emphasize throughout this section.

To develop a comprehensive personnel security program that determines and monitors an individual's character traits, both prior to hiring and once an individual becomes an employee, the personnel security process should involve three primary steps:

1. Conducting preemployment screening processes prior to the actual hiring of any potential employee
2. Investigating current employees suspected of violating company rules and regulations
3. Protecting all employees from discriminatory hiring or termination as well as guarding against unfounded allegations of illegal or unethical activities and conduct

To develop this overarching process, it is absolutely critical that an effective personnel security program includes proper documentation—meaning formal documentation of company policies and procedures regarding your organization's personnel actions. Developing this documentation is a critical task in establishing an effective personnel security program and ensuring all personnel actions are consistently followed for each and every individual throughout the entire organization—in fact, this is true not only for the personnel security program but also for any other area that is part of an organization's safety and security program. This documentation must detail methods for implementing the various processes and procedures that are vital to an overall personnel security program. These parts include your organization's human resources processes, details on the conduct of preemployment screening, the process for hiring new employees, and how your organization reacts to allegations and conducts investigations for inappropriate behavior. By having written documents and then consistently following these processes with the help of these formalized policies and procedures, you are much more likely to ensure that supervisory personnel located throughout various sections within the company can consistently follow all human resources processes. This not only will ensure that all potential and current employees are the best fit for the organization and that they meet your company's interests, but also will protect your organization against lawsuits and other legal issues that can arise from employees' actions. All of these formally documented procedures ensure greater consistency across the entire organization and ensure supervisors can make the best informed decisions regarding their employees.

Now that we have reinforced the need to formally document personnel processes and procedures, we look at the three primary steps that should be included in your organization's personnel security process over the next several sections.

Conducting Preemployment Screening

Prior to even considering whether to hire an individual, it is critical that your organization conduct some type of screening to begin assessing whether that particular individual's character traits fit those of your company. The primary purpose in conducting preemployment screening is to identify potential employees who may be bad risks or do not fit with the team before they are even hired and working. To help simplify the process and break it down into manageable tasks, it is useful to look at preemployment screening over the course of the following four-step process.

1. Define what character traits, experience, and other factors your organization wants the screening process to look at in a prospective employee. These areas can include specific job qualifications, character traits, education, level of experience, or other areas that are important to your specific organization's personality and work ethic.
2. Develop specific methods and processes that test the abilities and characteristics that you want to measure.
3. Compile the information in a uniform and measurable way to determine the candidates who best meet your organization's requirements for the position in question but also how their personality fits with that of your company.
4. Use and maintain this information when making an informed hiring decision.

These screenings must follow an established and consistent set of standards within your company for each and every individual being considered for a position in your organization. As we have previously discussed, the way to ensure consistent application across the entire organization is to formally document these standards in an easy-to-follow process for any individual who conducts hiring within your company. Once you have established these steps into an overall set of procedures, you can move forward with your hiring choice.

Employee Investigations

The next area to include within a comprehensive personnel security program is the process of employee investigations. These investigations can include background checks along with investigations that may need to be conducted after an individual has been hired in the event there is inappropriate behavior. We will first cover background checks and then discuss methods to accomplish other types of investigations.

The purpose of the employment background investigation is to identify individuals who may be a risk with regard to employee theft, lawsuits, or losses to the company and prevent these actions before the individual is hired and they could occur. There should be no exceptions and a background check should be conducted on all potential employees, as it verifies the accuracy and completeness of an applicant's statements, develops additional relevant information on the candidate, and determines the individual's suitability for employment. The background investigation should also look for inconsistencies between an applicant's statements made in his or her application or interview. The following is a complete list of information and items that should be included as part of any employment screening background investigation:

- Check any local security incidences and police files to determine if the individual has any derogatory information
- Obtain details on any gaps in employment history
- Check previous residences
- Research the applicant's consumer report and financial status
- Check civil court and criminal court records
- Contact the candidate's personal references
- Verify education background
- Conduct interviews with former employees and work associates
- Check military history, professional certifications, and social security number

The other type of investigation occurs after an individual has been hired and if there are charges of misconduct by the employee. These investigations are conducted in the event of any suspicions or allegations that an employee may be violating company rules or regulations. If it is determined that an employee investigation be conducted, it is imperative that the results stand up to the necessary scrutiny of the legal system or any union agreements your company is subject to. This makes the employee investigation process a vital part of ensuring your organization can maintain discipline and provide a safe and secure work environment while still meeting any requirements to protect the individual. To ensure any investigations of employee misconduct meet these requirements, it is best to use a formal process that includes the following tasks:

- Designate qualified investigators within your organization. These individuals should be unbiased and objective and have some experience and training on the conduct of investigations.
- Continually develop investigative resources to quickly and accurately obtain information on individuals involved in the investigation or the incident in question.

- Follow established methods to collect, handle, and store evidence. The basic rules for collecting and handling evidence must follow the same chain of custody that is required and used in a court of law because it is never known at the outset of an investigation if actual criminal action occurred. In this manner, the investigator can be assured that any evidence collected will be able to be used by law enforcement if necessary.
- Investigators should be trained and able to follow proper interview techniques with any eyewitnesses, supervisors, and suspects so that they can obtain as much information as possible from other persons who were eyewitnesses. This enables the investigator to determine the circumstances and facts surrounding the incident under investigation, as one of the best methods of obtaining this information is through interviews.
- Complete investigation reports in the proper format to ensure full documentation of the results of the incident.

Protecting Employees from Discrimination and Unfounded Allegations

The last area we will cover within the personnel security realm is providing protection to your organization's employees from discrimination and unfounded allegations. There are many requirements that any organization must comply with during both the screening and the investigation processes. These considerations and restrictions are derived from a number of laws and regulations that your human resources point of contact should be intimately familiar with and include the following:

- Age Discrimination in Employment Act–1967
- Americans with Disabilities Act
- Civil Rights Act–1964
- Consumer Protection Act–1976
- Department of Justice Order 601-75
- The Electronic Communication Privacy Act of 1986
- Employee Polygraph Protection Act of 1988
- Fair Credit Reporting Act
- National Labor Relations Act
- The Omnibus Crime Control and Safe Street Act of 1968 (Title III)
- The Privacy Act–1974

Conclusions on Personnel Security Measures

We have covered the three primary areas that form the basis of an effective personnel security program—preemployment screening, investigations, and ensuring your employees are protected from discriminatory hiring and unfounded allegations of improper conduct. To ensure your organization meets the many requirements within this program, it is critical that you develop formalized documentation that outlines all these areas to ensure consistency and minimize any possibility of placing your organization in a situation that violates the myriad of laws and acts covering human resources actions.

Emergency Response Roles and Responsibilities

We will cover many of the specific details necessary to delineate duties necessary to respond to an emergency incident in Chapter 7 in much greater detail when we discuss the structure and makeup of Crisis Management Teams; however, in relation to our discussion on mitigation measures for emergency response it is helpful to briefly discuss some of the individual roles and responsibilities at this point. By establishing these duties prior to your organization's actual response to any emergency, you will greatly assist your organization's ability to respond to and help minimize the effects of any potential emergencies.

To ensure an organization's emergency response is properly conducted there are various roles that must be identified and defined. A consideration for these duties is the organizational structure of your company and how you divide responsibilities on a day-to-day basis, so we will discuss only the basic positions necessary in general terms. First, you will need to identify an incident commander. This person is in overall charge of the response to any emergency incident and will normally match the individual who is in charge of your organization on a daily basis. Other roles that must be established include focal points for communications, media relations, and information systems and an individual responsible for coordinating any facility or maintenance issues. There may be additional roles and responsibilities that are necessary based on the nature of your business and the various functions within your organization, such as a specific information technology representative or safety point of contact. As stated earlier, we will go into much greater detail on all the various roles and responsibilities that must be identified to assist in mitigating against any potential emergency incident during our discussion on Crisis Management Teams; however, it cannot be emphasized enough that it is critical that you identify a responsible individual prior to any emergency to ensure each necessary task will be planned for and accomplished.

Emergency Response Plans and Procedures

As we have discussed previously, the best method for implementing any program is a well-written organizational plan along with any associated procedures included in this plan. This requirement for formal plans and procedures is no different when dealing with your organization's emergency response program. Although we cover many of the details necessary to address in any emergency response plan in Chapter 4 and include a complete template for this plan in Appendix A, as these plans relate more to the emergency response planning factor of preparedness, these plans also have an impact on your organization's ability to mitigate against potential incidents. As with individual roles and responsibilities, we will provide some brief information regarding these plans during our discussion of mitigation measures in this chapter prior to the more detailed coverage of these plans and procedures later in this book.

There is some necessary information that should be included in and form the foundation of any emergency response plan. This information should be tailored to fit the specific requirements within your organization based upon your location, your facility, your security measures that are currently in place, the type of business, and even your company's culture. Although we provide some general verbiage for an emergency plan that discusses each of these topics in Appendix A, the following areas should be included in any comprehensive emergency response plan:

- Discussion on the four major planning factors for emergency response—mitigation, preparedness, response, and recovery
- Makeup of your organizational Crisis Management Team and your organization's chain of command for response to various emergency incidents
- Procedures that detail evacuation and shelter-in-place responses
- Emergency medical operations that provide for treatment of the injured
- Procedures to account for all personnel, including employees and any visitors to your facility at the initiation of an emergency
- Internal rescue operations, should emergency response personnel be overwhelmed and unable to deal with your organization and personnel
- Checklists that detail your organization's response to specific emergencies (we provide templates of actual emergency response checklists in Chapter 8 for you to use that can be tailored within your organization)
- Actions to provide recovery from an emergency, including damage assessment, cleanup and salvage operations, business restoration, methods to retain customer and client information, and mutual aid and agreement activities

When you develop and write these emergency response plans, it is ideal that individuals knowledgeable with security, emergency response, and specifics regarding your own organization be involved in the development of any detailed plan to ensure the document is complete and meets the specific needs of your organization. This will help provide a plan that not only meets the myriad of items that need to be included with regard to emergency response but also is tailored to the unique aspects within your company. By discussing the items detailed above, as they relate to the specific information regarding your organization and location, you will ensure your emergency response plans provide some of the basic information necessary to provide instructions to your employees on their actions and response in the event of an actual emergency, which will ultimately help to mitigate against an actual emergency.

Summary of Mitigation

There are several different security measures that will effectively mitigate against any potential emergency incident. The first mitigation measure is for an organization to develop and implement a comprehensive security program with formalized plans and procedures. Within any safety and security program, there are three primary areas that should be addressed—physical security, information security, and personnel security. By implementing security measures within these areas and incorporating the security principles and fundamentals as you design these measures into an overall security system, you can provide mitigation against a variety of potential emergency incidents. By ensuring your organization has provided security and mitigation measures, your company will be much better able to at least minimize the impact of any potential catastrophe and possibly even stop an incident from occurring through deterrence or the ability to detect an incident.

During our discussion regarding mitigation, we initially covered the principles of security to protect your organization's critical resources. These principles included a discussion of the preparatory actions by any perpetrators that are conducted prior to any incident, which include reconnaissance and assessing your organization's security and the effectiveness of your processes and procedures. We also covered the nine fundamentals of security, which include:

- Identification of critical resources
- Defense in depth
- Notification
- Response
- Simplicity
- Securing the weakest link
- Use of choke points
- Unpredictability
- Separation of duties

The last security principle we discussed was the need to balance safety and security requirements, along with the inconvenience and disruption that can occur through their implementation, with the need to maximize your organization's efficiency and effectiveness in its day-to-day operations. Within this principle, we introduced the Security versus Business Operation Triangle to better illustrate the competing forces that you must balance to provide a safe and secure environment that best protects your personnel and resources but still allows for effective and efficient business operations.

Next, we covered physical security measures that help to mitigate any potential emergency incidents. We discussed various options regarding perimeter security; doors and windows, typically one of the weakest links in any facility's physical security system; exterior and interior lighting; access control processes; alarm systems; and safes and vaults. These physical security measures provide the most visible deterrents and mitigation factors to any potential emergency incident.

We then looked at information security and mitigation measures that work to protect the hardware, software, and communications that compose your organization's information systems. To implement an effective information security program it is necessary to focus on the three main pillars—confidentiality, integrity, and availability—of any information system. We looked at these areas and briefly covered some basic methods to implement measures that enhance this program and help mitigate potential emergencies.

The last security and mitigation measure we discussed dealt with personnel security. One of the primary purposes of personnel security is to ensure that potential employees will meet your organization's interests and be productive employees. This is accomplished by conducting preemployment screening, investigating personnel prior to hiring and any employees who have violated company policies, and protecting employees from discrimination.

After our discussion on the various security and mitigation measures within the three areas of a safety and security program, we briefly covered the roles and responsibilities necessary to properly respond to any emergency incident. Although we cover these responsibilities in much greater detail in Chapter 7, suffice it to say that to mitigate against any potential emergency, it is necessary to clearly define everyone's role and their responsibility prior to the kickoff of an actual incident and your organization's response.

The last major area within mitigation of any possible emergency incident that we covered was the development of emergency response plans and procedures. These documents are critical to any effective emergency response program as they provide the necessary guidelines and instructions across the organization to ensure consistent methods and procedures in how your company's emergency response program is implemented, and we have included a complete template for an organization's emergency response plan in Appendix A.

End Notes

1. A&E Television Networks. 9/11 Attacks. (November 27, 2013), http://www.history.com.
2. John M. Kean, ed., The 9/11 Commission Report. 9/11 Commission Chairman, www.9-11commission.gov.
3. Chad Brooks, Employee Theft on the Rise and Expected to Get Worse (Business News Daily, June 19, 2013), web. 10 December 2013, www.BusinessNewsDaily.com.
4. David Hoelzer, Teach Your Boss to Speak Security: Separation of Duties. (Forbes. Forbes Magazine, April 26, 2010), web. 10 December 2013.
5. Military Handbook 1013/10. Chapter 2.3. Design Guidelines for Security Fencing, Gates, Barriers, and Guard Facilities.
6. International Standard ISO/IEC 17799:2005(E). Information Technology – Security Techniques – Code of Practice for Information Security Management.
7. Cryptome. Fundamental Security Concepts, www.cryptome.org.
8. International Standard ISO/IEC 17799:2005(E). Information Technology – Security Techniques – Code of Practice for Information Security Management.

Preparedness

4

Preparedness is the next emergency response planning factor that we will cover. To ensure that your organization is prepared to respond and recover from any potential emergency, there are several areas that should be considered. These areas within the preparedness planning factor can be divided into the following five items: communications, command and control, collection and distribution of resources, coordination, and congestion. We look at each of these areas separately as we discuss how to accomplish the necessary preparation over the following sections.

Communications

Communications is possibly the most important aspect of your organization's preparation for any type of emergency incident. If you have not communicated how your organization responds to any given situation and if you have not properly planned for methods to communicate procedures and instructions during an actual event, the ability of your company will be severely hampered and this is likely to result in more severe consequences from the incident.

Emergency Response Plans and Procedures

The first item within communication and preparedness is the need to have formal documentation and plans to disseminate the information and procedures throughout your organization. We have previously emphasized the need to implement an organizational emergency response program through a well-written plan that includes any associated procedures and checklists. These formal plans provide the best means to communicate how your employees should respond and react in the event of an emergency.

We have included a fairly comprehensive template that includes the various topics and sections that should be included within a typical emergency response plan along with some standard and generic verbiage that should be included in this plan in Appendix A. This template forms a terrific starting point for you to begin to develop a plan that is specific to your organization and meets your needs. With the information and template for an organizational emergency response plan within Appendix A, we next discuss specific equipment requirements along with other methods and procedures that can assist with communication during an actual incident.

Communicating during an Actual Emergency Incident

There are several considerations that any organization must address to ensure they have adequate communications in the event of an emergency incident. The first consideration is having equipment that provides the ability to communicate across the entire facility and ensure all work areas can be immediately notified. The next consideration is procuring any necessary communications equipment required for your staff, and in particular members of your Crisis Management Team, so that they can talk with one another despite the aftereffects of the incident. The final consideration is how your organization will coordinate with outside agencies during the emergency. These methods should be detailed within your emergency response plans and procedures so that your organization understands how you wish to respond to emergencies and how individuals will be notified.

The first consideration we mentioned is how your organization plans to notify employees at the onset of an incident. How you accomplish this notification is critical because it ensures not only that all employees are aware that an incident is occurring but also that they receive instructions on what actions they should take. This can occur through a notification tree using telephones and cell phones or it can be accomplished with a facility-wide notification system such as an audible alarm or loudspeaker (or a combination of both). The easiest and quickest of these notification methods is the use of a facility-wide intercom or alarm system; however, many facilities may not have this option available to them. There are some disadvantages to the use of an intercom system. One disadvantage is that many personnel will assume everyone has received the appropriate notification of an emergency incident. To overcome this issue, there should be procedures in place to check that all personnel have received the notification. Also, there should be a process to identify employees who are not in the facility at the time of the incident and a method to contact these personnel. The notification tree—a procedure that dictates individuals to contact personnel within their supervisory chain by telephone or personal contact—is slower; however, it can be accomplished without any special equipment (other than telephones, of course) and it provides greater assurance that all personnel have been notified. A notification tree will normally start at the top of the organizational chart and work downward as it provides instructions for each employee on who he or she contacts and it moves down to the lowest-level employees. Whereas the notification tree will take longer than making one intercom announcement, this method (when done properly) will better account for all personnel within your organization, including any employees who are out of town at the initiation of an emergency. Whatever method your organization plans to use for the notification of all your employees, it is important that everyone knows how this will be accomplished prior to an actual incident.

The second consideration that your emergency response plans must cover is what communications equipment is necessary to have to properly respond to an emergency. This determination must ensure you have procured the equipment necessary to allow your staff to talk to one another in the event of an emergency before disaster strikes. Your organization should allow for any limitations and capabilities of the various communications systems that are available to ensure you are not dependent on one piece of communications equipment—for example, cell phones—that can fail during many types of emergency incidents. During many major incidents that have occurred, such as natural disasters, it has been found that entire cell phone networks will typically fail because of the amount of cell phone traffic. This overload can cause the network to become overwhelmed and crash, or the natural disaster could conceivably destroy cell phone relay towers, creating further constraints on the network. Based on these concerns, it is not a good idea to become too reliant upon one single type of communications equipment during an emergency. The solution to these issues is to ensure your organization has several different viable communications systems with some type of redundant equipment. In addition to, or even in lieu of, cell phones, plan on using landline telephones; or better yet, purchase a radio and walkie-talkies for use during emergencies if your facility is small enough to utilize them. Other communication methods that may need to be utilized, and should be considered when developing your particular procedures, could include FAX machines, local area networks, or, in the worst case, designating employees to act as individual messengers or even the use of hand signals. Whatever types of equipment you choose, your plans and procedures should detail this so that all personnel understand how you plan to work through the incident.

The last consideration involves communications procedures that provide guidance on how you will coordinate with outside agencies during an emergency incident. At a minimum, it is critical that your plan identify what individuals, by position, will be talking with the three primary external agencies: emergency responders (e.g., police, fire, etc.), the media, and external relief and aid agencies—it will probably be necessary that different personnel coordinate with these various agencies based on several factors. During the initial stages of an emergency, coordination with emergency responders will probably take all of an individual's time, so any person tasked to liaise with these agencies will probably be unavailable for any other tasks during this initial response. With regard to the press, the larger your organization, the more likely it is that any emergency experienced by your business will result in media interest. With this in mind, it is imperative that you consider how your organization will react and respond to the press and community. By identifying which individual will accomplish this coordination, you will not only enable other individuals to concentrate on their jobs and provide a more effective response to the emergency, you will also provide a more positive impression to the media and ultimately the community that your company operates in. The last group of agencies will involve those that can provide assistance—in terms of either material and equipment or money—and an individual who can work with these organizations will enhance your organization's ability to receive this aid.

Command and Control

In any situation, people must know who is in charge. This is even more imperative during a response to an actual emergency incident. It is likely that the overall leader within any organization during day-to-day business operations will remain as the person in charge in the event of an emergency. This is not only realistic but also recommended, so that all employees know who they need to listen to; however, within your senior management team the rest of your chain of command may change based on the type of emergency situation and the particular requirements involved in the response.

To ensure you can properly respond to different types of situations appropriately, your emergency response plans should delineate who these key personnel are going to be based upon various types of emergency incidents. For example, in a situation involving damage to the facility itself—such as a fire or major hazardous material spill—your facility manager or maintenance supervisor may be the key person that the senior leader needs to coordinate with; however, in an actual attack against your organization (e.g., active shooter or unauthorized personnel entering your location) your security expert may be the primary focal point. To establish command and control for all the various types of incidents that could occur at your organization, your emergency response plans should be prepared so that they designate these key personnel for each incident.

Another area to assist in establishing the command and control necessary to respond to any emergency incident is the designation of a Crisis Management Team for the various types of incidents you may see. The Crisis Management Team will be the primary group of personnel from within your organization that forms during any emergency incident and will work the myriad of tasks required to adequately respond to the situation. While we discuss the composition of this team, along with the specific roles and responsibilities for each individual team member, in Chapter 7, these details must be prepared prior to the initiation of an actual incident. It is important that the membership of the Crisis Management Team should always remain the same to make the response to any situation easy to understand for all personnel and to speed up your organization's ability to respond; however, the key personnel to be consulted for the various types of incidents may change based on the nature of the emergency.

Collection and Distribution of Resources

Another area that is important in ensuring the preparedness of your organization's ability to respond to an emergency is to identify, collect, and distribute the necessary resources that will be required during the response to any type of incident. Trying to identify what resources are available, along with locating and storing them, cannot be accomplished once the emergency has begun. There will be too many other tasks that require everyone's attention at this point in time. Instead, it is necessary for you and your team to determine this information prior to the initiation of any type of emergency situation that could realistically arise.

Before the resources necessary to respond to an emergency incident are organized, however, another task involving your organization's resources must be accomplished as part of the preparation phase of emergency response planning. This is to ensure you maintain an up-to-date inventory of not only your critical resources but all of your organization's high-dollar equipment. We have already discussed the need to accomplish this task, not only for the company's critical information resources, but also, for much of your resources, so that you have the ability to identify what items may have been damaged or destroyed as a result of the incident and to help you better identify any necessary repair or replacement actions to be accomplished when you enter the recovery phase of emergency response. Without an accurate knowledge of what equipment and resources you have on-hand at the onset of an incident, it will be virtually impossible to determine what items are needed to resume your normal business operations.

Other than these inventories of your organization's critical resources, there are other items that must be identified, obtained, and stored during your preparation for any emergency response situation. These items include critical information necessary to your company's continuation, transportation considerations, medical procedures and supplies, emergency food items, and equipment kits necessary for your Crisis Management Team to operate effectively. We look at each of these items over the next several paragraphs.

The first resource that must be identified and safeguarded is your organization's critical company information. As we discussed in Chapter 3 in our overview of security principles, critical resources—including information and data—are essential to the function of your business and their loss will result in business failure. We have highlighted our original definition here because many people will designate too much of a business's information as critical. If this occurs and a huge amount of information is identified as important to maintain, the task of identifying and collecting this information can become overwhelming—perhaps even impossible. Instead, by limiting the amount of information that is truly necessary for your organization to continue operations, the task is not so insurmountable. Once this critical company information has been identified, there are many means to ensure backup of this information at a safe location. Use of off-site data storage centers is likely to be one of the best options and there are a variety of services that not only can store your organization's critical information but do so automatically. Based upon the threats and vulnerabilities to your company there may be simpler courses of action such as placing this information on your own backup devices and storing these in safes that are both fireproof and waterproof. Regardless of what option you consider, if your organization has not prepared for the collection and storage of critical company information prior to an incident, the results can be catastrophic, as research has shown that two of five small business enterprises that experienced a disaster went out of business within five years after the loss of their critical information.[1]

Transportation considerations must be identified and arranged prior to the kickoff of an actual emergency incident. In the event that evacuation becomes necessary and your employees are unable to use their own vehicles, either because of the nature of the emergency incident or because of damage to the parking areas and vehicles around your facility, it may become necessary that an individual must arrange some type of group transportation. This individual should be designated within your emergency response plans and he or she should explore various options—perhaps even obtain the necessary transportation if the risk is high enough—prior to, or immediately upon initiation of, the actual emergency incident. In many organizations, the need to arrange alternate transportation for your personnel may not be required; however, if you have not explored this possibility and prepared for it, and then find that it is necessary during an actual emergency, other organizations will have probably used the limited transportation methods available within your area and there will be none available for your own personnel.

Another consideration that should be planned for is medical supplies. Many organizations will simply assume that first responders will be able to care for any injuries that could be sustained in the event of an emergency incident. Because many different types of emergency situations will affect not only your own organization but many others within your local area, this assumption could result in an increase in the number of personnel hurt along with the potential for serious complications to those initially injured because your organization has not provided for some basic medical equipment and because your own personnel could have administered some basic medical care shortly after initiation of the emergency. Fortunately, there are some simple solutions that can minimize this possibility. One solution is to ensure your organization's emergency response plans address medical care in the event that paramedics or emergency personnel cannot immediately respond to your location. Within your plans, you should identify locations that can be used to care for any casualties and procedures that provide for the transport of any injured personnel to these areas—these areas are typically called casualty collection points (CCPs). Consolidating the injured personnel to CCPs will enable any personnel who are trained in first aid or emergency medical assistance to move to specifically identified locations and provide care as needed. To prepare to implement these procedures, it will also be necessary to obtain and store medical supplies to provide initial first aid for injured personnel prior to the arrival of medical responders. These medical supplies should include first-aid kits and portable stretchers that can be used to move any injured personnel. Many of these medical supplies should be consolidated at your organization's CCPs because these areas will be the primary locations where injured personnel will be taken. With these medical procedures and supplies prepared prior to any emergency incident, it is likely that you will not only minimize but also prevent serious medical consequences occurring to any personnel injured at the onset of the situation.

In the event that your employees are forced to shelter in place and they are unable to leave the facility for an extended period of time, it is important to plan and prepare for emergency food supplies to be available. There are an almost unlimited number of options that can meet this requirement—the only important factor is to ensure you have planned for this contingency by purchasing these supplies, storing them, and ensuring that your employees understand that these emergency food supplies are available through your emergency response plans.

The last resource that should be considered prior to the kickoff of any emergency incident are "go bags" for your organization's Crisis Management Team. These bags should be prepared ahead of time with any equipment necessary for each member to accomplish her or his duties during an actual incident. Equipment will typically include local area maps, diagrams of company facilities (to include interior and exterior plans), emergency communications equipment, and a copy of the emergency response plan and any applicable checklists. These go bags should be organized by each individual member of the Crisis Management Team and kept in her or his work area so that they can rapidly deploy to their designated locations at the initiation of an emergency.

All these items—considerations for critical information necessary to your company's continuation, transportation of your personnel, medical procedures and supplies, emergency food rations, and go bags for your Crisis Management Team—must be identified and consolidated prior to the start of an emergency. For each of these items there should also be a responsible individual identified who will ensure they are procured and stored, or coordinated, in accordance with the instructions detailed in your emergency response plans. These actions will greatly enhance your preparedness for a potential emergency incident.

Coordination

The next area we will cover in our discussion of preparation for an emergency response is coordination. This area works in concert with the command and control area, as it deals with the identification of roles and responsibilities during an emergency incident within the organization and with external groups—similar to the various responsibilities that form the overall chain of command in the event of an emergency incident. To ensure coordination occurs, both within your organization and with outside agencies, it is necessary to identify the tasks that should be accomplished and designate the responsible authority in the event of an emergency. It is also critical that your organization form the Crisis Management Team as rapidly as possible once the emergency has occurred. Because your Crisis Management Team oversees all your activities involved in your response to the emergency incident, coordination among the numerous agencies involved during the response will be difficult to initiate without this team's interaction and guidance. In addition to forming the Crisis Management Team, it is also necessary to conduct periodic training and exercises so that not only your organization but the key members of this team can practice and develop the necessary processes to enable them to work together to effectively coordinate their actions during an actual incident.

Congestion

The last area within preparedness that we will look at is the concept of congestion. Congestion refers to bottlenecks in the work flow of your organization. It is meant to identify areas of congestion within your organization and eliminate them to the maximum extent possible prior to the occurrence of an emergency incident.

Within your organization, there are likely to be *single-point failures* where critical tasks flow through one individual or a particular work section and which create some of this congestion. In many cases, these single-point failures are going to be your superb performers—the employees that can get virtually any task done quickly and efficiently, and owing to the qualities of these individuals, many work processes may become overly dependent upon them. During normal operations, this reliance may not be much of a problem (except when these individuals are on vacation or out of the office for any extended period of time); thus there may be no need to provide for allowances or redundancies so that other work sections can become able to accomplish some of these critical tasks as a backup. In the event of an emergency, however, these individuals who are single-point failures can quickly become overwhelmed owing to the significant amount of work that must be accomplished in a limited amount of time. By being overwhelmed, these individuals could create severe consequences to your organization's ability to respond if you continue to rely on these congestion points during your response to an incident. To alleviate some of this congestion, it is best to ensure there are methods to duplicate some of the effort, to assist with any critical tasks that may normally be accomplished by these key employees.

Overall, the best method to mitigate congestion—particularly in the event of an emergency—is to identify all the critical tasks that would be necessary to be accomplished within your organization and provide some redundancy to these efforts. By ensuring there are alternate people or work sections identified and trained so that they can not only assist with certain tasks but even accomplish the work should the primary personnel become unavailable or unable to accomplish that particular task, you will greatly enhance your preparedness for any emergency situation and alleviate much of the congestion that occurs during an incident.

Conclusions Regarding Preparedness

We have reviewed the five areas that should be considered when looking at your organization's preparedness: communications, command and control, collection and distribution of resources, coordination, and congestion. In addition to these areas and the discussion within this chapter, there are a variety of resources that will further assist you in preparing for an emergency—one of the best being the Ready.gov Web site created and maintained by the U.S. Department of Homeland Security. This Web site provides a significant amount of additional information and references that will help you in this preparation.

One of the primary ideas to take away from this chapter, however, is the need to have a formal set of emergency plans and procedures that cover all of these areas so that everyone within your organization understands the chain of command during response, the resources that will be available to assist during this response, and the roles and responsibilities of all your personnel in the event of an actual emergency incident. Again, we have provided a complete template of these plans in Appendix A. By combining this template with the information contained throughout this book, your organization will have a great starting point to develop these plans.

End Note

1. Emazzanti Technologies, *Selecting a Backup Solution for your Critical Information.* Retrieved from web on September 2, 2014, www.emazzanti.net.

Response

5

The next major planning factor that we discuss within emergency response is arguably the most important of all—how your organization actually reacts to an emergency as it occurs. This planning factor covers the actions that your personnel should take at the onset of the incident and throughout the initial phases of the situation. Response refers to the actions, processes, and procedures that should occur during the emergency to contain and control the situation. Once the incident has been contained and all necessary actions have been taken to stabilize the situation, the final emergency response planning factor—recovery—begins. Depending upon the type of emergency incident and the ability of your organization to accomplish the necessary actions, the process of response could take as little as minutes or it might take several days to complete. We cover this process of response over the course of this chapter and provide information on how to develop the necessary actions you should focus on within your emergency response planning so that it will assist you in containing a potential incident before the company can begin to work on recovery and restoration of its business capability.

The Two Primary Types of Response

Earlier in this book, we briefly discussed that there are basically only two primary types of response for any given emergency incident: either an evacuation or a shelter-in-place operation. Although there will be differences in the specific actions required by certain individuals or groups based upon the nature of the incident (i.e., natural disaster versus human-caused situation), limiting the response to only two types of actions will make it much easier to ensure your entire workforce acts appropriately if an emergency incident were actually to occur. With only two types of actions, the vast majority of your employees will need to remember only what they need to do in the event of either of these operations (evacuation or shelter in place). This will make it much easier for your organization to properly plan, train, and understand their roles; which will be critical to minimizing damage in the event of an emergency.

Deciding to Evacuate or Shelter in Place

The primary factor in deciding whether to order an evacuation or to have employees perform a shelter-in-place operation is always based on the type of incident and how to best ensure the safety of personnel—this includes not only your employees but also any visitors or individuals under the care of your business. Based on the type of emergency and the situation, your organization will need to decide whether it is safer to evacuate personnel who are located inside the affected facility or to shelter in place. Whereas some situations are fairly straightforward—for example, a fire always demands the immediate evacuation of personnel—decisions for other types of emergency situations may not be so obvious. For example, it was thought for many years that in the event of an active shooter incident, the correct decision was for all personnel within the building to shelter in place and lock down the facility. Owing to lessons learned and experiences gained with several active shooter situations, however, it has become apparent that this response action is not the safest or best option for all personnel. The vast majority of active shooter situations are resolved when the perpetrator either takes his or her own life or is killed by responding security or law enforcement personnel—and the end of these situations is almost always the former—and the time it takes the shooter to run out of ammunition or motivation and turn the gun upon himself or herself is relatively short. With this outcome in mind, the original accepted response of having personnel shelter in place and lock down the facility to prevent others from entering until law enforcement arrives simply allows for the active shooter to have unimpeded access inside the facility for an extremely long period of time—something that the perpetrator was looking for anyway. Based upon this analysis, the response to an active shooter incident has been revised to consider that individuals who can evacuate in a safe manner by avoiding contact with the intruder should get out of the facility as quickly as possible. This revised response calls for only a minimum number of personnel—specifically those in close proximity to the shooter who cannot safety evacuate the facility—to seek shelter and go into lockdown. Although these personnel are still at risk, because they must remain inside the facility with the perpetrator, their safety precludes any attempts to leave the building. Additionally, by evacuating all the other people within the building, it is hoped that the number of personnel in immediate danger is significantly lessened. Again, based on experience from these types of emergency incidents and the fact that active shooter situations are almost always resolved when either the shooter runs out of ammunition or first responders arrive and locate the shooter, this revised response action to this type of scenario has now become the more accepted practice. Although this is only one example to give you an idea of the need to have an accepted process to help determine whether you evacuate or have your personnel remain in place, you will need to quickly make the decision within your own organization to ensure the safety of the maximum number of personnel within your facility.

Although each individual situation is different, there are fortunately some guidelines to assist you in your decision whether to evacuate or shelter in place based on the type of emergency situation. These guidelines include not only the type of incident but other factors such as any available information regarding the emergency itself, use of that available information, the type of facility affected by the emergency (e.g., how secure and strong the building itself is), public notifications or warnings, and recommendations by first responders. It cannot be emphasized enough that a similar type of emergency could result in different decisions to evacuate or shelter in place based on some of these other factors; however, certain emergencies should consider one response action over the other during your initial decision-making process. For example, many types of major storms should cause evacuation to be considered as the first option to ensure safety of all personnel. If there has been a chemical hazard in your area and large amounts of debris in the air are observed, or if local authorities say the air is badly contaminated, it may be advisable to seal off your facility and shelter in place. The type of facility your organization is located in and how it is affected by the emergency will factor into your decision to evacuate or remain. For example, if your facility is in a bunker made of concrete and steel, your building will be able to withstand a severe storm, as opposed to if your organization operated out of a temporary structure, and you may decide to keep all your critical resources within the facility during a natural disaster. Listening to the television or radio, or frequently checking the Internet for information or official instructions, will also assist in your decision. A final factor that will assist in your decision is based upon any instructions by law enforcement, fire department personnel, or health department officials. If they instruct you specifically to evacuate or seek medical treatment, do so immediately. As we look at each of the two response actions—evacuation and shelter in place—we will discuss different types of emergency incidents and provide some specific guidance on what actions and procedures should be included in your organization's emergency response plans based upon those particular events.

Evacuation

When considering whether to evacuate personnel, the most obvious question to ask is whether people are safer outside the facility as opposed to remaining in place. We discussed many of the items that should assist in your decision, so once the determination to evacuate has been made, the next step is to determine where your personnel will need to evacuate to (Figure 5.1). To ensure your evacuation plans account for all scenarios, these plans should include procedures that involve both short- and long-distance scenarios. Let us explore what we mean by these two types of evacuations. Short-distance evacuations are normally accomplished in the event that immediate evacuation from the building is necessary but personnel do not need to move any great distance from the building to ensure their safety. Examples of this type of evacuation

Figure 5.1 Evacuation.

include fire drills or equipment breakdowns that could create hazards within a relatively small immediate area. Long-distance evacuations are necessary when larger
hazardous areas could cause danger to personnel over greater distances. These types
of evacuations may be due to bomb threats, radiological concerns, or chemical contamination, and in many cases, long-distance evacuations should be considered when
walking is impractical owing to distance or weather considerations. The obvious disadvantage to a long-distance evacuation is the need to travel, which creates the potential requirement for alternate transportation to move personnel to safe areas. These
added logistical requirements cannot be overlooked in your planning for long-distance
evacuation scenarios.

As part of your evacuation planning, you should also include procedures that assist
with movement control for individuals leaving the facility, shutdown of any equipment, and assembly areas. All these areas should be considered within your emergency response plans and should also be considered when developing your evacuation
plans. Movement control procedures should provide guidelines to assist in evacuating
a facility in the most rapid, safe, and effective manner. These procedures should ensure
any routes and exits are clearly delineated and marked, both in your plans and, if possible, with clearly visible signs along the primary evacuation pathways. These routes
should be kept clear of debris and any office equipment that could hinder movement
at all times because one never knows when an evacuation will be necessary. These
routes should also be wide enough to accommodate the large numbers of personnel
who would need to evacuate the facility. Procedures for this movement control should
also include the designation of personnel to act as wardens to assist with the evacuation of personnel as they depart from their work areas and building. These evacuation
wardens have the responsibility of being posted in specific locations that could create
backups of individuals as they evacuate the facility and helping to move employees
through these areas to remove them from danger into safe areas. Generally, one warden for every 20 employees is an adequate rule of thumb to use when identifying these
individuals within your emergency response plans. These movement control procedures can greatly assist personnel who may be nervous and scared, preventing any
potential injuries from panic in the event of an actual emergency.

Depending on the nature of the emergency and the time personnel will take to evacuate from the facility, it may be advisable to shut down certain equipment or manufacturing processes if individual safety is not compromised. This process should entail
designating certain employees to briefly operate fire extinguishers or shut down gas
and/or electrical systems and other special equipment that could either be damaged if
left in operation or create additional hazards for first responders (such as the release of
hazardous materials). For these potentialities, your procedures should cover instances
in which this may be necessary for your particular operation along with what specific
systems and equipment should be shut down.

Once an evacuation has been initiated, the last consideration is the need to identify
the locations of gathering points or assembly areas for both short- and long-distance
scenarios. Obviously, the need to identify assembly areas is a critical item because
personnel must know where they are going once they have moved outside the facility,
but this process must be emphasized to all personnel so that once they move to these

preestablished locations your organization can proper account for all personnel. It is also important to designate assembly areas not only outside the facility but also inside your workplace, in the event that a long-distance evacuation becomes necessary. Necessary space is another consideration when determining assembly areas, so you must make sure any designated assembly areas have sufficient space to accommodate all of your employees. Exterior assembly areas, used when the building must be partially or completely evacuated, are typically located in parking lots or other open areas away from busy streets. Consider the possibility that employees could interfere with rescue operations and work to minimize this possibility when designating your evacuation assembly areas by keeping these areas away from likely approaches for these emergency responders. An additional consideration is to try and designate assembly areas so that you will be upwind from your building (based upon the most common or prevailing wind direction) to minimize the threat from any hazardous material spill. A final consideration is based upon the need for a long-distance evacuation, in that procedures must be established for further evacuation in case the incident expands. This may consist of sending employees home by normal means or providing them with transportation to an offsite location. With these considerations in mind, you should be able to tailor evacuation plans for your organization that can be included into your overall emergency response plan.

Shelter in Place

The other response action we will look at is the shelter-in-place operation (Figure 5.2). As discussed earlier, this is done when it is necessary to have personnel remain. There are two primary types of shelter in place that should be considered within your emergency response plans: lockdown and sealing off areas of a facility. A lockdown is accomplished to protect individuals from some type of threat—this could be protection from the effects of a natural disaster or to avoid detection against some type of hostile intruder. In a lockdown, all personnel hide in the room they find themselves in at the onset of the incident, lock and barricade any entry points, and attempt to remain hidden within a room. The other type of shelter-in-place operation is designed to provide the ability to seal off specific areas of the facility using equipment and

Figure 5.2 Shelter in place.

procedures to provide some level of protection against any type of hazardous material containment.

There are several considerations that should be accounted for in any emergency response plan to provide adequate procedures for a lockdown. If a lockdown is implemented through notification of the facility, the first step personnel must take is to immediately move out of hallways or open spaces and into rooms that can be secured with a door or by blocking the entrances. This does not mean that people should move to their individual offices, because this could require longer distances to move, but instead employees must be trained to move to the nearest room that can be secured. In the event of a severe weather emergency, personnel should remain in the center of the room, away from exterior windows, and remain in place until emergency personnel have notified everyone that it is safe to leave. For emergencies involving workplace violence or a hostile intruder, once people are inside an available room they should attempt to protect themselves against these threats by locking the door, blocking any windows that provide observation into that room, and using furniture to barricade the doorway or entrance. Once these actions have been accomplished, the next step against a hostile intruder is for personnel to use any remaining furniture as shelter and cover, placing themselves against these items to protect them against any hostile threats and remain hidden and quiet. If it is safe to leave the building without detection by any hostile intruders, personnel should do so; however, if this is not possible, employees should not attempt to leave the room until emergency personnel have entered the room and checked the area.

In the event of a shelter-in-place operation requiring that areas of the building be sealed off to contain any hazardous materials, the following procedures should be implemented.[1]

- Shut and lock all windows and doors.
- Turn off all air-handling equipment (heating, ventilation, and/or air conditioning).
- Establish a predetermined sheltering room (or rooms) and ensure personnel know these areas so they can proceed to them upon notification of this type of shelter in place.
- Ensure plastic and duct tape are procured and stored in these locations, so that employees can seal any windows and vents using these materials.
- Seal the door(s) with duct tape around the top and sides and place a wet towel at the bottom of the door.
- Turn on a television or radio and listen for further instructions.
- When the "all clear" notification is announced, open windows and doors, turn on the ventilation systems, and evacuate the facility until the building's air has been exchanged and refreshed.

Some additional items involving shelter-in-place sealing procedures should also be considered. First, employees cannot be forced to shelter in place, so it is important to maximize cooperation of all employees in your shelter plan. The next consideration is that specific employees should be assigned duties involved in the sheltering plan and alternate employees should also be assigned to these responsibilities. By including these procedures and considerations into your sheltering steps within your emergency response plan, you will be much better prepared to keep your personnel and organization safe in the event of a hazardous materials incident.

Key Elements of Emergency Response

The key elements of response to any emergency incident are the protection of human life; accountability for your personnel in the event of an emergency; reduction of the exposure, damage, and loss to your organization's critical assets; and the prevention or minimization of personal injury to individuals. To ensure your planning meets these elements, it is important to consider the following areas for any type of emergency response:

- Command and management of emergency operations
- Accountability
- Fire management operations
- Security and traffic control operations
- Internal rescue operations
- Emergency medical operations
- Staff care

We will look at each of these areas separately over the next several sections.

Command and Management of Emergency Operations

Managing emergency operations provides for the overall implementation, conduct, and coordination of your organization's emergency response plan over the course of a situation. This not only involves the management and control of your organization's personnel within the facility but should also cover the necessary coordination of your organization's various functions with outside agencies that are assisting with any response activities.

We have already touched upon the best method to command and manage emergency operations—designation and formation of your Crisis Management Team—and we delineate specifics for this team, along with each member's tasks and responsibilities, in Chapter 7; however, there are some general items to consider in relation to commanding and managing an emergency. Once any type of incident has initiated, it is necessary to determine where the Crisis Management Team will operate during the incident so that this information can be clearly communicated to the entire group to enable them to begin to manage the organization's overall emergency response activities. Some additional actions that are important in commanding and managing the response are to determine and develop procedures within your emergency response plans regarding how the organization's staff will conduct personnel notifications, recall any key employees not included in the Crisis Management Team but that are required to respond to the incident, and accomplish communications to the organization's employees and the public throughout the response. You must clearly identify the specific individuals who will perform the recall and have alternate plans in case the local phone system is down. As discussed earlier, you must have the ability to notify personnel within all your facilities and work areas to ensure employees can take the appropriate actions in accordance with your plans.

Another area regarding command and management of an incident that must be considered prior to the onset of any emergency is communication with the media and community. We discussed earlier the need to designate a point of contact who will handle all the communication with the press. This task moves into the next responsibility that helps manage your organization's response to an emergency—that of communication and coordination, both within the organization and with the public and the community and with external agencies. As we discussed earlier, these tasks will be probably need to be carried out by different people. The responsibility of communicating and coordinating within the organization and with the public will typically fall to the same individual responsible for public information or public relations and who would be coordinating with the media. It is important that this individual be designated and all employees understand that this person should be the sole employee in communication with the press so that there is no miscommunication or confusion occurring during the actual response to an incident. If your emergency response plans do not specifically cover these aspects of communication and coordination with the media and public, it could result in a great deal of damage to the perception of your organization as you progress through response action to the emergency situation. Other functional experts will probably be the best people to coordinate with external agencies that provide aid or relief, and these communications should fall within their typical areas of responsibility. For example, the individual responsible for maintenance of the facility should identify and work with agencies that provide financial relief and support to repair the building and its infrastructure. By designating these personnel, along with any procedures regarding contact with the media, your organization and employees will be much better prepared to manage the response to any type of emergency incident.

The final task that is part of commanding and managing the emergency response operations is to develop and implement a reporting system with the purpose of providing information to the Crisis Management Team over the course of the incident. This process should not only provide updates on the ongoing situation but also include feedback and any areas of concern that are identified throughout the response phase of the incident. One of the responsibilities that should be included within the Crisis Management Team, but that is sometimes overlooked, is the need for personnel performing administrative support. With these personnel, you will be able to conduct accurate record-keeping of any information obtained throughout the response phase of the incident and, as a result, your organization should then be able to conduct an after-action review once all response activities have been accomplished. The purpose of this after-action review is to review the overall response to the situation, review all actions and feedback, evaluate any problems that exist within your current emergency response procedures, and correct these deficiencies in your emergency response plans. It should be noted that this task can be extremely difficult to accomplish at the conclusion of an actual emergency, as personnel will be motivated to simply move on after the emergency and resume normal business operations; however, this after-action review is an important aspect of your emergency response program and not only will improve your ability to respond to emergencies but also can make your entire organization better.

Accountability

Although this item is listed as only one of the key elements within the response phase of emergency operations, accountability of personnel is arguably one of the most important tasks your organization will need to accomplish over the course of the entire incident. No matter what type of business your company performs, at the initiation of any type of emergency incident the first question on everyone's mind—including families of your employees, citizens in the local community, and the media—will be focused on the number of injuries and of any personnel who are missing as a result of the situation. An example of the need to have a process that accurately accounts for your employees can be found during the events of 9/11. The majority of the communication surrounding this tragic event focused on the casualties and obtaining the status of friends and family members that were injured or missing during the attacks on the World Trade Center and the Pentagon. Without a process to provide accountability for your organization's employees throughout the emergency situation, however, determining these numbers will be an impossible task. Furthermore, even if you have a process in place to accomplish this task, if it does not perform this accountability in an accurate and exact manner, you will create further issues both during and after the incident by creating a negative impression of your organization that will affect future prospects for your business. To ensure you have the necessary tools for this accountability, we now look at processes to ensure it can be accomplished, even during the confusion of an ongoing emergency, and next, we provide some methods to ensure this process works effectively so that you can be confident you will provide accurate counts of personnel in the event of an incident.

To accomplish a thorough accountability of personnel within your organization, you must first ensure that you have a known and accurate baseline number of all employees and visitors to your facility at any given time. Regarding your employees, if your organization does not conduct daily checks of the number of employees who have come to work and report these numbers to a centralized point of contact, it is difficult to know how many people are out of the office on a daily basis. These reports not only ensure the ability to accurately account for all your employees in the event of an emergency but also allow your organization to be aware of all employees that are on duty, on vacation or leave, out on a business trip, or missing. By having this awareness, it will be easier for your entire team to conduct business operations in an efficient and effective manner. If you do not already accomplish some type of daily workforce assessment, it is a necessity to establish such a process, not only for your daily work effort but also to account for employee numbers during an actual emergency. In addition to your own workforce, the other aspect that must be accounted for are any visitors to your facility. In the event of an emergency, your organization will be held responsible by the public and media for accounting for any visitors that were within your facility at the time of the incident and reporting their status (e.g., injured, missing, etc.). As with your regular employees, your organization must have a process that is practiced at all times to account for any visitors and the ability to know when these individuals have entered and departed your business location. This can be done in a variety of methods. One method is to provide every visitor to your facility with an escort—this escort should be an employee who will be responsible for the visitor during her or his entire stay within the facility and will maintain contact with the individual over the course of her or his visit. In the event of an emergency, the escort will be responsible for instructing the visitor on the proper actions and will report the visitor's presence when the numbers accountability for all other personnel is being conducted. Another method to account for visitors is to have some type of a sign-in/sign-out log. As visitors enter and leave the facility, they provide some basic information in a log, including their name, their organization, the time they arrived, and the time they departed. An alternate method to the sign-in/sign-out log is the use of visitor badges. This method does not require the individual to sign in as he or she enters the facility, but instead an employee who monitors entry and exit into your facility issues numbered visitor badges and your employee annotates when the visitor badge has been issued and returned. Both the sign-in/sign-out log and the visitor badge are methods of accounting for nonemployees within your facility that provide the numbers of and accountability for these personnel that were under the care of your organization in the event of an emergency. A disadvantage of these two methods is that your business must have an individual that acts as an entry controller into your facility, which results in the addition of an employee within your organization (if you do not already utilize an individual in this position). This employee can be a security guard or simply a receptionist; however, these personnel must be located at any unsecured entry point that provides unimpeded public access into your facility to ensure they are able to account for all personnel entering and departing the building. As we discussed during our coverage of access control, it is best to limit these entry points to only one location to better control the personnel who enter and exit the facility; however, these methods will still require an employee to monitor this entry and maintain any logs or visitor badges as required.

Once you have developed your accountability methods to provide an accurate baseline for both employees and any visitors, you can now focus on processes that provide for the accountability of personnel in the event of an actual emergency. Although there are some minor variations in these processes depending on the type of response action—either an evacuation or shelter in place—there is a basic process that provides a foundation for any variations in reporting this accountability based on the specific type of response. This basic process should mirror your daily workforce accountability reporting system that we discussed earlier. Normally, the best process is to simply have the lowest-level work sections and supervisors within your organization conduct a count of personnel and report any missing individuals, along with their status (e.g., injured, missing, etc.), up their chain of command to a centralized individual—normally your organization's human resources point of contact who is a member of the Crisis Management Team. This human resources point of contact will then consolidate the information and report the results to the organization's Crisis Management Team. For visitors, the same process applies. If you choose to use an escort system, these visitors would be included in the reports submitted by any work sections the escort belongs to; and with the use of a sign-in/sign-out log or visitor badge system, the entry controller would report any visitors still under your organization's care so that their status can be determined.

With this basic foundation for determining accountability of personnel in the event of an emergency, we now discuss any variations based on the type of response action. During an evacuation, this accountability should take place once personnel have reached their designated assembly areas; the accountability process should not slow down the rapid movement away from any areas that could pose a danger. This can become challenging as the evacuation distance increases, so it is important to ensure you consider the accountability process within your emergency response plans, particularly in the event that a long-distance evacuation becomes necessary to ensure safety of all personnel. As we have already discussed, the importance of the task of accomplishing this accountability cannot be emphasized enough, as most of the initial questions—and many of the issues you will probably deal with over the course of the situation—will deal with the number of employees missing, injured, or dead. Again, accounting for all employees after an evacuation is critical, as confusion in the assembly areas can lead to delays in rescuing anyone trapped in the building or to unnecessary and dangerous search-and-rescue operations.

In the event of a shelter-in-place response, accountability can become a little more challenging because personnel will be moving to the nearest safe area at the initiation of the incident—this area could very well be in a location different from their normal work space. If the sheltering occurs owing to a hazardous material incident, accountability should be easier to accomplish because communication with the sealed-off areas is possible, either by landline telephone or cell phone, to determine the status of all personnel. In the event of a shelter-in-place response owing to a hostile intruder, communication will be much more difficult, possibly even impossible, with any personnel who were unable to evacuate the facility. In this case, accountability of all evacuees should be conducted using the standard methods discussed earlier. For any personnel that are unaccounted for, the organization should then begin to determine if they are still inside the facility or if they are safe from harm. Additionally, personnel who are trapped inside the facility with a hostile intruder will contact an outside agency (normally law enforcement), so your organization should continue to coordinate with these external agencies to determine if they have any contact with your employees and you can ascertain their status and update your accountability information. If communication with individuals inside the facility is impossible or you do not have firm information on the status of any other missing employees, this accountability will have to wait until the situation is resolved.

Once again, we cannot emphasize enough the importance of being able to conduct an accurate accounting of personnel—for both your own organization's employees and any visitors to your facility—in the event of an emergency. To accomplish this accountability, your organization must conduct daily personnel counts during normal business operations to ensure you have an accurate baseline and then have adequate procedures to ensure this accounting can be conducted during an actual emergency incident.

Fire Management Operations

Fire management operations are another area that addresses the key elements within emergency response and assists with the command and management of any incident. Adequate planning within this area limits the loss of life and property that could occur to your organization, and to effectively accomplish this, it is important that your organization liaise with local fire departments prior to an actual incident to ensure that both your company and the local fire department are aware of each other's plans in the event of an emergency. This coordination will also ensure that your evacuation planning meets any local requirements and regulations. Another consideration within your organization's fire management operations is to provide for specific personnel who would assist any rescue units, if requested by fire department officers. A final area should include a description of the building layout and available fire suppression systems within the facility. All this information should be included within your evacuation plans and procedures, which should be coordinated with your local fire department officials.

Security and Traffic Control Operations

Security and traffic control operations are another element necessary for emergency response management. These operations should enforce applicable orders and company policies within your facility grounds to provide the orderly movement of personnel in and out of the facility and its property in the event of an emergency. Of particular concern within this emergency response element are two key functions: crowd and traffic control. We have already covered the methods to assist with crowd control, which include the designation of routes and evacuation wardens, but there are some additional considerations regarding traffic control and assisting with the movement of personnel away from the facility once they have exited the building.

In the event of an actual emergency and notification of an evacuation, many employees will want to get away from the facility as quickly as possible, so traffic control is an aspect that your organization should plan for. Added to the evacuation of your own employees is the presence of emergency responders and other agencies that will need to simultaneously gain access to assist with the response efforts and this could result in some major traffic issues. These conflicting traffic flows can result in congestion and potentially create more complications to an already critical situation. For this reason, it is critical that your organization have plans to ensure that employees wishing to leave the area do not hinder access by the inbound emergency responders. This can be accomplished by assigning employees to provide this traffic control to help with both the evacuation and the emergency response actions.

As a result of the necessity of providing this traffic and crowd control, there are a couple major tasks that should be considered within your emergency response plans. First, it is necessary to assign personnel responsible to conduct security and traffic control and coordinate their activities with local law enforcement agencies. Next, the ability to communicate with any personnel tasked to conduct this movement control is necessary to provide direction as needed to their activities, and any communication equipment, along with any additional resources needed to accomplish security and traffic control operations, must be procured, stored, and made available to applicable personnel fulfilling these duties in the event of an emergency.

Within your emergency response plans, you need to identify specific personnel that will provide traffic and crowd control, along with where they should report at the initial announcement of an evacuation. Many organizations are hesitant to directly task certain personnel with duties in the event of an emergency, thinking that these responsibilities can be divided out at the onset of an emergency; however, nothing could be further from the truth. Once an emergency incident kicks off, the Crisis Management Team will be overwhelmed with details associated with that particular incident and they will be unable, or they will forget, to task out this and the many other duties that must be performed. By including this information and any roles and responsibilities tasked out prior to the onset of an incident, it will be ensured that these tasks are performed and thus prevent other issues from arising over the course of the emergency response. Once these individuals have been identified, it is recommended that you coordinate with local law enforcement prior to establishing your detailed procedures regarding security and traffic control. By coordinating your proposed plans with local law enforcement you will not only ensure that your actions do not detract from their ability to respond to your facility, but you should also prevent any potential congestion mishaps from occurring. Your discussions with these law enforcement professionals prior to finalizing your plans will also provide you with valuable information and perspective from other areas to improve your traffic and crowd control procedures.

Once these plans have been finalized, your organization will need to ensure you have the ability to communicate with any mobile personnel tasked to conduct this traffic and crowd control. This is important because these traffic control monitors will be located outside the facility and in congested and busy locations. This communication can be accomplished by ensuring you have adequate radios for these personnel (remember that cell phones should not be depended on in the event of an emergency, as discussed earlier), along with any associated equipment such as batteries and charger units. There may also be additional resources and equipment necessary to accomplish these security and traffic control operations, including traffic cones, barricades, and other associated equipment, to assist in the smooth flow of personnel and vehicles during an emergency incident.

By having plans and procedures to assist with crowd and traffic control in the event of an evacuation, your organization should be able to minimize any damage or injury that could occur. This can be accomplished by designating individual employees to act as traffic control monitors, providing them with the communications and other necessary equipment, and coordinating these plans with local law enforcement agencies.

Internal Rescue Operations

If the emergency situation extends well beyond your own company and facility it will affect other agencies and personnel within your area and possibly even the entire region. This can occur with a natural emergency such as earthquakes, severe storms, or floods. In these types of incidents that affect large areas, emergency responders will probably be overwhelmed and possibly unable to respond to your location in a timely manner. To ensure your organization is prepared for this eventuality, your emergency response plans should prepare employees to conduct your own internal rescue operations within the facility and immediate area.

The Crisis Management Team should be prepared to designate specific individuals to carry out these internal rescue operations. These tasks should include coordinated search and rescue operations for the facility and the surrounding area, providing immediate care for any injured personnel (we cover this item in greater detail in our discussion on emergency medical operations below), and safely removing employees from any damaged areas within the building. To conduct these rescue operations, it is necessary to determine and develop a process to locate and mark areas where there may be trapped individuals and establish safe zones to remove personnel to from areas where the facility is severely damaged. To assist with these tasks, ensure that maps and floor plans are available for searches, and designate employees to serve as guides for rescue teams. It is important to note that employees cannot be forced to partake in these rescue efforts, so care must be taken when designating these individuals. It is also important to coordinate these plans with local rescue agencies, particularly fire officials, to ensure you do not violate any requirements these agencies may have when they are eventually able to respond to your location.

Emergency Medical Operations

Including emergency medical operations within your emergency response plans will ensure your organization can provide for the treatment of personnel injured as a result of the incident. We have already reviewed some basic emergency medical operations, including designation of casualty collection points and consolidation of any medical equipment in these areas to assist with immediate care to injured personnel prior to the arrival of paramedics or other medical personnel. Your medical planning should also include coordination with a coroner in the tragic event of a death involving one of your employees as a result of the incident. Emergency medical operations must plan for actions in the event of multiple casualties, including locating, collecting, and transporting injured personnel for treatment until the arrival of medical professionals. Two major tasks are involved in this function: employee accountability and establishment of first aid and casualty collection points.

The first task involved in emergency medical operations is accounting for your employees and identifying causalities. We have already discussed the importance of employee accountability and how the human resources point of contact within your Crisis Management Team should manage this effort; however, the importance of this task cannot be overstated. Accounting for all your employees and visitors is critical because the primary focus of many emergencies rapidly moves from affects of the incident itself toward identification of all involved personnel. The particular emphasis on these individuals will focus on the exact numbers and names of individuals who have sustained any significant injuries or death. This focus is inevitable and will occur in every type of emergency that involves the potential for injury and so we cannot emphasize enough the criticality that your organization develop, and be able to accomplish, a thorough process to ensure accurate accounting of all personnel who were in your facility at the time of an incident.

To assist with the task of locating and collecting any casualties, prior to their transport to medical facilities and trauma centers, it is necessary to establish a minimum number of centralized locations where your organization will conduct immediate medical care. As we have discussed earlier, by establishing a casualty collection point

Figure 5.3 Emergency medical care, casualty collection, and triage.

(CCP) in an area within your facility and prepositioning first aid kits and other medical equipment, this will greatly assist in your organization's ability to respond and treat any medical injuries. Prior to any incident your organization should identify a specific location, or several locations depending upon the size of your facility, where injured personnel would be brought—again, these areas are termed casualty collection points (Figure 5.3). These areas allow for personnel with medical knowledge and training to gather at the initiation of the emergency to provide care to the injured personnel. By having these CCPs within your emergency response plans, you will enhance the possibility of saving some critically injured personnel by providing a plan, as opposed to having employees try to move through the entire facility themselves to find any individuals requiring medical care. These CCPs should have basic first aid kits and medical equipment to help in initially treating the injured and also have equipment to transport the injured, such as folding stretchers. It is also advisable that you coordinate the location of your predesignated CCPs with first responders, so that they are aware of where to respond so that they can concentrate their care on the critically injured.

In the event of any death, the primary assistance for your organization is to provide the coroners with information regarding the identification of the remains and the disposition of personal effects. Identification of the remains should be accomplished by conducting the accountability of all employees through the methods discussed earlier. Another consideration is the disposition of the deceased's personal effects. This task will very likely fall upon your organization, although this should be confirmed prior to an incident by research into your area's requirements and procedures of your local law enforcement department. If this task does fall to your company, it is important to take an inventory of any items found that belonged to the deceased, collect them into a sealed package, and store them in a secured area—much like any procedures that would be involved with collecting and storing evidence. In this manner, when the employee's next of kin is ready to pick up his or her effects, they can be provided with both the inventory and the sealed packet containing all the items so that they are assured they are receiving all their loved one's property.

Preventive medicine is another consideration of emergency medical operations and provides for public health and sanitation services during the incident. Two primary considerations within preventive medicine are to ensure drinking water is available and sanitation services are provided in the event that personnel must remain in the facility for any lengthy period of time and public water and sewage are inoperative owing to the incident. Storing bottled drinking water and determining a source of chemical toilets, should the need arise, before the actual emergency resolves these concerns. We discuss storage of water and other items necessary to assist your staff in the next section.

Staff Care

As discussed, some types of emergencies can last for a lengthy period of time and, as a result, there may be some basic human needs that should be planned for in the event of these types of incidents. These needs include food, water, lodging, and even child care, to name just a few items. Based on the nature of any emergency that would require these necessities, it must be remembered that every other organization within your area would also require these resources once an emergency situation has kicked off, so it is best to plan ahead and procure and store a minimum amount of these types of supplies well before any incident.

With regard to food, water, and other necessities required by personnel over the course of an emergency, it is best to put together a disaster supply kit and store these items in various locations throughout the facility. Items that should be included in a disaster supply kit are as follows:

- Medical supplies and first aid manual (unless you have already provided for these and stored them in designated CCPs as part of your planning)
- Hygiene supplies
- Portable radio and extra batteries
- Flashlights and/or lanterns with extra batteries
- Camping cook stove and fuel
- Sterno cans
- Matches in a waterproof container
- Blankets
- Useful tools to dig or break out of a location, such as a shovel, ax, sledge hammer, pick, and saw
- Can opener, utensils, and cookware

Several of these items will need to be checked on a periodic basis to ensure that they are in good working condition and, where applicable, that they have not reached their expiration date. In addition to these disaster supply kits, having an ample supply of clean water in the event of an emergency is a top priority. A normally active person needs to drink at least two quarts of water each day—people in hot environments, children, nursing mothers, and ill people require even more.[2] In addition to drinking water, storing water for hygiene and food preparation may also be required based on your organization's particular risks and concerns. If you consider storing water for these additional purposes, people will typically need one gallon per day. In the event of an emergency, if supplies of water are running low it is best to not ration water. Instead, people should drink the amount of water they need for that day and attempt to try and find more water the next day. Individuals can always minimize the amount of water their bodies need by reducing activity and staying dry and cool. Food is the other primary item that should be considered, in addition to the items within a disaster supply kit. There are many emergency food options that should be considered and can be used in the event of a situation. These emergency food options will store for lengthy periods of time and are relatively inexpensive. Some examples include military Meals Ready to Eat, or MREs, along with many other emergency food packets that are readily available to purchase. Regardless of what emergency food option you decide upon, all these items—disaster supply kit, water, and food—should be procured and stored in a location that is accessible to most employees in the event of an emergency. It should be noted, however, that you will need to ensure that employees understand these supplies are not to be tampered with or used until an actual emergency and develop a process to periodically check these items to ensure they are available in the necessary quantities and condition to meet individuals' needs during an actual emergency.

As mentioned earlier, there may be other staff considerations that your emergency response plans should address based upon your organization's goals in the aftermath of an emergency. These considerations can include providing for transportation, lodging, and child care for your employees. Many emergency response plans will not address these issues, as many businesses feel these issues would fall under the purview of an individual's insurance policy; however, it may be something you should consider based upon your company's culture, the region you are located in, and the types of risk that could result in certain types of emergencies.

All of these items will assist in caring for your staff in the event of an emergency incident and what requirements you choose to address within your emergency response plans will depend on the nature of the incidents your organization may experience and the length of time the emergency and its effects may last, along with your company's culture regarding the level of care for your employees.

Summary of the Response Phase

Over the course of our discussion on response, we initially covered the two primary types of response actions: evacuation or shelter in place. Although specific actions will always differ based on the unique circumstances surrounding that particular situation, one of the initial decisions for your organization is whether to implement one of these two primary response actions and if so, which one. By limiting your response actions to either evacuation or shelter in place, the task of preparing your emergency response plans becomes much easier, as does the task of training your employees to better understand their roles and responsibilities in the event of an actual incident.

We also discussed the key elements of emergency response, which are protecting human life, preventing or minimizing injuries, reducing potential damage to your organization's critical resources, and accountability for your organization's employees and visitors. To ensure these elements were addressed, we looked at several different areas that assist in covering these items. These include command and management, accountability, fire management, security and traffic control, internal rescue operations, emergency medical operations, and staff care. By addressing each of these areas within your organization's emergency response plan, you should ensure coverage of the key elements involved in your emergency response.

End Notes

1. National Institute for Chemical Studies, *Shelter in Place at Your Office: A General Guide for Preparing a Shelter in Place Plan in the Workplace*, (November 1999). Retrieved from web on September 04, 2014, www.nicsinfo.org.
2. Federal Emergency Management Agency, *Food and Water in an Emergency*, (Department of Homeland Security, August 2004). Retrieved from web on September 05, 2014, www.fema.gov.

Recovery

6

Recovery is the fourth and last emergency response planning factor that we will cover. This phase covers the planning and considerations necessary to reestablish full functionality of an organization and its business capability after the incident has been contained through response efforts. The unfortunate aspect of recovery is that this process can be lengthy. Although most emergency incidents will normally last a relatively short period of time, the recovery from such an event could take days, weeks, months, or even years, in extreme cases, until your organization is able to match production levels achieved prior to the emergency. The need to plan for recovery is critical, however, because many businesses that fail to prepare for an incident are unable to ever recover and they eventually fail. For this reason, it is vital for your organization that you include recovery in your emergency response plans.

To move the recovery process along as rapidly as possible and reestablish full functionality of the business, there are various actions that must be accomplished. These include:

- Damage assessment
- Cleanup and salvage operations
- Customer and client information
- Mutual aid and agreement activities
- Business restoration

Many of these tasks can be done in concert with one another and each of them can require specific and separate expertise to ensure they are accomplished properly, so it is best to organize teams to carry out each of these functions within your organization. Although many of these teams may require the same functional expertise, having separate and specific teams will help to divide up much of the work and synergize these recovery efforts so that your organization can achieve its full business capability as quickly as possible. There are several functions within each of these actions that can be accomplished prior to the actual recovery phase of an incident to help speed up recovery. Over the following sections, we look at each of these tasks and cover what is involved, to help you not only to understand what should be accomplished but also to ensure these functions are completed in a comprehensive manner. Once we have covered the first four recovery actions, we then look at business continuity planning. Although this subject relates to both preparedness and recovery, we have included this area within our discussion on emergency response recovery, and its importance deserves a detailed and separate discussion.

Damage Assessment

This action should be the first accomplished by an organization as it enters the recovery phase—in fact, it can sometimes even be started while response actions are still taking place. The purpose of damage assessment is to estimate the damage and collect related information and data highlighting equipment and areas of the facility that require repair or new construction to resume normal business operations. Damage assessment is a preliminary evaluation of damage or loss caused by the incident and is meant to assist in the determination of what can be replaced, restored, or salvaged. The information and data gained from an accurate damage assessment not only help to guide other recovery actions through the establishment of priorities and goals, but also will be used as you progress to the other actions that form the recovery phase of emergency response. With the information obtained from the damage assessment, you will be able to determine time estimates required to repair, replace, and construct areas that are necessary for the overall recovery of the business. Additionally, the cost estimates and information regarding productivity losses are necessary when requesting assistance from government agencies and insurance companies that can provide resources to aid in recovery.

Before discussing the specific areas involved in accomplishing damage assessment, we first look at some preparation tasks that are critical to obtaining the required information. The most important area of preparation that will aid in your organization's damage assessment process depends upon accurate record-keeping of your building facility. This includes an up-to-date inventory and detailed information of all equipment (i.e., number, make, model, etc.). It should also include structural drawings of the facility and infrastructure. Without this initial baseline of what resources your company started with prior to the actual incident, it will be virtually impossible to determine what damage has been done as a result of an emergency. For this reason, it is critical that your organization maintain detailed inventories and surveys of the facility and your critical business equipment. With accurate inventories, it will be much easier to develop itemized lists of all damage, including photographic documentation that occurred as a result of the emergency. In addition, these detailed surveys will also assist and streamline the reimbursement process with insurance underwriters and government officials.

Another preparatory item to consider for the damage assessment is to define roles and responsibilities for the various tasks that will need to be accomplished within your organization's emergency response plans. There are several different areas of expertise that are required and should be tasked to the team and its individual members conducting the damage assessment. A critical functional expertise within this process comes from facility and maintenance personnel who can assess damaged areas within the building or various equipment items that will need to be repaired or purchased. Another work area to include in this team is human resources personnel. These experts should be included in the damage assessment process to identify required duty positions that have become unavailable in the aftermath of the incident owing to injuries or loss of employees as a result of the event. Another functional expertise that should be included in this group is financial personnel. These employees must be involved in the damage assessment process to provide the cost analysis necessary to assist with many decisions involved in the reestablishment of business operations. A last function that should be considered for inclusion in the team conducting your organization's damage assessment would be health and safety personnel. These individuals not only can provide assistance to ensure the facility is rendered safe for employees to work after any repairs have been made, but also can assist with many of the requirements that go along with workplace safety throughout recovery. Your emergency response planning should clearly define specific personnel to accomplish these tasks as you enter the recovery phase and perform damage assessment.

Once these preparatory actions involved with damage assessment have been accomplished (again, these actions include maintaining established inventories prior to the initiation of an incident and forming a team with defined roles and responsibilities of specific personnel to assist with this recovery task) your organization will be better able to perform the necessary functions that ensure a comprehensive damage assessment has been accomplished. These functions can be divided into four general tasks to assist in the ease of planning and division of responsibilities. These tasks include an initial situation overview, an initial damage assessment, a damage assessment and needs analysis, and a damage and loss assessment. We look at each of these items over the following sections.

Initial Situation Overview

The initial situation overview task within damage assessment is carried out as quickly as possible after resolution of the emergency. This task is meant to provide a broad picture of the extent of damage sustained by your organization and assist in planning for the subsequent tasks to follow. To provide an idea of how quick this process should be, a typical overview should be carried out and completed within the first eight hours after conclusion of the actual emergency. The primary focus of this initial situation overview centers on issues involving the number of casualties and their positions, displacement of personnel, and damage to critical company resources. The goal of this initial assessment overview is to determine the scope of the disaster through several basic questions:

- How many people and work areas are affected?
- What areas of the building are affected?
- How bad is the damage to the facility and equipment?

This overview is best conducted by personnel within their respective work areas—these employees will be the most capable personnel to rapidly assess the work space and equipment to quickly and accurately determine the significance of the damage and how it will affect their ability to operate in the future. With this in mind, it is a sound practice to have the damage assessment team work with individual supervisors to have them assess their respective work spaces and provide a brief synopsis in response to the questions listed above. As the group obtains this information, they should consolidate the data and forward their overall evaluation report to the Crisis Management Team. In this manner, this overall decision-making body dealing with the emergency situation can better determine what type of assistance is warranted and to what extent any additional resources are needed. Once all work areas have had their initial situation overview, the next step is to perform an initial damage assessment, which provides more detailed information regarding the extent of the damage.

Initial Damage Assessment

The initial damage assessment has a broader scope, is more detailed, and will take a longer period of time to complete than the initial situation overview; however, its purpose is much the same. It is still evaluating the damage and loss of personnel and resources within your organization to determine what areas require work to reestablish the preemergency condition. The initial damage assessment begins the detailed process of annotating specific items requiring repair or construction and should provide a much more detailed report of the work areas along with each item of equipment that sustained damage within your facility and organization. This assessment also provides an evaluation of what areas are currently usable and can immediately begin normal operations. As with the initial situation overview, it is useful for the damage assessment team to work with individual supervisors to obtain this information, which they will eventually filter up to the Crisis Management Team. Last, the initial damage assessment task helps the overall business to begin to prioritize what work areas are necessary to focus resources on, in order to resume full functionality of the organization.

To accomplish this portion of the damage assessment process, it is useful to utilize a standardized form to assist personnel. This document is meant to provide information to the damage assessment team with data that are consistent and can be easily understood from all the various work areas within your organization. Figure 6.1 shows an example of such a form and provides you with an overview of the information that should be compiled.

This document defines and identifies the level of damage sustained to certain work areas and provides a list of various facilities and/or work areas that have sustained damage. It also provides an estimate of that area's ability to accomplish and sustain work in its current condition—this information will help not only to determine your organization's immediate capability to conduct business operations but also to prioritize what repairs and purchases should be conducted first.

Damage Assessment and Needs Analysis

Once information from the initial damage assessment has been consolidated, it is now possible to work toward identifying the needs and requirements that are necessary to begin work to recover your organization's full business capability. This area not only helps to identify these needs but also helps to prioritize what tasks should be completed to bring the business back into full operation. To efficiently accomplish this process and be able to separate these tasks to accomplish them simultaneously in an organized manner, it is best to divide up the requirements into major areas that are necessary for your organization to conduct operations. There are several different major areas into which most businesses can categorize these items: facility infrastructure, organizational processes, personnel, and equipment. We look at each of these major areas over the next several paragraphs.

The facility infrastructure area ensures that the buildings and work spaces are safe and able not only to meet basic human needs but also to support normal business operations. These issues include any structural damage to the facility, which would

INITIAL DAMAGE ASSESSMENT FORM

Level of Damage Defined	
Level I	No Significant Damage – Usable / Operational
Level II	Minor Damage – Needs repair to be usable / operational
Level III	Major Damage – Structure / Work Area is unusable and cannot be occupied
Level IV	Destroyed – Unusable and cannot be repaired

Facility / Work Area _____

Assessor _____ Date Assessed _____

Facility / Work Area	Level of Damage				Comments / Observations
	Level I	Level II	Level III	Level IV	

Figure 6.1 Initial damage assessment form.

have been identified as areas designated levels I, II, or III during the initial damage assessment. Facility infrastructure also assesses the building and its utilities to support people in a safe and comfortable work environment. Even if the structure of the facility is sound after an incident, people cannot work if the water, sewage, heating and cooling, electrical, or information and networking systems are inoperative. This area will normally be the responsibility of the facility and maintenance personnel working alongside safety experts within your organization to identify needs and help prioritize what tasks must be done in their appropriate order.

It is possible that some emergency incidents will result in the loss of some employees. These losses may have occurred as people decided that they are unable to come back to work because of the effects of the incident or they may have even been causalities of the event; regardless, your organization will need to determine how, or even if, their positions should be filled. The initial tendency of many businesses may be to simply fill all open slots owing to these losses; however, the first decision involved with this task is decide whether these positions should even be filled. This decision falls in line with the previous task of determining if there are any modified organizational processes you may have chosen to implement, because these changes may have resulted in fewer positions or modified duty positions prior to the incident. Once you have finalized the positions to be filled along with their specific responsibilities, the next step is to work on hiring new personnel to perform these duties. Any revision or modification to your personnel should be reviewed by your senior management team based upon the impact these changes will have upon your entire company. Once these workforce changes are approved, the human resources point of contact along with the applicable supervisor can work through the normal hiring process.

Based on damage to work spaces or personnel losses as a result of the emergency incident, your organization has the opportunity to make your business more efficient through modifications to your organizational processes. Not only should your company consider changes to your manufacturing processes based on damage or loss to certain equipment items, you should also consider overall changes to your work flow to make your company more efficient. In this manner, you can use recovery to implement change within your company that simply results in a better way to do business. As you focus upon the methods and processes you utilized to accomplish business goals prior to the incident, your overall management team should identify any mitigating factors that will prevent these same processes in the aftermath of the incident. These mitigating factors could be the loss of a key employee or significant damage to a particular work space. As the organization's senior management team (normally all these personnel should be members of the Crisis Management Team) works through the processes previously used prior to the emergency incident and identifies any mitigating factor associated with that particular method, you should work to find alternative processes that may actually result in more efficient and effective operations. Even if there are no losses to key personnel but you have identified changes to your organizational structure or work flow, these can be implemented as you begin your recovery efforts. As a result, you can use this area of recovery—making modifications to your organizational processes—to benefit your business. Using this thought process, you may ironically discover improvements within your organization as a result of the emergency, because you may either identify a process or work flow that was inefficient or be able to implement an improvement that was too controversial for your employees prior to the incident that greatly improves the efficiency and effectiveness of your organization.

Obtaining the necessary equipment to reestablish business capability is the last area we discuss within the damage assessment and needs analysis task. Although many organizations will accomplish this task by simply referring to inventories accomplished prior to the incident and procure any shortfalls, it will be wise to take a step back and look at the results of your other work. Your organization should take into account any modifications you may be considering within your organizational processes and workforce. As your leadership team works to implement these changes based upon your previous analysis, it may not be necessary to purchase each and every equipment item to ensure resource levels are brought back up to predisaster inventories. Instead, you should ensure that any equipment replacements take into account any changes you have implemented in any modified business operations. Only then should the organization produce a finalized list of equipment purchases. Once this equipment list is finalized, your purchasing point of contact can begin working the necessary details to procure and obtain these equipment items.

Damage and Loss Assessment

This item is the final task we will cover within the area of damage assessment and, fortunately, it should also be the easiest to accomplish. This task is simply a compilation of all the costs associated with any repairs and construction, along with the price of any equipment that requires replacement because of loss or damage during the emergency. This accounting is necessary to document any business losses for tax purposes and insurance claims. It should be a relatively simple endeavor because these costs would have already been calculated as part of the previous tasks within the overall damage assessment process—now these financial data need only to be consolidated. To ensure this task is accomplished properly, it is necessary that any personnel making purchases associated with construction, repair, or new equipment coordinate and provide all necessary data to the financial bookkeepers and accountants within your organization so that this information is maintained by one single point of contact within the company.

Cleanup and Salvage Operations

This recovery task oversees all cleanup of the incident, to include decontamination of work areas if necessary (Figure 6.2). As with the damage assessment portion of recovery, there are several considerations that should included as part of your preparation and within your emergency response plans and procedures. Procurement of equipment to assist with the cleanup operation should also be considered when planning for this area, including obtaining protective gear for personnel performing any decontamination tasks if your company works with hazardous materials. Other preparatory actions include planning to obtain dumpsters for debris and conducting or contracting for decontamination services if you are unable to accomplish this task yourself. The cleanup and salvage operation may also be required to seek contractor support to repair damaged utilities and fire protection systems to bring these services back to operational status. In addition to these preparation items, we will look at several

Figure 6.2 Cleanup and salvage operations.

additional considerations that you should include in your recovery planning, such as general precautions, clothing and personal protective equipment, electrical hazards, and fire protection. By incorporating these tasks prior to the onset of any incident, your organization will be much better prepared to conduct cleanup and salvage operations in a safe manner.

General Precautions during Cleanup and Decontamination

Before beginning any cleanup operation, it is critical that your emergency response planning include several general precautions. First, a preliminary inspection of the area should be done. The purpose of this inspection is to ensure the stability and structural soundness of the space so that cleanup personnel can conduct their work safely. It is also important to have a plan to contact medical personnel in case of any injury sustained during the cleanup operation. Another precaution is to ensure that individuals are aware that they should report any obvious hazards observed during cleanup—including downed power lines, frayed electrical wires, or gas leaks—along with a process to provide reports to the appropriate authorities. Based on specific hazards that can accompany cleanup efforts created by standing water or other water damage created by flooding, there are some additional general precautions that should be considered in these types of operations. A wooden stick or pole should be used when checking flooded areas to identify any pits, holes, and protruding objects before entering any underwater areas. Another precaution around these areas is to ensure that personnel do not use any electrical power equipment in or around standing water—this includes fuel-powered generators, which should be left outdoors. A last general precaution is to consider the use of life vests if deep water is present within the damaged areas.

In the event that decontamination is necessary your emergency plan should have personnel contact local authorities or the Environmental Protection Agency to accomplish this task properly; however, there are some basic precautions that should be included in your procedures. Extreme caution must be taken when handling any

Figure 6.3 Decontamination.

containers holding any substances that are known or suspected to contain hazardous materials. Before entering areas where they will be working, employees conducting cleanup should be notified if there are any known hazardous materials in the area so that they will be aware of any potential hazards. Additionally, emergency response plans should ensure that any employees who may come into contact with any hazardous materials wear personal protective gear to protect them from possible hazards (we will look at specific protective gear in the next section). Although it is best to await the arrival of experts in hazardous materials and decontamination, in the event that individuals or areas are contaminated and immediate action is necessary, the following actions should be covered in your organization's plans and procedures. Water-based cleaning methods (scrubbing, shampoo, steam-cleaning, and soap) will greatly reduce the risks of contamination. When using these methods, it is important to use a great deal of water to flush out any possible contaminants. Pressure hosing an area is an option to consider to decontaminate a room or other work space. Continuously applying water at high pressure, will help wash away much of the contamination. When using any washing method for decontamination, it is best to start high and work downward to ensure the contaminants are washed away from the person or area (Figure 6.3).

Personal Protective Clothing

Your emergency response plans should ensure you have personal protective clothing and equipment on hand prior to any actual incident. These items are necessary during any cleanup operation and should include standard industrial safety items such as steel-toe boots, long pants, and safety glasses. A hardhat should also be worn if there is any danger of falling debris. Dust respirators may also be necessary when working around mold or vegetable matter. In the event that hazardous materials may be present additional personal protective clothing is necessary. This includes chemical resistant clothing worn over standard protective work clothes such as a hooded two-piece chemical splash suit and disposable chemical-resistant coveralls, along with inner and outer chemical-resistant gloves and booties.

Electrical Hazards

In the event of any recovery action, there is likely to be potential electrical hazards present as personnel begin cleanup operations. Some basic considerations should be included within your emergency response planning to protect employees. Personnel should treat all power lines as energized until it has been confirmed that they are not powered. Regardless of this confirmation, individuals should never touch any downed power lines or any object in contact with such lines in any standing water. Care must be taken to be aware of any overhead or underground lines when clearing debris as these lines may have become exposed during damage sustained from the emergency incident. If damage to the electrical system is suspected, turn off the electrical system within the facility and follow lockout/tagout procedures before beginning work (it is best to have the system inspected by a qualified electrician prior to turning the system back on). Use ground-fault circuit interrupters in all wet locations during cleanup operations to provide improved safety for personnel conducting the cleanup. By adhering to these considerations, individuals conducting cleanup and salvage operations will be safe from any potential electrical hazards.

Fire Protection

The final area we look at within cleanup and salvage operations deals with fire protection. If a gas leak is detected while conducting cleanup, evacuate the building and contact the authorities. As you are conducting cleanup, ensure that there are fire extinguishers and provide procedures for fire evacuation based on any obstructions to the facility that occurred as a result of the emergency incident. If possible, work to clear debris from any fire exits to provide the maximum possible number of evacuation routes.

Customer and Client Information

We briefly discussed this recovery task when we covered the preparedness phase of emergency response; however, because of its importance we will go into some more detail in this section. During this phase of your organization's recovery operations, this task comes to fruition when you begin to reestablish contact with your business's customers and clients. As covered previously, ensuring you have a complete list of contact information for your organization's customers and clients after an emergency is an obvious part of this task and should be a relatively simple process with the proper planning and preparation. Maintaining and keeping this information in a secure location that will be safe from any destruction can be accomplished by storing this information on a flash drive or external server within a fireproof/waterproof container or maintaining the data at an offsite location.

As part of your recovery operations, it is a good idea to include this information as part of the equipment that is maintained by your Crisis Management Team. This will enable your organization to know where this information is so that you can reestablish communications with your customers as rapidly as possible once the incident is over and possibly even provide them with updates throughout the incident if your relationship with a particular client demands. Keeping the information with the Crisis Management Team is relatively easy to do if you store some basic customer information (name, address, and type of service provided) on some type of portable device and include this item as part of the kit for the communications point of contact within this group. Once you begin recovery operations, having this information readily available will enable to you to provide updates to these customers and clients and provide them with piece of mind that you can not only continue to meet any obligations but also continue to provide service to them in the future.

In addition to providing updates to your immediate clients, another portion of this task should be to provide updates to the public and community in general. With general information provided to the public regarding the best way to use company goods or services and your progress in restoring services during the recovery phase, not only can your organization establish contact with potential customers, but you will be better prepared to continue business as normal after the emergency situation has been resolved. Additionally, these public updates should include accurate information regarding service hours, locations, or any changes in procedures as you reopen your business operations. By not only ensuring you are able to provide your normal customers and clients with updates on your recovery but also including the entire community in communications, you may be able to gain additional customers for the future by the perception in the local area of your ability to quickly move forward after a disaster and by demonstrating your ability to rapidly recover from an incident.

Mutual Aid and Agreement Activities

Mutual aid and agreement activities help to identify and determine what outside agencies can provide assistance to your organization in the aftermath of a disaster and coordinate support and aid from these respective agencies. There are literally hundreds of agencies that can provide this support, including charitable organizations along with state and federal government agencies. Prior to any actual emergency, it is important that your organization work to identify the agencies that can actually provide your organization with the type of assistance you may require based on the nature of the emergency.

A good starting point to prepare for this assistance is to establish contact with the Federal Emergency Management Association, or FEMA. Prior to an incident, the FEMA Web site will be a good source of information to identify many of the organizations that are available to provide assistance in the event of an emergency. Once an incident has actually occurred, it is a good idea to start your effort to obtain some of this assistance by contacting FEMA initially. In addition to aid to your business itself, this assistance can also include money for employee's housing and essential expenses, including food and clothing and critical personal expenses such as medication. Another federal agency that can assist with your organization's recovery is the Small Business Association and the U.S. Department of Labor. In many cases, these organizations provide disaster and economic injury low-interest loans to businesses and individuals to repair or replace real estate, personal property, machinery and equipment, inventory, and other business assets that have been damaged or destroyed in a declared disaster.

Another federal government agency to look to for assistance is the Internal Revenue Service. In the event that your organization experiences an emergency incident; there are a variety of tax breaks associated with disaster relief and recovery. If your organization assists your employees with some expenses in the aftermath of a disaster, there may be some considerations or even exemptions for these payments that should be researched and identified. Additionally, any relief funding that your organization receives will also have some tax exemptions that may assist with your recovery operations. Any qualifying disaster payments from any source in connection with qualified disasters are not taxable as income and are not subject to employment taxes or withholding. According to the IRS, a qualified disaster is defined as[1]:

- Terrorist or military action
- Accidents involving a common carrier
- Presidentially declared disaster
- Event that the Secretary of the Treasury determines to be catastrophic
- Disaster determined by a federal, state, or local authority that warrants governmental assistance

In addition to these federal government agencies, there are also a variety of agencies at both the state and the local government levels that can provide assistance to your organization throughout the recovery phase of emergency response operations. Because these agencies are unique to your specific region and city, we will not cover them here; however, your organization should work to identify these agencies for your emergency response plans and ensure you have updated points of contact.

Along with the many different governmental agencies that provide relief, there are several charitable organizations also available to provide relief assistance. The American Red Cross and the Salvation Army are two of the more familiar agencies; however, there are hundreds of other organizations that can provide a variety of assistance options after an emergency incident. Whereas many of these organizations are focused on individual needs, several of these agencies will probably be able to assist your business in ensuring that care can be provided to each of your employees. As is the case with state and local governments, what organization and the type of assistance they can provide will depend on your location, so your emergency response planning should work to research and identify these potential sources of aid prior to the onset of an actual incident.

Business Restoration

The first four areas we have covered within recovery operations, damage assessment, cleanup and salvage, customer and client information, and mutual aid and agreement activities, are all aimed at helping with the restoration of your organization's business. The information and effort from these recovery areas will be used as we work toward this last section, which is directly involved with recovery operations—restoration of your organization's business capability so that it can be brought back online to levels seen prior to the incident. This task of business restoration not only starts this process, but will ultimately tie into your Business Continuity Plan, which we will cover in the next section of this chapter.

Tasks involved in the restoration of your organization's business should be based on the information and results obtained during your damage assessment. When you carried out the damage assessment and needs analysis, you would have identified any needed structural repairs or construction to the facility, positions to be filled, and equipment that must be purchased. Furthermore, this damage assessment would have determined the priority of what items should be obtained based upon their criticality to your organization's business operations. As we discussed, you will be able to begin work on the initial tasks to procure these needed services with this prioritized list.

During business restoration, it is necessary not only to look at the highest priority tasks but also to take a comprehensive look at all the necessary portions of your overall organization—facility, workforce, and equipment—and conduct backward planning to ensure these tasks are finished in accordance with their priority rather than simply started in a certain order. It is best to look at some of the higher priority tasks that will take the longest to complete or implement and begin any necessary planning and initial actions to accomplish these efforts in the appropriate order. Once you have determined the necessary order to begin the various tasks, you can begin to take the various actions necessary to recover from the incident, including facility repair and construction, making the decision whether to relocate some or all of your employees during these repair projects, and any hiring actions to fill vacancies of key positions as you begin these efforts.

One area within business restoration that requires significant planning and lead time involves any required repairs or construction to the facility or within specific work areas. There are several tasks involved in these efforts that require lengthy planning and preparation, all of which add to the overall schedule necessary to complete these actions. Prior to any major renovation or construction, it will be necessary to obtain engineering and architectural drawings that detail these projects. Once these drawings are developed, they will be used to obtain any necessary permits and building approvals. These documents are also necessary to determine any specifications and requirements that must be documented to enable potential contractors to determine price bids to accomplish the work. Once this information has been provided, the organization will need to make a decision whether it is necessary to relocate—either temporarily while these projects are ongoing or, possibly, permanently—to continue business operations. This decision will be based on the length of time necessary to accomplish the renovation and construction process, along with a cost–benefit analysis that compares the money required for any renovation and new construction versus moving into leased facilities. As you obtain prices for the various repair and construction projects, it may become evident that it is more cost-effective to relocate or rebuild, rather than make repairs to the facility. If a relocation of some or all of your employees becomes the apparent solution, there will be additional costs and considerations based on the many complexities that involve moving some or all of the business.

In the event that all or a portion of the organization must relocate, these financial considerations should include any potential transportation costs to provide for the long-distance movement and relocation of persons from the damaged areas of the facility in order for them to continue with their tasks. Several other considerations are involved with facility relocation and should be accounted for when looking at the various costs involved.

- Where will your organization relocate?
- What will it take to accomplish the relocation?
- Who will work at the new location?
- Will any special equipment or services be required at the new location?
- How will these work areas communicate with other functions within the organization that have remained in place?

Transportation is a key consideration within the facility relocation operations, because a process to transfer personnel to other job sites may be needed. Another consideration is communication—if only a portion of your workforce must relocate while repairs are made to their office areas, how will they communicate and interact with other portions of your organization so that you can continue to accomplish your overall business objectives throughout the business restoration? The addition of utilities and computer services in multiple locations should also be accounted for when you make your decision of whether to relocate portions of your business operation. These factors must be taken into account when you analyze relocation versus repair or construction.

If your organization must hire new personnel to fill vacant positions, this process can also take time and should begin early during the recovery phase. Revising the job description (if your organization has reorganized some work processes as a result of the emergency), advertising the vacant position, obtaining applicants, and conducting the hiring process can take several months depending upon the position's qualifications and the number of available applicants.

By beginning work on decisions and tasks involved with facility repair, relocation, and hiring actions during the business restoration effort, your organization will be better positioned to implement your Business Continuity Plan.

Business Continuity Planning

Business continuity planning is an important area involved in recovery operations. In fact, it so important that many individuals believe business continuity encompasses the overall emergency response planning process. Whereas I have chosen to give this area its own separate section within recovery operations, this should not dilute the importance of this planning. There are also differences between other portions of emergency response planning and business continuity planning, since several major aspects of emergency response—specifically response and recovery operations—are conducted in reaction to a situation; however, business continuity planning is a proactive process that ensures that critical services or products within your organization can continue to be delivered during an incident that could cause a disruption.[2]

This business continuity process should thus be a major aspect of any organization's emergency response preparation to better accomplish recovery operations. In addition, it can also combat other types of disruption issues, including supplier issues or departure of key personnel that can occur without any ongoing emergency situation. This business continuity planning process then becomes a critical part of an organization's emergency response program—in fact, it is so important that there are numerous books and articles published on the preparation and development dealing solely with this particular planning process. Although we will not be able to go into the detail covered in these many books and other resources, we will briefly cover the aspects involved with this process over the next several pages to provide an overview of this subject.

First, let's discuss the similarities and differences between business continuity planning and business restoration and emergency response planning. The objectives of all these planning processes are much the same—they provide methods that attempt to minimize the disruption to your organization's business operations, caused by minor issues common to any organization (e.g., a major subcontractor going out of business or the retirement of a key manager within the company) up to and including a major catastrophe. The major difference between these various planning methods is that, whereas business restoration and emergency response planning provide actions to implement once an emergency has occurred, a Business Continuity Plan is meant to enable services to continue being delivered. Instead of focusing on reactive measures to accomplish recovery after a disaster, a Business Continuity Plan attempts to ensure that critical operations continue to be available by identifying some of these issues prior to their occurrence. Another difference—particularly between business continuity planning and business restoration—is that business restoration includes any immediate or short-term actions that will enable your organization to achieve initial operational capability if an incident occurs that could not be foreseen. These actions will provide the necessary foundation, but they are not comprehensive, whereas a Business Continuity Plan is designed to deal with all aspects of this planning. In other words, business restoration provides your organization with much of the data and documentation, along with some initial groundwork, but there will be additional effort required to implement the more comprehensive business continuity planning process that is designed to be accomplished over the long term. In short, business restoration forms a part of the overall business continuity planning process, so we have looked at this area separately to make these initial and short-term methods easier to understand and put into action. A final difference between these planning methods is based on the proactive methods involved in business continuity planning. Whereas there are many types of emergency incidents that will have little or no warning, some events that can cause disruption to a business can show signs that they will occur prior to actually happening. Proper implementation of business continuity planning should help to identify metrics and measurements that it is hoped will identify some of these early warning signs before a disruption actually occurs so that the organization can take appropriate action before the issue becomes a significant problem.

As alluded to earlier, there are many experts who consider emergency response to be part of business continuity planning. I believe the opposite is true—that emergency response forms the overall construct for all aspects of emergency response and recovery, including business continuity planning. Although this specific planning process is a portion, it is a very significant portion that is meant to assist with the recovery of an organization from many types of incidents. To explain my reasoning for this belief; the ultimate cause that initiates the vast majority of these planning processes—emergency response, business restoration, or business continuity planning—is an emergency incident, or the precursors to such an event. As stated previously, there may be some events that can be foreseen based on indicators and measures. In these cases, business continuity planning provides an excellent tool to accomplish workarounds or alternative business operations to overcome these disruptions. In the event of many types of emergency incidents, however, such as severe weather, terrorist actions, or violent criminal activities, there will be little warning, and the mitigation measures that we have discussed and that your organization should have taken during the preparedness phase and response actions will be the primary procedures you must utilize to react to these events. Thus, the actual implementation of most portions of an organization's emergency response plan does not occur unless there is some type of significant event—typically an emergency incident or major disaster—that requires action to avoid or minimize disruption of the organization's business capacity. The Business Continuity Plan deals with a small portion of these events that can be identified before they become a significant problem. In either planning process, the lack of a significant event will render any type of emergency response or business continuity action unnecessary. The bottom line is that regardless of how one wishes to categorize business continuity planning and emergency response, it is necessary to ensure you have plans for all types of incidents and disruptions.

Now that we have discussed the interrelationships between business continuity planning, business restoration, and emergency response planning, let's look at what considerations and necessary steps are involved in the development of a Business Continuity Plan.

Development Steps for a Business Continuity Plan

When your business is disrupted, it can cost money. Revenue is lost because of the inability to fill orders for your customers. Add to these losses the extra expenses associated with the damage or loss of equipment or personnel owing to an emergency and this will mean that your organization is likely to see a drastic reduction in profits after any type of disaster. Unfortunately, insurance and various aid packages will not always cover these costs nor can they replace customers that may defect to other competitors in the event your services are disrupted, so it is critical that your organization develop a Business Continuity Plan as part of your emergency response program.

A Business Continuity Plan should maintain the continuous delivery of critical services and products. It should also include the identification of critical resources that support the continuity of your business operations, which could include personnel, information, equipment, financial allocations, legal counsel, and infrastructure protection. By measuring the inflow and outflow of these critical resources, your organization may be able to identify disruptions to or problems in the delivery of its services and products before they occur. There are several benefits to having a Business Continuity Plan. One benefit is that it enhances the organization's image with internal and external stakeholders by the demonstration of a proactive attitude. Other benefits include improvement in the overall efficiency of the organization and the identification of the relationships between various resources and the critical services and deliverables within your business. This information can better assist you in implementing mitigation measures that will help prevent issues before an emergency incident or other type of disaster occurs.

The process to develop an organizational Business Continuity Plan includes the following four steps:

1. Conduct a business impact analysis to identify time-sensitive or critical business functions and processes, along with the resources that support these items.
2. Identify, document, and implement plans necessary to recover these critical business functions and processes.
3. Organize a business continuity team and develop a formalized Business Continuity Plan to manage a disruption in business operations.
4. Conduct training for the business continuity team and testing and exercises to evaluate recovery strategies and the current plan.

In many cases, the effort to accomplish these steps may be less than you realize, as many of these tasks have been started or even completed if you have already worked through many of the planning and preparation efforts we have previously covered as part of your overall emergency response program. We will look at each of these steps as we discuss the development of a Business Continuity Plan and what is necessary to accomplish each of these steps to ensure these efforts are fully understood.

Business Impact Analysis

The first step in the development of a Business Continuity Plan is to carry out a business impact analysis. The purpose of this analysis is to identify the organization's mandate and define critical services or products, rank the order of priority of services or products to ensure their continuous delivery or rapid recovery, and identify internal and external impacts of potential disruptions. Furthermore, this business impact analysis should predict the consequences of any type of disruption involving a business function or process within your organization and gather information needed to develop recovery strategies to overcome these potential disruptions.

We have already discussed the primary means of identifying these potential disruptions: completion of a risk assessment, the development of which we covered in the Introduction chapter of this book. As part of this risk assessment, your organization should have developed a Risk Assessment Matrix that provides a prioritized list of various risks or disruptions that could hinder your business operations. With this list of risks, your organization should identify and implement various security measures and corrective processes to provide mitigation and minimize the possibility of these events happening. Unfortunately, based on limitations in funding and resources it is unlikely that most of these potential risks and disruptions can be fully mitigated—and there are probably several that could not be addressed at all. As a result, your business impact analysis should look at all of these risks and vulnerabilities and develop plans that account for them and provide some method to ensure your business continues its operations.

In addition to identifying the various risks and disruptions that could affect business operations, your business impact analysis should also identify your organization's critical business functions and processes. This task cannot be accomplished until your organization first defines what goods and services must be obtained, produced, or delivered to continue remaining in business. This information can be obtained from your organization's mission statement and from any requirements or agreements to deliver specific services and products. Once you have identified these critical goods and services, you must next identify the critical aspects of the organization, such as specific processes, resources, or personnel. This can be done through discussions with employees who have detailed knowledge of how their specific work area operates and how their function contributes to the objectives of the overall business. These key personnel should be able to identify the critical tasks and processes, along with the impact on the operation if these functions are interrupted.

Once you have identified the critical items, the next step within the business impact analysis is to prioritize these critical services or products. These must be prioritized based on minimum acceptable delivery levels and the maximum period of time the service can be down before the organization begins to experience severe damage. This item, the maximum tolerable downtime for a particular service, will become the primary factor in determining the ranking of critical services. To obtain this factor, information is required to determine the impact of any disruption to a specific service delivery, loss of revenue, additional expenses, and intangible losses. Again, much of this information can be obtained from the individuals in their respective work areas, as they should be the most knowledgeable to estimate the maximum time that the critical process they identified can be unavailable before it will affect the rest of the operation. Many business continuity planners use the term MTD, which was mentioned earlier as the maximum tolerable downtime, to describe this. The MTD should help to further clarify the impact of any disruption to a critical service by defining how long the organization could function without that particular service and how long the client would accept its unavailability. This time period quantifies all of the various critical services into one standard measurement and is helpful to better prioritize each of these resources.

Once you have identified the critical aspects within your organization and prioritized these areas, your organization can then begin to establish workarounds to enable your business to continue to function based on these sources of disruption coupled with critical business functions. These workarounds are the beginnings of the recovery plans for these critical business functions and processes.

Develop Recovery Plans for Critical Business Functions and Processes

Once your organization has completed its business impact analysis, you can begin to develop specific recovery plans to address each of the critical services or products that were identified. These plans should be focused on your critical business functions and processes and they should be based on MTDs. The functions and processes that have the shortest MTDs—which will equate to the highest priority—should provide you with guidance on where to focus your initial efforts in developing these recovery plans. Failure of the areas with short MTDs will result in the quickest roadblocks and disruptions to your overall business operation. As you develop your specific recovery plans, you should ensure they address risk mitigation measures already in place, along with current recovery capabilities of business operations and response preparation.

As we have stated earlier, the threats and risks you should work to mitigate are identified in both the Risk Assessment Matrix and the business impact analysis. Through the implementation of security measures—whether they be physical, information, or personnel security measures within your overall safety and security program—your organization should have worked to mitigate many of the higher priority threats. As mentioned earlier, it is impossible to bring the threat of each and every potential vulnerability to zero; however, working to moderate these risks is an ongoing process and should be performed even when the business continuity planning process is not active.

Once you have detailed the various mitigation measures already in place, the next step in developing these plans is to look at the current recovery capabilities of business operations within your organization. These business operations refer to the various processes and work flows within your organization that have been identified as critical to your ongoing success. In the event that there is a disruption in this area, your plans should identify current arrangements that are already in place and ensure their continued application to overcome these potential risks. For example, if an emergency incident disables a key supplier, your organization's recovery plans may have already identified other possible vendors for these materials so that you can continue to receive the necessary supplies and continue on with your normal business operations. If there are no current arrangements, your planning should develop methods to overcome any of these disruptions to ensure you can continue with these critical processes and work flows.

Development of a Formal Business Continuity Plan

We have already covered the need to document a formalized plan in other sections of this book, and this is no different in the case of your organization's Business Continuity Plan. Whether you include the business continuity planning process and its associated documentation within your overall emergency response plan, or whether you decide to develop a separate and stand-alone blueprint for business continuity, this plan must be written down and key personnel in your organization should be familiar with it to ensure your organization can successfully carry on after an emergency incident or other type of concern that can cause disruption to your business. Furthermore, it is beneficial to have separate business continuity plans to address each individual risk or disruption. This is not only helpful to ensure the organization implements only the actions dealing with the particular disruption that is occurring, but it also makes the document easier to understand and follow.

A good first step in developing a formal Business Continuity Plan is to designate a team to lead and support this effort. We have already discussed many of the advantages of having a specific team of individuals to accomplish tasks involving your organization's emergency response program. These teams ensure tasks are properly delegated to individual experts and as a result the overall process will be much more efficient and effective. This is no different from the development and implementation of a Business Continuity Plan, as this document must include many different work functions to ensure it can address not only the potential disruptions but also the necessary mitigation measures across the entire organization. As a result, these team members should be selected from trained and experienced personnel who are knowledgeable about their responsibilities. In addition to identifying membership, it is necessary to define the duties and responsibilities along with the authority structure to ensure the team has the necessary leadership and that individual team members understand their specific role as it relates to the development of the formal Business Continuity Plan.

With a designated group to author the Business Continuity Plan that is incorporated into your organization's overall emergency response program, it is now possible to work on the actual plans for each individual risk or potential disruption. These plans are based on the results of the business impact analysis that identified these disruptions along with the risk mitigation measures already in place along with your current recovery capabilities. It is also beneficial to ensure that these plans are designed to deal with increasing levels of severity of impact from a disruption. For example, if limited flooding occurs next to an organization's building, sand bagging may be used as the initial response. If the flooding persists and water rises to the first floor, the next action would be to move critical work functions to another facility or to a higher floor in the same building. If the flooding becomes even more severe, the relocation of critical parts of the business to another area until flooding subsides may be the best option. In this manner, your recovery plans will provide for a graduated response to the many types of emergencies. It is also a good idea to consider the risks and benefits of each possible option within the plan to keep costs to a minimum and ensure flexibility in your recovery actions as various disruption scenarios are analyzed. Individual Business Continuity Plans should also include facility and support functions within each individual continuity plan, as many types of incidents can result in damage to your building or to equipment that is critical to your operation. We have already discussed the need for recovery actions to begin repair and construction projects early because of the lead time that can be required to reestablish these critical functions—other options may be to subcontract out critical components if this enables your organization to continue operations. We have also discussed recovery plans for personnel, through the identification of key personnel in your business operations and provisions to hire new individuals in the event any of these critical employees are lost, either through normal retirement or separation or as a result of an emergency incident. The last planning area to consider within your individual Business Continuity Plans deals with information systems. A key consideration for any Business Continuity Plan is to ensure coverage of your information technology resources and components. These items, which include networks, servers, desktop and laptop computers, and wireless devices, are critical to running any business operation in today's environment. With the importance of these services in mind, recovery strategies for your critical information technology resources must be included in your overall business continuity planning so that technology can be restored as quickly as possible to meet your organization's business needs. For each critical service or product within your organization, it is best to choose the most realistic and effective options when creating the overall plan.

Business Continuity Training

As with any important issue within your company, you need more than just a formalized plan to ensure people are able to implement actions and responsibilities. You must also have training to reinforce and emphasize individual actions and to enhance understanding of the overall plan. This training should be provided for both the individual members of your team involved in business continuity planning and for the entire organization. This practice applies not only to this one area, but should incorporate the entire emergency response program. We look at training and the conduct of simulations involving your organization's overall emergency response program in greater detail when we discuss training in Chapter 9 and exercises in Chapter 10.

Summary of Recovery Operations

In this chapter, we covered the various aspects that form recovery operations within emergency response planning. The four main areas of recovery—damage assessment, cleanup and salvage operations, customer and client information, and mutual aid and agreement activities—all focus on your organization's ability to reestablish your company to full business capacity. The last subject we discussed, business restoration and business continuity planning, is an additional planning effort that enhances your emergency response planning. Business continuity not only helps to identify additional disruptions that could occur to your organization, but also works to prevent some of these disruptions from happening altogether. As a result, this planning further refines your overall emergency response program.

End Notes

1. Internal Revenue Service, *Disaster Relief: Providing Assistance Through Charitable Organizations*. Retrieved from web on September 9, 2014: www.irs.gov.
2. Public Safety Canada, *A Guide to Business Continuity Planning Government of Canada*. Retrieved from web on September 21, 2014: www.publicsafety.gc.ca.

The Crisis Management Team

Now that we have covered the four emergency planning factors—mitigation, preparedness, response, and recovery—along with the associated processes and actions that assist in their planning and implementation, over the next several chapters we will look at some of the specific tasks that are included in each of these areas but are important enough to warrant additional explanation. All of these planning factors help to form a comprehensive emergency response program, which will ultimately ensure your organization can continue beyond any type of emergency situation. This chapter details the primary team that assists in planning and directing the response of your organization to an emergency incident—the Crisis Management Team. In subsequent chapters, we will look at the proper and accepted response to various types of incidents along with the emergency response training program. This training includes not only formal training within your organization but also the conduct of exercises and simulations that help your employees to better understand their actions in the event of an actual incident.

The formation of a Crisis Management Team is a valuable method not only to help personnel better react during the response of an organization during an actual emergency but, if used properly, it can also assist in the preparation and planning of the overall emergency response program. This group of personnel will enable you to divide the various tasks involved in identifying risks and vulnerabilities, determining and procuring the appropriate mitigation measures, developing and writing plans and procedures, and ultimately making what could become a gargantuan job of implementing your organization's emergency response program a little easier by delegating tasks among various personnel through the establishment of the various roles and responsibilities. Over the course of this chapter, we will look at the various functional tasks that the Crisis Management Team must accomplish, both prior to and during an actual incident, along with individual members' roles and responsibilities, and finally we will look at how this group should function.

Crisis Management Team Tasks and Composition

Before we look at the various tasks that an organization's Crisis Management Team should accomplish, we will cover the membership of this group along with each individual member's role to ensure this group's effective operation. To set the stage for discussing the necessary functions that compose this team, let's first focus on the primary tasks and who should assist in their accomplishment.

Roles for the Crisis Management Team

Overall, the primary role of the Crisis Management Team is to ensure the organization is adequately prepared and has planned for potential emergency incidents. This aspect of the Crisis Management Team's tasks is typically overlooked by many organizations, as the normal focus of this group is to simply respond after an emergency has started. The team's ability to assist in preparation and planning should not be forgotten, however, because it is only logical that this group of individuals can and should accomplish the necessary groundwork and develop the organizational emergency response program—particularly because they will be the primary group to act in the event of an actual incident. As we discussed in the Introduction, this preparation and planning starts with the development of the organizational risk assessment and accomplishment of the Risk Assessment Matrix. By their involvement in this process, it is guaranteed that the Crisis Management Team will be well-versed in all the potential threats that could occur to their organization, along with the priority of their probability of occurrence. This knowledge provides a baseline for the next preparation and planning task—the development and writing of the organization's formal emergency response plan. It is also advantageous that this group develop the organization's written guidance and formal plan with regard to its emergency response program, particularly because this group of individuals will be the unit that must actually implement its procedures during high-stress situations that are going to occur with any type of emergency. In addition to accomplishing the risk assessment and developing the actual plans, it is also beneficial for this group to be the major decision-making body in regard to the approval of any projects that involve security and mitigation measures intended to minimize any potential threats. Whereas many organizations will view their Crisis Management Team like a fire-axe—stored in a glass case with the instructions "break in case of emergency"—ensuring that this group accomplishes these preparation and planning tasks can greatly assist a company in getting through any type of emergency incident with minimal loss or damage owing to the knowledge and expertise of this team based upon these initial tasks.

With these preparatory and planning roles firmly established within the Crisis Management Team, let's look now at the roles this group should accomplish over the course of an actual emergency. The first role is to rapidly detect the early signs of a crisis. Many organizations can be unwilling to admit an emergency situation is actually occurring (much like an ostrich with its head in the sand); however, the willingness to rapidly recall and form the Crisis Management Team as early as possible can greatly assist in an organization's ability to effectively respond to an incident. It should be noted that the organization should not view the formation of the Crisis Management Team with a sense of panic, as this can spread among the employees familiar with the company's emergency response procedures; so it is better to recall this group if an incident *could* occur, rather than wait until the situation is already on top of everyone—at that point in time, this team will be unable to proactively affect the organization's response to the incident and the company will be hard-pressed to minimize the effects of the incident.

The next role for the Crisis Management Team is to obtain information as a result of the incident. One of the first items of information is to identify the immediate problem areas that are being created, or will occur, as a result of the emergency situation. This may take some time as the team will probably need to obtain this information through communication with all necessary functional work areas within the organization. Much like a naval captain on a vessel at sea, who must rely on status reports from various sections within the ship in the event of a crisis, this team will also be dependent on gaining perspective on the various problem areas throughout the facility and organization as a result of the incident and must develop a process to ensure it obtains this information as quickly and accurately as possible. It should be noted that accuracy may be the more important consideration regarding this information because sugar-coated assessments during the actual event could ultimately hurt the organization. These overly optimistic assessments will not provide an accurate picture of the ongoing events, which in turn will not allow the Crisis Management Team to be fully aware of all the facts. Ultimately, this could result in poor decisions based on improper information. With this in mind, it is critical that your business promotes obtaining accurate data at all times and it does not "shoot the messenger," even during normal business, because employees will conduct themselves during an emergency as they would during their typical day-to-day activities. Another task in relation to obtaining information is to develop processes that ensure status can be received by the Crisis Management Team throughout the emergency incident. This can be developed by working with employees in their respective work areas and particular expertise to have them identify any areas of concern as the incident progresses. Obviously, this can be done only if time and circumstances allow, based on the situation and nature of the emergency and what type of information may be required. In virtually every instance this information is best gained from the employees themselves, because those who work in a specific functional area will be the most knowledgeable at identifying issues and providing solutions within their respective work areas. The Crisis Management Team should ensure there is a process to filter this information to the group and process the data as they arrive. With this method of obtaining the insight of employees within their own work areas, it would be possible to gain more valuable insight and provide updated status on the nature of the problem (if it has been resolved or become more significant) as the situation develops.

The next role for the Crisis Management Team is to take action to respond to the emergency. Based on the prior preparation and planning, this group should use the organization's emergency response plan as a guide and tailor any specific response actions to react to the exact situation. No plan is going to be perfect, however, and this should be understood during the development of your emergency response plan. Instead, the goal of this plan should simply be to identify guidelines in your organization's response but it should be understood that your plan should not hope to achieve a perfect set of response actions nor should the plan try to create an individual checklist for every possible scenario that could occur within every type of emergency situation. There is a quote attributed to the boxer Mike Tyson: "Everyone has a plan—until they get punched in the face."[1] This can be applied to writing and developing plans in general in that it is a given that any plan will need to be revised on the fly during the course of an emergency. Thus, it could be counterproductive to spend an inordinate amount of time trying to cover every single contingency and have a preestablished set of subsequent individual actions within an emergency response plan. Instead, ensure your plans simply provide the basic guidelines and actions to your employees. With the plan providing these recommendations of types of actions along with other aspects of your emergency response program, your Crisis Management Team will be able to do what it can do best—react to the situation and determine proactive solutions that best minimize damage and loss to the organization.

The last significant task—and possibly the most important—for your organization's Crisis Management Team is to provide calm and professional leadership during any type of volatile situation. Panic and the perception of confusion will be felt throughout the organization and this is particularly true during the high stress found as a business responds to an actual emergency incident. By dealing with the crisis at hand in a calm and cool manner though, this group of senior leaders will encourage all employees to face the ongoing problems with courage, determination, and a positive attitude. This role may be the most critical of the Crisis Management Team because properly accomplishing this task will motivate the entire organization and ensure they do not lose hope, and all individuals will deliver their best effort in working toward any possible solutions to the current incident. This task will not only help the group to minimize the effects of the current emergency, but it will also help the organization come out of tough times it finds itself in and prepare for the future.

Crisis Management Team Membership

Now that we have discussed the general roles and functions of the overall team, we will look at the specific work functions that should be part of your organization's Crisis Management Team along with some of their individual roles and responsibilities. An important item to consider as you choose which of your employees should sit within this group is that any member must have the appropriate responsibility and authority to make decisions within their respective functional area of expertise. These decisions should include not only the ability to resolve issues involving work processes or responses within their specific area but also the ability to make procurement and financial decisions. This authority is critical because most emergency incidents require immediate action. These decisions—whether it is necessary to obtain resources or redesign work processes or other methods—are necessary as a business responds to an ongoing event, so the membership of your Crisis Management Team must be able to make these decisions without having to check with others. As a result of this requirement, it is normal that this team includes the most senior managers within the company so as to ensure they have the proper responsibility and authority. An additional consideration for any Crisis Management Team will be based upon an organization's unique structure and setup. If, for example, an organization has several personnel responsible for several of the functional areas we will cover, it will probably be necessary that all these personnel are part of the Crisis Management Team. A final consideration is to attempt to keep the number of members to a minimum, because more people can make the decision-making process more cumbersome. Your emergency response plans should detail the specific membership of the Crisis Management Team based upon these considerations. We will cover each individual functional area that should be included in this group over the next several paragraphs.

It is a well-established practice that command and leadership must be held by one individual—this is normally termed "unity of command." This tenet of leadership ensures that everyone understands who is in charge and that there is no questioning of the leader's authority by other personnel within the organization. To ensure this type of command and control is maintained within your organizational Crisis Management Team, the logical choice for the leadership position of this group is your company's Chief Executive Officer (or the overall leader of the organization if there is no designated CEO). As is the case with any other task, someone must be in overall charge of the Crisis Management Team to provide direction and focus their efforts toward the necessary objectives and goals. This leadership position has several duties and responsibilities. The first duty occurs prior to the initiation of any emergency incident. In this role, the leader of the Crisis Management Team provides oversight throughout the preparedness phase of your emergency response program. The leader organizes, directs, and ensures that development of your organization's emergency response plan is accomplished; along with the designation, regulation, and coordination of the many responsibilities and tasks required as part of this planning process. This individual also ensures this preparation by directing and guiding the Crisis Management Team as they conduct emergency response training. This training ensures that both members of this group and employees better understand their roles and responsibilities in the event of an emergency. This training should include not only formal training conducted on a periodic basis but also practice of the organization's overall response to a potential incident through simulations and exercises. We look at this training later in the book. The second primary task of the leader is to direct response activities in the event that an actual emergency has occurred. This individual acts as the overall person in charge throughout the response phase and is typically referred to as the Incident Commander (IC). Although the IC could be any employee, it is best to make this position the overall leader of the organization because he or she must not only have the authority to make far-reaching decisions that could affect the entire business into the future but must also be able to direct all the other members of the Crisis Management Team to accomplish necessary tasks. Once an emergency has kicked off, the duties of the IC will include assuming overall command and control of the situation and assessing the severity of the incident. The IC will be responsible for determining when to recall the Crisis Management Team and where they will report so that all the members can coordinate their activities. This individual will also implement the organization's emergency response plan and determine what actions should be accomplished—as we discussed earlier, this includes the decision whether the organization conducts an evacuation or shelter-in-place operation to respond to the incident. The IC will also work with individual team members to ensure the business coordinates with first responders such as local law enforcement and fire department officials to synergize efforts with these agencies. This leadership position will also determine follow-up response strategies and oversee all incident-specific response activities within the organization. The last major task of the IC during the response phase of the incident will be to declare the incident as "over" and oversee the transition into the recovery phase for the organization. Once this transition has occurred, the final role and responsibility of the leader of the Crisis Management Team begins as he or she must oversee recovery operations for the organization. As we covered during our discussion on recovery operations, these tasks will include actions within the areas of damage assessment and cleanup and salvage operations, ensuring customer and client information is available, working with team members to identify mutual aid possibilities and coordinate agreement activities during recovery, and implementing actions to restore the business through business continuity planning efforts. As in other phases of emergency response, throughout these recovery efforts the leader should direct the other members of the Crisis Management Team to prioritize actions and allocate resources that enable the organization to reestablish critical business operations first and then work on follow-up tasks necessary to bring the company back to full operational capability. These tasks–throughout the planning and preparation phases of emergency response, as part of the response activities during an actual incident, and finally during recovery operations—must be guided by the overall leader of the Crisis Management Team, who is logically the leader of the entire organization.

Along with the leader of the Crisis Management Team, this group should include any administrative support that this individual or the group as a whole requires. This administrative support is an important, but often forgotten, task when organizations work to develop a list of members for their own Crisis Management Team. The members of this team serve a critical function as they work to respond to an incident and as a result, they will not have the time to work on many of the necessary administrative tasks such as drafting any needed correspondence or recording ongoing activities. By including personnel that can accomplish these administrative tasks, it will free up and enable the other team members to take the necessary action in making decisions and working with other personnel as they respond to the emergency. Some of the specific tasks of these administrative support personnel include recording and maintaining a chronological record of all events involved with the incident, assisting with internal communications, and drafting any necessary correspondence or statements to coordinate with external agencies. By having an individual, or several persons, to accomplish these administrative tasks, the remainder of the Crisis Management Team will be better able to focus their efforts and direct their actions within their own functional areas and minimize damage and loss to the organization as a whole.

Now that we have covered the duties and responsibilities of the leader of the Crisis Management Team along with the necessary administrative support for this group, we look at some of the major functions that should be included within this team. One key member is the organization's point of contact responsible for facility and/or maintenance issues. Throughout the entire emergency response process, an individual who is knowledgeable with regard to the facility's infrastructure along with the location and overall design of the utilities, any mechanical and electrical systems, and alarms within the building is critical. The roles and responsibilities of this individual include assistance during the development of emergency response plans regarding the abilities of the facility's infrastructure to withstand damage along with the identification of critical points in the design of these various systems. This identification of these critical points in the facility's infrastructure should occur during the preparation and planning phase of emergency response so that this individual may be able to develop additional protection or add measures that could help mitigate damage to some of these areas. During the onset of an actual emergency incident, the facility and maintenance point of contact will be required to assist with response actions involving the facility or any equipment within the building. These actions could include technical advice on the shutdown of certain equipment in the event of a natural disaster or how best to conduct efforts that seal off certain portions of the facility in the event of a hazardous material spill. Additionally, during the recovery phase of the emergency response, this individual will probably be one of the key members of many Crisis Management Team activities because many of the necessary actions during this phase will relate to accomplishing needed repairs to equipment or portions of the facility, which could include performing any necessary construction to enable the organization to resume full operations.

Another key function that should be included as part of the Crisis Management Team is the point of contact within your organization for information systems or computer networking duties. This individual will perform functions similar to those of the facility and maintenance functions, albeit relating to issues that involve computers, servers, networks, communications equipment, and other information system items. During the preparedness phase of emergency response, this individual will need to identify mitigation measures that help to protect the information system from disruption or attack. During the response phase to an actual emergency incident, and through recovery operations, the information systems expert will be required to assist the Crisis Management Team to ensure the organization is able to store critical company data, minimize damage to information systems infrastructure, and assist in the rapid reestablishment of the organization's information systems to fully recover from an incident.

The next work function that should be included as a member of the Crisis Management Team is the point of contact within the organization for logistical and transportation issues. In some companies these two functions may reside with different personnel. If this is the case in your organization it will be necessary to have both personnel as members within this group. The logistical point of contact should not only be able to address supply and inventory issues during preparation and planning, but also be able to conduct procurement and purchasing throughout response and recovery actions. The tasks that should be the responsibility of the logistics point of contact during response and recovery will be extremely important as you work to regain your business capability after any type of emergency response, because there will probably be many items that will need to be either replaced or purchased to reestablish your operations. The logistical expert will be a vital part of the procurement, delivery, and installation of any equipment. A point of contact for transportation is necessary if it becomes necessary to obtain and provide vehicle support in the event of a long-distance evacuation during either response or relocation efforts that could occur during recovery operations.

Another key individual that must be included in any Crisis Management Team is your organization's focal point for communications and public affairs. This individual will have two primary responsibilities. The first is to prepare for and accomplish the various communication efforts within the organization during any emergency incident. This includes establishing processes that will ensure all employees are notified of an event, coordinating the procurement of any necessary communications equipment with other stakeholders in the organization (such as the information systems and facility point of contacts), and ensuring any procured communications equipment will be available in the event of the loss of cell phone or standard phone lines during an emergency. The second primary responsibility for this individual is to accomplish any coordination with all media and perform public relations actions during an actual emergency. This task should begin prior to any incident by establishing a rapport with these agencies, acting as the primary conduit with local press and television agencies, and developing company-wide procedures to deal and coordinate with the media. This last task is critical as many emergency incidents have shown that if all employees within an organization are able to contact and communicate with the media during an actual emergency, this creates a lack of any coherent message from your company throughout the actual situation and results in a great deal of confusion and more problems. Instead, your communications point of contact must develop public relations policies and procedures to ensure your employees understand what they can and cannot say in the event of an actual emergency.

The last individual that should be included as part of the Crisis Management Team is the human resources point of contact. During both the preparation and the response phase of an emergency response operation, the primary responsibility of this individual is to provide procedures and ensure the organization can conduct accountability of all staff and any visitors in the event of an incident. As we have discussed previously, this task is critical during any type of situation but this issue becomes paramount in the event that the emergency involves injuries or loss of life because the identification of these individuals will rapidly become the primary focus of the media, other outside agencies, and ultimately the community where your organization is located. For this reason, it is critical that a well-established process is available and understood by all personnel to ensure that the rapid identification of any employees who have sustained any significant injuries or death can be accomplished and reported. Even after the conclusion of the emergency response, the human resources individual will be responsible for overseeing the hiring process during the recovery phase. This process will probably be established prior to any type of incident; however, the human resources point of contact on the Crisis Management Team may need to speed this hiring process in the event that any new employees are needed immediately to replace any personnel lost as a result of the incident.

Although we have discussed several different functional areas that should be included as part of the Crisis Management Team, there may be other departments that should be included within your own specific group. This membership should be based on your specific organizational structure and how you accomplish work flows and processes within your business. The personnel we have discussed are likely to be the minimum number of functional areas of expertise, but based on your own company, there may be other areas that should be included. In addition to ensuring all areas are included within the Crisis Management Team, it is also important to delineate each individual member's roles and responsibilities as they are added to this team. By formally establishing and directing the specific tasks of each member, you will define all the necessary tasks and ensure that the various members do not duplicate actions during an actual emergency—particularly because there will be far too much to accomplish in the event of any incident. Whereas the work functions we have discussed should provide you the basics of the various departments necessary to be included as part of a typical Crisis Management Team, it will ultimately be up to you to tailor this group to ensure it will meet the needs of your organization both during preparation and planning and throughout the response and recovery phases of any emergency.

Now that we have looked at the overall function of the Crisis Management Team, along with a discussion on the minimum membership along with each individual team member's responsibilities, we will look at the various actions of this group as a whole and considerations that will aid in the team's formation and recall after initiation of an incident.

Crisis Management Team Considerations

As mentioned previously, this group's primary function is to execute relevant plans and implement actions to assist in overcoming the emergency situation. We have already discussed the individual roles and responsibilities of key members that compose this group; however, it is worth reemphasizing the role of the entire Crisis Management Team, which is to analyze the evolving situation of the ongoing incident and use the existing plans as guidelines to formulate actions that are meant to save the organization. By saving the organization, we refer not only to its ability to conduct business but also to saving its reputation and standing in both the industry and the community. To accomplish these objectives, how exactly should this team function and act? Over the next several paragraphs, we look at methods to assist you in better understanding how your organization's Crisis Management Team should work during an actual crisis, which will translate into a better response across your entire organization.

Recall and Formation of the Crisis Management Team

One of the first considerations is when to actually recall and form the Crisis Management Team. The best answer to this is that an organization should recall—meaning that all the team members are contacted and directed to a rally point to meet and begin coordinating necessary response actions—at the earliest possible moment. An organization's Crisis Management Team should be recalled and formed to respond when there are warning signals of an impending emergency incident. It is always better to err on the side of caution and recall this group if there are any circumstances that could lead to an actual emergency; it is much more beneficial to conduct a recall of the Crisis Management Team as early as possible because it is better to have the team prepared rather than to scramble after an actual emergency incident has initiated and the group—and subsequently the entire organization—is now forced to try and catch up to the rapid series of events. Recalling the team should be a relatively easy task that can be done simply by the team leader's administrative support making contact with each member and informing her or him of the location at which to meet. There is no harm in recalling the Crisis Management Team and then finding out they are not necessary, as opposed to needing this group but not forming it until it is too late.

Crisis Management Team Equipment

We have briefly mentioned that each individual member should have some type of kit to bring upon any recall of the Crisis Management Team. We now cover some specifics on what particular items should be included in these kits. All members should have a kit, prepared in advance, in a small bag or backpack to ensure it is readily available and easy to carry, which contains the following items:

- Copy of the emergency response plan
- Maps of the area surrounding the organization's facility (preferably including all buildings within the map's boundaries)
- Floor plans of the organization's facility
- Employee contact lists that ensure 24/7 coverage for all personnel
- Cash and corporate credit cards
- Radio and extra batteries
- Water (two bottles) and food (small snack items or energy bars)

In addition to these basic items, each individual Crisis Management Team member should have any information or equipment specific to her or his particular function. For example, the facilities and maintenance point of contact will probably need detailed drawings of the building and its infrastructure schematics (i.e., electrical, heating and ventilation, and structural drawings). The human resources individual should have complete listings of manning and recall rosters for the organization. The communications and public affairs point of contact should have contact information for local media, and the logistical or financial point of contact should have any material and documentation necessary to accomplish procurement activities. These items are only a small list of examples—each individual member should be able to determine what specific information, equipment, or materials he or she may need in addition to the previous listings and ensure it is included in his or her crisis kit.

Functioning of the Crisis Management Team

Once the Crisis Management Team has been formed and has all their necessary equipment, they are ready to accomplish their function, which is to ensure the organization is able to respond to the emergency and rapidly recover to its full operational business capability. The team leader should bring the group together and immediately take charge of the situation so that the overall Crisis Management Team will work as a single unit. We will look at the various steps to ensure the group accomplishes these functions.

The first step for the Crisis Management Team is to understand the main areas of concern during emergency situations. This is similar to many issues in business—it is critical that the team determines the actual nature of the crisis so that they can act toward resolving that specific issue. This may sound easy, but during an actual incident it can be much more difficult because of the uncertainties and "fog of war" that can make it extremely difficult to determine the true nature of the emergency. The term "fog of war" is derived from Carl von Clausewitz's theories contained in his treatise, *On War,* and refers to the uncertainty in awareness experienced by participants during high-stress activities. Although this term is normally associated with military operations, it is valid across any stressful and fluid situation, including the response to an emergency. A perfect example to help illustrate this fog of war in a nonmilitary incident can be found during the response to Hurricane Katrina. Communications were severely affected by the hurricane and its aftermath. In fact these effects were so severe that Paul McHale, the Assistant Secretary of Defense for Homeland Defense, stated "the magnitude of the storm was such that the local communications system wasn't simply degraded; it was, at least for a period of time, destroyed."[2] The consequences of this massive communications failure resulted in something like the fog of war within the Gulf Coast region. To give just two examples, the New Orleans police department's communications system was inoperative for three days after the hurricane, and only a few backup channels were available to first responders as they descended into the area to help. As a result, the police were unable to determine where to prioritize their efforts nor were they able to provide direction so that their officers could effectively accomplish their duties. The other example is Mississippi's National Guard responders, who were unable to establish effective communications links with the governor or the state's emergency management agency for 48 hours after the hurricane hit.[2] Because of this lack of communication, authorities had little situational awareness—what was going on, who was where, what equipment was needed, and who was going where and when. This all resulted in an inability to effectively determine the priorities for response and how to best deploy the limited resources to assist the affected communities. Through these examples, I hope to have shown that it can be difficult to determine the exact nature of the problem and the evolving situation as your Crisis Management Team attempts to respond, but it is critical to see through this fog of war and ensure your team can determine the correct course of action as you develop your response.

Once the team has properly identified the problem, the next step is to prioritize the issues necessary to respond to the ongoing emergency. The Crisis Management Team should work together to rank the problems based upon their effect on the employees as well as the organization. It is important to note that the team should not only consider the immediate impact of the various issues, but also take into account the long-term consequences to the organization's business capability. Once this prioritization has been accomplished, it will enable the group to know which problems must be resolved immediately and which can be attended to a little later. Once this has been accomplished, the Crisis Management Team should work to develop solutions to negate, or at least minimize, the effect of each issue as the team moves down this prioritized list.

As the emergency situation moves along, it will be necessary to continually repeat these first two steps—determine the main issues resulting from the incident and prioritize their severity to determine in what order each issue is dealt with. In this manner, your organization can continually reassess the emergency, its effects to your business, and how best to respond to the situation as it evolves.

At the conclusion of the incident, it is important to note that the Crisis Management Team should make time to review the overall incident and their response. This will not only yield lessons learned to improve your organization's current emergency response plans but will also have several other benefits. First, by identifying areas in which things went wrong, or at least issues were found, team members will better understand how current processes within your standard business operation can be improved and made better for smooth functioning of the organization. If the crisis was caused by internal concerns within the organization, this review will also enable corrections to the various problems and shortcomings that led to a crisis within the workplace. A final benefit is that this review will help to develop alternate plans and strategies for the tough times. It should be noted that this review need not be accomplished solely by the Crisis Management Team—a single entity should not make all these decisions alone. It is wise to have team members sit with other employees on a common platform to help identify and discuss issues they experienced during the emergency and take each other's suggestions to modify and revise plans that are acceptable to all.

Summary Regarding the Crisis Management Team

Over the course of this chapter, we have looked at an organizational Crisis Management Team and how this group can assist in an overall emergency response program. This team is critical to a company's ability to properly respond to an emergency incident and also to the preparation phase of emergency response, as the team assists in the development of plans and procedures along with any recovery actions that will be necessary. We looked at what functional work areas should be included in the membership of this team along with their individual roles and responsibilities. We also discussed how and when to recall and form this group along with any equipment that members should have to more effectively respond to an ongoing incident. Last, we covered some broad steps to provide an overview of how the Crisis Management Team should conduct their efforts during the response phase of an emergency. This information should provide you with a baseline of how to form and guide your organization's Crisis Management Team actions prior to, and during, an emergency incident.

End Notes

1. Di Salvo David, *10 Smart Things I've Learned from People Who Never Went to College*, (Forbes, August 2, 2012). Retrieved from web on September 10, 2014: www.forbes.com.
2 Miller Robert, *Hurricane Katrina: Communications & Infrastructure Impacts*, (National Defense University). Retrieved from web on September 12, 2014: www.carlisle.army.mil.

Emergency Response Training

Now that we have covered the specifics of an organizational Crisis Management Team, we will look at methods of training an organization and its employees in emergency response, which can ultimately lead to improvements in the overall response capability of any business. One of the primary factors of your organization's emergency response training program is that any type of preparation in this area should not be an afterthought. Although there can be a tendency to place emergency response training on the back burner after the significant amount of effort that was required for the development of your overall plans and procedures, once these organizational emergency response plans are finalized they cannot simply be placed on the shelf as you move on to other tasks. Instead, the procedures and response actions that your employees must take in the event of an actual incident require a process that ensures they have internalized these methods—otherwise, your emergency response plan will simply become words on paper that gather dust on a bookshelf. For this reason, an overall training program to help educate your employees and emphasize these concepts is critical to the success of your overall emergency response program.

A viable training program has several functions; it is meant to ensure your employees understand their roles and responsibilities in the event of an actual emergency incident, but also the emphasis within the organization on safety, security, and emergency response will result in an increased security awareness among all individuals within the organization so that they may assist in mitigation of potential incidents. This last function—increased employee security awareness—can be difficult to achieve; however, we have discussed this concept several times throughout this book for the simple reason that it is the most effective security measure you can institute within your organization and will result in a much more effective emergency response program. Security awareness not only can result in exponential increases in your company's security posture but can also save your organization time and money. This is because of the increased protection that a security-conscious workforce can provide with respect to highlighting security concerns, notification of suspicious actions, questioning unauthorized personnel, or reporting any issue out of the ordinary. An organization that provides employees with an increased level of security awareness will not require the same amount of security precautions and hardware that a similar company without this heightened awareness requires. This is because each individual within the organization possessing greater security awareness has more of a mindset focused on safety and security concerns—simply put, they will act like a security guard in many instances—which will ultimately augment any physical security measures that are already in place. In effect, high security awareness among all your employees can increase the number of security sensors and add to other types of security measures, which in many cases can even replace the need for expensive protection countermeasures and equipment.

To develop an effective emergency response training program and begin the process of increasing your company's security awareness, it is necessary to implement three different opportunities to train your personnel. First, an initial safety and security training course should be included as part of your standard employee indoctrination or in-processing program. Second, recurring safety and security training should be periodically conducted for all employees within your organization. The last training method that should be included in any complete emergency response program provides for the conduct of exercises that practice the safety and security concepts and tasks. These exercises are such a critical aspect of your training program that we have dedicated the entire next chapter to a detailed discussion on the planning and conduct of these exercises. Over the remainder of this chapter, we look at each of the first two training methods—initial and recurring training.

Initial Emergency Response Training

This is probably the most important training that you conduct within your organization because it sets the foundation for and establishes your organization's commitment to emergency response along with ensuring that your employees understand the various aspects contained within your company's program. This initial training can be easily accomplished in an hour or two by your organization's primary security point of contact with a professional presentation as part of the standard company in-processing and indoctrination. It is best that this training is conducted through a formal classroom presentation, as this preparation will set the tone across your entire organization and promote the concept that emergency response and the ability to protect your employees is an important part of doing business within your company. This training also provides new employees with necessary information regarding their responsibilities and actions should an emergency incident occur before they can review the emergency response plan (if they will ever review it at all).

Some of the items that should be covered during this initial training are as follows:

* Discussing the security and emergency response goals and objectives for the organization.
* Defining and explaining the three major areas of security—physical security, information security, and personnel security—and how these areas apply to mitigation measures within your own organization.
* Outlining and discussing the employee security awareness program and its importance within the organization's safety and security program.
* Identifying the organizational emergency response point of contact, including office location and contact information.
* Informing new employees of their responsibilities and actions in the event of an emergency. This information should include directions on basic response actions that all employees should be familiar with, as they are contained within the organization's safety and security plan and procedures. At a minimum, these basic actions should include your organization's actions during the two primary types of response—evacuation and shelter-in-place operations. Employee responsibilities should also be discussed and should include any organizational requirements to report information; this can include reporting suspicious activity,

changes in an individual's status (e.g., name, citizenship, marital status, etc.), loss of an employee identification card, or other adverse information.

- Requirements and guidelines governing security clearances (if applicable within your organization).
- Defining what resources are designated as critical within your organization, explaining why these items are deemed critical, and discussing company regulations that govern access to these resources. It should be noted that this item may need to be tailored or redacted based on the turnover of employees within your business and how long you are able to keep your personnel, because it would be unwise to provide this information to a group of people who are unlikely to remain in your service for any length of time.

By conducting this training at the start of an employee's career with your organization, it is easy to emphasize not only the place that emergency response occupies, but also the importance your organization places upon the overall safety and security program—all of which should be included as part of every employee's duties.

Recurring Safety and Security Training

In addition to initial training, recurring emergency response training should be conducted for every employee within your organization. This training should be conducted on a periodic basis—once or twice a year should be the goal—and can include any number of issues pertinent to your organization's program. Subjects that you may consider for this recurring training can include emphasis on items that were covered during the initial indoctrination training, such as basic response actions or the critical resources within your business. Another excellent training topic can be specific response actions for a particular type of emergency or incident. The types of incidents you may choose to cover could be based on management concerns due to potential threats that may exist against your company or are possible in the region where you conduct business, or they may simply involve a discussion and analysis of the lessons learned from recent security emergencies and incidents that were in the news. This last subject—incorporating recent incidents and events—has the advantage making a specific recurring training session more interesting and making it have a greater impact on individual employees, which will result in achieving more buy-in among your employees. Regardless of what subjects you choose to include in this recurring training, it should be conducted at a minimum once each year so that you continue to place the appropriate emphasis on emergency response, along with your organization's overall safety and security program, and continue to work to increase security awareness among your employees.

Conclusions on Emergency Response Training

As with any subject, training is a critical aspect of your organization's emergency response program. Training ensures individuals are knowledgeable about and aware of procedures and it provides them with any actions they are required to take. Owing to the many other priorities any company experiences, this emergency response training can take a back seat to other operational issues within your business. With the information contained in this chapter, however, it is hoped that you can incorporate this training in this vital area with minimal effort. Particularly, by ensuring that your organization provides initial and recurring training you will be able to gain the maximum benefit from your emergency response program and significantly minimize the potential for damage, loss, or injury to your company's resources and employees.

Emergency Response Exercises 9

Exercises and simulations augment any training program, as they provide the most beneficial type of training you can conduct to enhance your organization's emergency response program. As we discussed in the previous chapter, all training is closely associated with your emergency response training program and conducting exercises is a tremendous method to highlight the introductory and recurring training that should be part of your overall program. In addition to highlighting much of the training you choose to accomplish, these exercises also reinforce classroom training because they provide employees an opportunity to learn their roles and responsibilities in the event of an actual emergency—which is ultimately the primary reason for any type of emergency response training. It must be noted, however, that the process of planning and conducting an emergency response exercise can be very involved and time-consuming. For this reason, we have dedicated a separate chapter on this aspect of emergency response training to provide you with all of the necessary information to enable you to accomplish these exercises. Over the course of this chapter, we will provide you with the necessary details to plan, prepare, and conduct emergency response simulations and exercises for your organization.

Any plan that exists only in a binder on the shelf, or on a hard drive or server, is not one that will be successfully put into practice when the need arises. Although exercises and simulations require a little more time and planning than other training methods, they provide several significant benefits to any organization's emergency response program. One of these benefits is that a good exercise provides the most accurate assessment of your organization's current emergency response plan for a particular incident, with the exception of the actual emergency, of course. Even though the exercise is meant to simulate the stress and fluidity of an actual situation, a properly organized exercise can provide the most realistic evaluation of your organization's response and, as such, will highlight any significant areas that need improvement within your current procedures so that the organization can make corrections prior to an actual emergency. Another benefit is that an exercise will identify any training deficiencies or confusion regarding your employees' actions during their response to an emergency. An exercise will make it easy to identify whether most personnel understand their particular roles and responsibilities in the event of an incident or whether they are hesitant about what actions should be taken. If there are any issues or if employees are unsure what should be accomplished during their response to the emergency, you have the opportunity to make corrections or better define the applicable portions of the emergency response plan to ensure it contains clear direction. An exercise may also highlight the need for management to consider additional training so that employees can better understand what actions they need to take. Another benefit is that exercises provide more valuable and realistic training opportunities—these training events are more likely to result in lessons that will be internalized much more readily by employees rather than by their

Emergency Preparedness for Business Professionals.
Copyright © 2015 Elsevier Inc. All rights reserved.

participation in any classroom presentation that they might receive. A final benefit that exercises and simulations provide is to help the organization determine if there are any equipment or procedural shortfalls within the business's current planned response to an emergency. For example, if communication was not addressed in the current response plans to a natural disaster, an exercise will highlight the need to obtain portable radios or walkie-talkies to ensure your business can communicate during the event. As we cover the methods to accomplish an exercise, your organization will be able to achieve these benefits.

Unfortunately these benefits are offset by the additional amount of effort and planning that is necessary to conduct an exercise. Whereas classroom training requires some preparation and effort, an exercise or simulation requires a great deal more work than other types of training. As a result of this effort, however, conducting an exercise will pay dividends to any organization's emergency response program and the benefits achieved are well worth the effort, as these simulations will ensure employees understand their roles, result in improved plans and procedures, and identify any necessary equipment needed. All these factors will ultimately help to minimize damage and possible injury in the event of an actual emergency to your organization.

Exercise Planning Considerations

There are several items to consider when beginning to plan and develop any type of exercise. One of the most significant considerations includes designating knowledgeable personnel that can develop the exercise scenario and conduct an objective evaluation of the exercise. These personnel must be unbiased in order to supply an untarnished account of your organization's response to the exercise. Only with a realistic evaluation will you be able to truly assess your plan and judge the effectiveness of your employees' response. In addition to the evaluators' objectivity, it is also necessary that these personnel have no responsibility in the actual response to the incident. This is critical because without observers who can watch and assess everyone's response during the event without worrying about their own actions and responsibilities, it will be virtually impossible to accomplish a valid appraisal of your emergency response plan and the response actions that have been directed by your Crisis Management Team. Simply put, all of the effort involved in planning and conducting an exercise may be wasted if personnel who are responsible solely for evaluating the exercise and who can accomplish an objective and valid evaluation are not provided.

To ensure the evaluation is thorough and remains objective throughout the assessment, it is necessary to designate a team of individuals who have the sole responsibility to be observers and evaluators during the exercise. As stated, they should not have any responsibility with regard to your organization's response actions nor should they have any additional duties or responsibilities that should be accomplished during the simulated emergency. This can be accomplished either by designating a group of individuals from within your organization who are not critical to the response activities for the particular type of incident you are simulating or by considering obtaining personnel from an outside agency to accomplish this assessment. In some cases, local law enforcement or fire departments may be willing to assist in this evaluation of your exercise at no charge, or you may wish to consider working with a consultant to provide this service. Regardless of how you decide to provide for these evaluators, it cannot be emphasized enough that they should not be part of the actual response; otherwise many of the issues and areas for improvement obtained during the exercise would be based upon an inaccurate or biased response or invalid information.

Another consideration when planning an exercise is to ensure you use a realistic scenario as the basis for this simulation. It is also advisable to begin your organization's exercise program with a fairly simple type of emergency response—something on the order of a fire drill or shelter-in-place drill. Although this should seem obvious, there are many organizations who conduct their first exercise using an extremely complex incident that also has an extremely low possibility of occurrence according to the company's Risk Assessment Matrix. Many organizations will conduct this type of exercise simulation based on recent events and concerns within the community. For example, many public agencies and schools will conduct active shooter scenarios, which are one of the most complex types of events imaginable, immediately after a real-world incident. This knee-jerk reaction to public perception not only makes it extremely difficult to accomplish a valid training opportunity but also does a disservice to the organization's emergency response program because it is unlikely that the exercise will be successful in accomplishing its objectives. Ultimately, attempting an extremely complex type of simulation will add to the amount of time and resources necessary to accomplish the exercise and dissuade the company from conducting another exercise in the future. This complexity will also make it difficult to identify areas for improvement within your organizational emergency response plans. Instead, it is best to take "baby steps" and start an exercise program with a fairly simple simulation and take the experience and lessons learned from this as you progress to more complex scenarios.

A final consideration is to ensure your planning includes a detailed scenario with a complete sequence of events. This sequence of events, normally termed a Master Scenario Events List, or MSEL, by experts who routinely conduct exercises, is a comprehensive list of each individual event that forms the overall scenario. The MSEL will typically include each and every individual event that would occur over the course of an emergency incident. This MSEL not only provides for an overall guide to the exercise, but it also provides a breakdown of each individual event, making what can be a very complex scenario (i.e., an active shooter exercise) into a smaller group of incidents, which makes it much easier to plan the simulation and help to break down the multitude of activities into separate response actions. In small-scale exercises, such as a fire drill, the MSEL will be relatively simple and short; however, in larger exercises this document can be fairly extensive. Although we provide an overview of the scenario here, we provide a detailed discussion later in this section so that you can develop an MSEL.

Exercise Planning Process

To conduct any type of exercise, whether it is a relatively simple table-top simulation up to a full-scale exercise, there is a similar process for planning and developing the particular simulation to be accomplished. As discussed earlier, each of the exercises involves a varying level of effort and so these steps will become more involved as you proceed from a fairly simple simulation to a larger type of emergency response exercise; however, the following steps provide an easy-to-follow exercise planning process that will allow you to conduct any type of simulation.

1. Organize and designate an Exercise Management Team to plan, conduct, and evaluate the exercise. This could be a permanent group of individuals or it could be formed at the initiation of any planning process for a particular exercise. The Exercise Management Team should include an exercise director, who leads the overall effort, along with any additional personnel to assist with all necessary tasks to conduct the exercise and evaluate the results.
2. Determine the goal of the exercise. This is a critical step for any successful exercise and you should ensure that senior management agrees and understands the goal prior to proceeding with any further planning. In the context of conducting an emergency drill exercise, the goal will be fairly limited, because the primary response action for this type of incident will require only a simple evacuation. Some example goals for this smaller-scale type of exercise could include ensuring all employees are aware of the alternate evacuation rally point, their actions during a long-distance evacuation, or accomplishing proper accountability of all employees.
3. Review the emergency response actions required within your organization's plans. Again, this step not only applies just to smaller-scale emergency drill exercises but to all types of emergency response simulations. This review ensures management and the exercise team are aware of the required actions within the plan and may help to identify some shortfalls or areas for improvement prior to the actual conduct of the exercise.
4. Develop the exercise scenario. The scenario should be as detailed as possible and should include any necessary notifications to ensure the scope of the exercise stays on track to meet its specific goals. As we discussed earlier, this scenario development includes a detailed list of all events included in the overall emergency. Again, we will cover the development of the MSEL after covering the other tasks involved in the exercise planning process.
5. Conduct prior coordination with any applicable emergency response agencies. In the event your exercise could initiate some type of alarm within the facility or gain the attention of the public, who may raise the alarm, it is best to accomplish any necessary coordination with all local emergency response agencies prior to the exercise to provide them notification of the simulation. This notification may also provide the added benefit of obtaining their assistance and expertise as you plan and prepare for the exercise.
6. Conduct the exercise. The Exercise Management Team should conduct the exercise and ensure they have adequate numbers of individuals located in key areas to assess and evaluate employee response to the incident. We will discuss the various personnel necessary to conduct an exercise along with their roles later in this chapter, but for now these personnel include evaluators at the incident location itself, spread throughout the facility to assess employee reaction, and colocated with your organization's Crisis Management Team at their on-scene control location.
7. Conduct an exercise hot-wash. Immediately upon conclusion of the exercise, the Exercise Management Team should conduct a hot-wash of the exercise with your organization's

Crisis Management Team along with other members of your senior management team. This hot-wash will typically include a brief rundown of the exercise scenario, what the required response actions should have been, what actual reactions to the simulation were observed, and any areas for improvement. The hot-wash should also include key participants in the exercise to obtain their input and perspective.

8. Complete an exercise report. The Exercise Management Team should complete a formal exercise report that contains background on the exercise, areas for improvement, and any recommended changes to the current organizational safety and security plan.

By accomplishing these steps, your safety and security exercise will provide a superior training event to identify any issues within your current emergency response plan. The next aspect that is involved in planning an exercise is a discussion of the various roles necessary to conduct the simulation.

Exercise Roles and Responsibilities

There are a variety of individuals to fulfill certain roles necessary to conduct an exercise. These not only include the players, and any actors to add realism to the event, along with the exercise evaluators, but there are also several other types of participants to conduct all the necessary aspects that help to move the exercise scenario along and accurately depict the ongoing emergency situation. Depending upon the scope of the exercise, it may be possible to combine many of these roles we will look at, especially with regard to smaller-scale simulations, but most larger-scale exercises will require significant numbers within each group of participants. We will look at each of these groups of participants, along with their particular roles and responsibilities, in the following bullets.

- Players. Players are the employees within your organization that are responding and reacting to the exercise in accordance with emergency response plans and procedures. These personnel have the most important task in the exercise because they will be performing their regular roles and responsibilities as they would during an actual emergency and this response will provide the eventual evaluation of the organization's emergency response plans. Ideally, players should not require any prompting from exercise evaluators but instead be able to discuss or initiate actions based on the situation and their own knowledge of the organization's response procedures.
- Simulators. Simulators are personnel who role-play the activities of nonparticipating organizations or individuals. This can include the local law enforcement desk or a federal agency that would be required to respond to a particular type of emergency situation. Simulators will most often operate out of a control center that is out of sight from players. Instead, the primary contact with these simulators is via telephone; however, there may be occasional circumstances in which they are required to have face-to-face contact with players based on the type of scenario or constraints in the exercise. Simulators function semi-independently under the supervision of exercise controllers and they are supposed to enact roles in accordance with the actual procedures of the agency they are pretending to be. These roles should be detailed with instructions provided in the exercise scenario or MSEL.
- Controllers. Controllers are the main participants that are responsible for organizing and conducting the exercise. They plan and manage the exercise scenario, set up and operate the exercise location, and act in the roles of external organizations or individuals who are not

playing in the exercise. Controllers direct the pace of the exercise, provide key data to players, and may prompt or initiate certain player actions to ensure continuity of the exercise as detailed in the MSEL. In addition, controllers will issue information to players as required, monitor the exercise timeline, and supervise the safety of all exercise participants.
- Evaluators. Evaluators are the personnel who assess the players and the organizational procedures. They normally evaluate and provide feedback within a designated functional area of the exercise (e.g., human resources, operations, maintenance, security, etc.) with respect to their area of expertise. Evaluators observe and document performance against established capability targets and critical tasks.
- Actors. Actors simulate specific roles during the exercise play, typically victims, media, or other bystanders; however, their performance is normally not evaluated.

Although your organization's employees will constitute the players within the exercise, it is advisable to obtain knowledgeable personnel to perform the other necessary functions within the exercise scenario. In many smaller-scale exercises, it may be possible to combine the roles of simulators, controllers, evaluators, or actors to save labor; however, larger-scale exercises will probably need to have separate individuals to perform these various duties. The main consideration is to look at the exercise scenario you wish to accomplish and ensure the roles necessary to accomplish the exercise are filled.

Development of the Master Scenario Events List

Any type of exercise should try to approximate a real-world emergency to the maximum extent possible. To achieve this amount of realism, it is necessary that the exercise scenario has the necessary detail so that the events are apparent to everyone involved. This is one of the greatest challenges in any exercise, because the vast majority of the situation behind the emergency must be imagined by all the participants. If there is not sufficient detail, or if the sequence of events does not make sense to the players within the exercise, it will be difficult to make the scenario realistic. This detail ensures that the exercise is able to place stress on the participating players, which will in turn provide improved feedback on your organizational emergency response plans. How then can this detail be achieved? The best method is to ensure the exercise scenario has all of the necessary detail by including each and every event and notification that would normally occur over the course of an actual emergency.

To accomplish this within an exercise scenario, it is helpful to develop a list of each of these events and place them into chronological order. As was mentioned previously, this exercise list is commonly called an MSEL. The MSEL provides the overall script that drives the entire exercise. As the MSEL is developed, it is useful to remember the following steps:

- Review exercise objectives and the overall scenario to ensure they match with the desired goals.
- Identify a chronology of key actions that must occur. These actions can normally be categorized by work function or area (e.g., personnel, facility, intruder, etc.).
- From this chronology, develop a timeline of anticipated player actions.

- Develop the overall MSEL from this chronology and timeline to consolidate all the events into a single list.
- Vet the list with controllers and evaluators to ensure it provides the necessary detail and refine the MSEL as necessary. If personnel have read through the events list and do not understand the overall scenario, it will probably require more detail.

This list is composed of individual events that are provided to players to provide the necessary input to move the simulation along. These individual events are the critical part of the MSEL and they are commonly called injects. Exercise injects are scenario events meant to prompt players into action. This action should normally be in accordance with plans and procedures that implement response actions that the particular exercise scenario is designed to test. A good analogy that will better describe exercise injects are that they can thought of as specific lines in a play—a play that describes the overall exercise scenario. Through these injects, exercise controllers and evaluators provide players with updates of the situation and provide ongoing information regarding the incident as these players are participating in the exercise. For example, the initial exercise inject used to begin an active shooter simulation may state "An individual carrying an AK-47 walks into the main entrance of your facility." This inject would be handed to the receptionist at the main entry point. There are several elements that should be included in any exercise inject:

- Designated scenario time that the inject should be provided to a player
- Intended player who should receive the inject
- Synopsis of the event—what is supposed to occur at this point
- Controller responsible to deliver the inject
- Expected action by the player in accordance with the organizational emergency response plan
- Specific exercise objective demonstrated by the inject

Players will normally see only the first three items of the inject, as the rest of the information is meant to assist the controllers and evaluators. As these injects are provided to the applicable exercise players, the controller should take notes of actions taken by the players and any other items that may assist in their evaluation of the exercise.

To better illustrate the development of this overall scenario list, we will complete a brief example MSEL using an active-shooter exercise scenario. We will work through the various steps in the development of the MSEL, starting with a review of the objectives and scenario.

Review Exercise Objectives and Overall Scenario

Using the example of an active-shooter exercise, the objective of the simulation is to test and evaluate the response procedures for this type of emergency. Our overall scenario can be described as follows. A former employee, recently fired owing to poor performance, enters the main entrance of the facility at midmorning on a weekday. He is carrying an AK-47 with a military vest that contains several ammunition magazines and he appears to have other weapons on his person. He shoots the receptionist on duty in the building's foyer and proceeds to the Human Resources department on the second floor. He shoots employees that he comes into contact with as he moves toward the HR department, and when he reaches the Human Resources area, he directs all the personnel in the department into the HR director's office and barricades the door. In our example, the conclusion of this scenario is dependent on the speed with which the organization contacts local law enforcement and their response to the facility. If police are contacted quickly and they respond to the building in a rapid manner, the situation will end with police entering the room and disabling the perpetrator; however, if the organization does not contact police or they respond slowly (based on the judgment of the exercise controller or other predetermined conditions), the perpetrator will kill all the hostages and then commit suicide.

Identify Chronology of Key Actions

Based on the overall scenario detailed in our example, here is a brief chronology of key actions that must occur:

- Tuesday, 4 August, 10:15 a.m.: Shooter enters the main entrance of the building. This action should include a description of the equipment the shooter will have on his person, so that you can properly equip the actor who portrays this individual with simulated weapons and clothing. This action can also include the name of the individual, if your organization is small enough that a former employee would be recognized by most personnel.
- 10:16–10:20 a.m.: Shooter proceeds toward the Human Resources department on the second floor of the facility. The timeline should accurately represent the amount of time it would take for an individual to walk this distance with some added time should the perpetrator come into contact with any other employees.
- 10:20 a.m.: Upon reaching the Human Resources department, the shooter directs all personnel still in this area into the HR director's office.
- 10:22 a.m.: The shooter closes and locks the door, then moves some furniture into position to barricade the door. Note: if any damage may occur by moving furniture, this action would be simulated (or imagined) to ensure that no harm to the facility or any associated equipment occurs as a result of the exercise.
- 10:25 a.m.: If local law enforcement has not been notified by this time, it will be assumed that they will not respond before the shooter loses patience and commits suicide.
- 10:41 a.m.: If police were notified in a timely manner, they will enter the barricaded office and disable the perpetrator.
- 10:45 a.m.: If police were not notified in time, the shooter will kill all the hostages and then turn the gun on himself.

Develop Anticipated Player Actions

Now that we have developed a rough timeline of the exercise events, we can look at what actions players should take in response. In many cases, the development of these anticipated player actions will be based on your particular organization's emergency response plans and checklists. Using our example scenario, here would be some of the anticipated responses:

- Event: Shooter enters the facility.
- Anticipated responses:
  - Many employees will hear gunfire and move into hallways to see what is happening (this may occur even after the notification of an active shooter).

- ◦ Personnel inside the facility are alerted via building intercom of active-shooter situation.
- ◦ Local law enforcement is notified.
- ◦ Individuals able to evacuate should do so, others will shelter in place and barricade themselves.
- Event: Shooter reaches Human Resources department and takes hostages into office.
- Anticipated responses:
  - ◦ Hostages will be moved into room and stay in one general location as directed by the shooter.
  - ◦ Crisis Management Team is formed and begins to verify all necessary procedures have been accomplished to this point.
  - ◦ Emergency medical services are notified.
  - ◦ If notified, law enforcement is responding to the facility.
  - ◦ Local media finds out about the situation and begins to contact the public relations officer within the organization.
- Event: Shooter barricades himself and hostages inside office.
- Anticipated responses:
  - ◦ If notified, law enforcement arrives on scene.
  - ◦ Crisis Management Team point of contact coordinates with law enforcement personnel to pass on any known information. (Note: the amount of information provided will depend upon the organization's ability to pass on information from previous injects.)
  - ◦ Accountability of evacuees should be ongoing.
- Event: Law enforcement enter facility and barricaded room to neutralize shooter.
- Anticipated responses:
  - ◦ Crisis Management Team begins to obtain information on accountability of personnel.
  - ◦ Local law enforcement contacts medical services to respond to injured personnel and casualties.
  - ◦ Crisis Management Team coordinates with local law enforcement to obtain information on injured and dead.
- Event: Shooter is neutralized.
- Anticipated responses:
  - ◦ Crisis Management Team continues to obtain information on accountability of personnel and begins to receive reports of any missing, injured, or dead.
  - ◦ Crisis Management Team initiates procedures to determine the status of any missing personnel.
  - ◦ Local media reports the incident on local television and radio and continues to contact public relations officer for information.
- Event: Incident is reported on television and radio.
- Anticipated responses:
  - ◦ Crisis Management Team continues to obtain information on accountability of personnel and begins to receive reports of any missing or injured.
  - ◦ Organization is flooded with calls from local community to obtain status on family members who work or were visiting the company.

Develop the Overall MSEL and Refine with Controllers and Evaluators

The final step in developing the exercise MSEL is to complete the list based on the events and anticipated responses that have occurred over the previous steps. A standard format for an exercise MSEL is contained in a table with columns that denote

Table 9.1 **Example Master Scenario Events List (MSEL) Format**

Event #	Event time	Event description	Responsible controller	Recipient player(s)	Expected outcome of player action

time, a description of the event, what controller and player should provide and receive the specific inject, and the expected outcome based on actions by the exercise players. Table 9.1 shows an example of this MSEL format.

Now that we know what the format of an MSEL should look like, we will fill out this list using the information we have developed to this point in time for our example scenario of an active shooter. By referring to both our chronology and the list of events and anticipated actions, we can fill in the various events. These events become the necessary injects that will be provided to the exercise players to move the exercise along its desired path. Table 9.2 shows the completed MSEL for our example.

From this completed MSEL, the exercise team can now begin to work the specific requirements necessary to accomplish the exercise. These should include the exact amount of equipment and the number of personnel needed to provide the actors, controllers, and evaluators, and the exercise team can begin work to complete the necessary inject cards (normally placed on 3×5 cards that are presented to the appropriate player).

Conclusions Regarding MSEL Development

Depending on the size and scale of the exercise you plan to conduct, the MSEL can be fairly simple and broad in nature when used for a small-scale emergency drill, or it can be a very detailed script that prompts exercise participants to take some type of response action in the event of larger-scale exercises. Regardless of what type of exercise you are conducting, it is a good idea to develop the MSEL to ensure nothing is forgotten in the planning and preparation of the simulation. Additionally, the MSEL helps to ensure the exercise is testing the desired objectives, as this document identifies the timing and summarizes all key events, messages, inputs, and contingencies that need to occur within the exercise.

Another consideration with regard to the MSEL is that because this document contains the entire exercise sequence, the MSEL should be prepared in secrecy so that employees who will participate in the event will be unaware of what type of emergency will occur, so that they will not be able to preplan what actions should be taken. This secrecy will ensure that the exercise provides a more valid assessment of the organization's emergency response plan. To maintain this necessary confidentiality,

Table 9.2 Completed Master Scenario Events List (MSEL)

Event #	Event time	Event description	Method of inject	Responsible controller	Recipient player(s)	Expected outcome of player action
000	10:15	Shooter enters the main entrance of building. Shooter is armed with an AK-47 and two handguns in belt holsters. Shooter is wearing a military vest with several ammunition pouches containing several ammo magazines.	Actor	Exercise director	Employees near entrance	• Employees sound alarm
001	10:15	Shooter fires at receptionist. Receptionist falls to ground.	Inject	Exercise director	Receptionist	
002	10:16	Shooter moves toward Human Resources department on the second floor. Any personnel shooter comes in contact with are shot.	Actor	Exercise director	Employees along route	• Intercom notification of active-shooter incident • Employees do not move into hallways to look but instead they evacuate or shelter in place • Notify law enforcement
003	10:20	Shooter reaches Human Resources. Any employees in area are taken hostage and moved into HR director's office.	Actor	Exercise director	Employees in HR	• Intercom notification of active-shooter incident may continue • Employees continue to evacuate or shelter in place • Recall and form Crisis Management Team • Notify law enforcement and emergency medical services (if not done so already)
004	10:25	Shooter has barricaded himself and hostages in office and remains in place.	Actor	Exercise director	Hostages	• Employees continue to evacuate or shelter in place • Crisis Management Team begins accountability

Continued

Table 9.2 Completed Master Scenario Events List (MSEL)—cont'd

Event #	Event time	Event description	Method of inject	Responsible controller	Recipient player(s)	Expected outcome of player action
005	10:26	If notified, initial law enforcement arrives on scene.	Inject	Police exercise controller	Incident commander	• Crisis Management Team representative coordinates with law enforcement with any available information
006	10:27	Media representative from local television station contacts organization's Public Relations officer.	Inject	Media exercise controller	Public Relations officer	• PR officer responds to media as appropriate • Crisis Management Team is notified of contact
007	10:30	If notified, additional law enforcement personnel arrive.	Inject	Police exercise controller	Incident commander	• Employees continue to evacuate or shelter in place • Crisis Management Team continues accountability
008	10:35	If notified, law enforcement will move into facility.	Inject	Police exercise controller	Incident commander	• Employees continue to evacuate or shelter in place • Crisis Management Team continues accountability
009	10:45	If law enforcement was not notified by 10:25, shooter will kill all hostages and then commit suicide.	Inject	Police exercise controller	Incident commander	
010	10:48	Local media begin to report the incident. As a result, the Crisis Management Team is inundated with phone calls from the community.	Inject	Media exercise controller	Public Relations officer	• PR officer coordinates necessary response to the media as appropriate • Crisis Management Team works to minimize these requests or delegates additional personnel to assist the Public Relations officer

011	10:55	If notified, law enforcement will kill the shooter. One hostage will have sustained injury from the shooter before being neutralized.	Inject	Police exercise controller	Incident commander	
012	11:00	Law enforcement will declare the building safe and medical services will begin removal of injured.	Inject	Police exercise controller	Incident commander	• Employees who sheltered in place are notified they can proceed outside • Crisis Management Team continues accountability to include personnel who sheltered in place
013	11:10	Emergency medical services notify Crisis Management Team of the identities of injured and dead personnel.	Inject	Police exercise controller	Incident commander	• Crisis Management Team continues accountability
014	11:20	Once accountability is accomplished and Crisis Management Team is able to accurately assess the status of all employees and visitors, the exercise ends	Inject	Exercise director	Incident commander	

the MSEL is typically developed exclusively by the team responsible for planning and conducting the exercise. This group should ensure extremely limited distribution of the information within the MSEL so that the simulation can better gauge all participants' response over the course of the scenario—this distribution should even exclude senior management and members of the Crisis Management Team. The lack of any prenotification of the exercise—or what the simulation is designed to test—ultimately makes the event more realistic. Remember that employees would not have prior warning of an actual emergency incident so they should not have an idea of what will occur during the exercise.

Completing the Exercise Planning Process

Now that the overall scenario and the MSEL have been developed and formally written down, it is possible to accomplish the remaining steps in the exercise planning process. The next step is to ensure you conduct any prior coordination with any applicable emergency response agencies—this may result in their direct assistance with the exercise, but it will also ensure that if they receive notification from someone in the community who misinterprets your exercise as an actual emergency, they will be able to understand the nature of the incident. Once this notification and coordination have been accomplished, you should be able to proceed with the exercise and then accomplish the remaining steps in the exercise planning process, which include conducting the exercise hot-wash and finalizing the report to discuss any lessons learned and areas for improvement within your organization's existing emergency response plans.

Major Types of Exercises

Now that we have covered the process necessary to plan and organize an exercise, we will look at the types of exercises that an organization can conduct to assist with your emergency response training and planning. There are three major types of exercises that can be categorized to assist with training and evaluation of your safety and security plans and procedures. These exercise types include emergency drills, table-top scenarios, and full-scale exercises. Each of these exercises and simulations requires varying levels of effort; however, each provides many of the benefits any type of exercise has to offer. An emergency drill is the simplest and easiest exercise to plan and prepare for, followed by the slightly larger amount of effort necessary to accomplish a table-top scenario. At the end of the spectrum of involvement and preparation for these types of exercises is the full-scale exercise—this type of simulation is the most complex simulation to plan and conduct but it also allows for the maximum amount of testing and evaluation to an organization's emergency response plan. Over the next several sections, we will look at each of these types of exercises and explain what each type of simulation encompasses along with the actions to be taken to conduct each of these emergency response exercises.

Emergency Drills

An emergency drill is the simplest type of emergency response exercise and can be accomplished with minimal planning while still evaluating portions of your organization's plans and procedures. As with any type of exercise, the purpose of an emergency drill is to familiarize personnel with the safety procedures and ensure everyone is aware of the actions to take in the event of a real emergency; however, these types of simulations are typically limited in nature and they normally test only a small portion of an organization's emergency response plan—usually one or two specific response actions. The best example of an emergency drill is a fire drill. Owing to local, state, or federal requirements, almost every facility owner or operator must conduct fire drills and other similar types of exercises on a periodic basis. Even though many of these types of emergency drills are mandatory, that does not mean they should simply be done to "check off the box" in meeting that particular requirement—instead, organizations can take advantage of these required drills and maximize the benefit they provide with just a small amount of additional planning. This not only will ensure you meet the regulatory requirements to accomplish a particular emergency drill, but additionally will allow for your organization to practice some emergency response actions in conjunction with the event. Regardless of what type of response action you may choose to exercise during an emergency drill, you should ensure you follow each step within the emergency response exercise planning process, even including the development of an MSEL. Although the MSEL should be very brief for these types of drills, it is a good idea to utilize the same process for any type of simulation you conduct to ensure nothing is forgotten.

Emergency Drill and Evacuation Considerations

The first response action, and the one that is more typically associated with emergency drills, is an evacuation. Because evacuation from the facility is one of the two standard responses for employees and other visitors in the event of an emergency and most personnel will be familiar with their responsibilities, it is good practice to use these drills to test other possible scenarios for this type of exercise. Instead of always conducting the same type of immediate evacuation from the facility, your organization may want to consider conducting a long-distance evacuation or moving personnel to alternate rally points during one of these emergency drills. Whereas short-distance evacuations are the quickest method to get personnel out of the building and into specific areas, once personnel are knowledgeable about this action it is a good idea to practice some of the other evacuation drills. This is especially true if there is a potential danger located in close proximity to the facility that could produce occasions on which long-distance evacuations may be warranted.

Although we have briefly mentioned long-distance evacuations, we have not done a thorough explanation. Long-distance evacuations are defined as evacuations that result in personnel being located no closer than 400 yards from the building once they are in their designated rally or assembly point. These types of evacuations should be conducted periodically to ensure your employees know what they must do in the event a long-distance evacuation is necessary. Additional factors in conducting an emergency drill that involves long-distance evacuation could be the identification of issues such as alternate transportation if walking is impractical owing to the distances involved, the location of your facility (i.e., if the building is on a major thoroughfare or highway), or weather considerations in your region. Some types of situations that may warrant these longer distance evacuations include gas leaks, bomb threats, chemical/biological incidents, or other emergencies that could result in a hazard in the immediate area of the facility. Because of the potential logistical difficulties, long-distance evacuations should be directed only by a designated individual within your organization, such as the Security Manager or other suitable executive, or may be ordered by local law enforcement or fire department officials. These considerations involving long-distance evacuations should be taken into account in your planning of any emergency drill in which you will be testing this type of scenario.

Another consideration prior to conducting any type of emergency drill involving an evacuation is that your organization should designate multiple rally or assembly points for individual work sections or employees. These multiple locations where personnel should gather after exiting the facility provide flexibility and also ensure that employees are prepared to evacuate to alternate locations in the event that the primary rally point or area is unavailable. Once an alternate rally point has been designated, the easiest procedure is to make staff aware of both the primary and the alternate locations. Normally, personnel should be advised to move toward their primary assembly area unless they have been notified that the use of an alternate location is necessary upon initiation of the evacuation.

Another consideration for any type of evacuation—particularly in the event of an actual emergency—is the ability to ensure accountability of all your employees and visitors to your facility at the time of the incident. We have discussed this need throughout many of our previous discussions of emergency response planning; however, it cannot be emphasized enough. Even in the case of a simple fire drill, this accountability is a critical process and should ensure not only that your organization can account for all individuals assembled in their respective evacuation area during these relatively simple response actions but also that the business can identify any missing visitors or employees who were located within your facility at the time of the emergency.

A final issue to consider when looking at emergency drills and prior to an actual evacuation is to determine your organization's decision-making process for when release of employees is a better option than a simple evacuation. Factors in this decision include how long the evacuation is anticipated to last, the time of day when the evacuation occurs (if the evacuation occurs 10 min prior to the end of the workday, it will probably be better to just conduct a release), or if there is any potential of long-term contamination or eventual damage to surrounding areas around your facility. In the last two instances, you would have some very upset employees if you failed to allow people to remove their vehicles during the evacuation and, several hours after the incident, authorities determine that all those vehicles are now damaged because of their proximity to the building structure. Regarding any long-term contamination, it is advisable to coordinate with local authorities before allowing employees to remove their vehicles because they may simply be spreading the potential contaminants throughout the area. Typically, this decision-making process should involve senior management within the organization and ensure they have the authority to make this decision. In the case of contamination, this decision may fall outside the purview of the CEO or whomever your organization may designate to make this decision, so your appropriate emergency plans and procedures should include these considerations within any decision-making process.

Emergency Drill and Shelter-in-Place Considerations

The second primary response action we have previously discussed is the shelter-in-place operation. An emergency drill can also be used to test this type of event within your organization. There are two major types of shelter-in-place operations that we have covered—one involves sealing areas off within the facility to limit the spread of any contaminants and the other is to protect personnel trapped inside the building from an armed perpetrator. There are some considerations in the event you choose to exercise a shelter-in-place process that seals off certain work areas. One such consideration is to determine if your organization has viable hazards that could result in some type of contamination. If your business is an accounting firm and is not located near any agencies that deal with hazardous materials, it is not necessary that you plan an exercise to test such an unlikely scenario. If, on the other hand, your organization does work with such materials, this may be a good emergency drill to conduct. Another consideration is the need to ensure your employees are aware of what areas should be sealed off and that adequate materials are available (e.g., plastic sheets, duct tape, towels, etc.) to accomplish this procedure. A final consideration is to ensure maintenance personnel are aware of their actions. As mentioned previously, this can include shutting down ventilation systems and closing ducts to minimize spread of contaminated air throughout the facility. In the event that you choose to exercise a shelter-in-place operation that involves barricading rooms against a perpetrator, the first consideration must be that employees understand this should be done only as a last resort. If they are able to evacuate the facility without risk from the culprit, they should do so. If this is not the case, employees must be aware of the actions to take, including covering any windows in the room, using furniture to block the entry, and hiding in locations that provide cover and concealment from the individual.

Once you have planned for these considerations involved with either an evacuation or a shelter-in-place scenario, your organization is not only ready to plan for an emergency drill exercise but, more importantly, prepared to respond to a real-world emergency.

Table-Top Scenarios

Conducting a table-top exercise is a little more involved than planning an emergency drill; however, this minimal amount of added effort provides several more benefits to your organization created by taking a more thorough look at the necessary emergency response and the opportunity for greater involvement among your staff. Furthermore, you can test emergency scenarios that would not be possible during a simple emergency drill. Last, a table-top scenario offers the ability to tailor the extent of the simulation based upon your specific exercise objectives and available time your staff can dedicate to the scenario. Again, even though this type of simulation does not involve the effort necessary to accomplish a full-scale exercise, it is still best to use the exercise planning process. There are also some additional considerations to assist in preparing for this type of exercise beyond those involved with an emergency drill. Let's assume that you have already determined the type of emergency incident you wish to use in your table-top scenario and have conducted a review of the emergency response actions detailed in your organizational plans and procedures as we look at these additional areas.

Preparation Considerations Involved in a Table-Top Scenario

The first step is to ensure you have an adequate area or work space to conduct the planned table-top exercise. It is not necessary to accomplish a table-top exercise at the actual site of the emergency as this could make planning and accomplishment more difficult—remember that an advantage of a table-top scenario is that it is much easier to conduct than a full-scale exercise. Instead, the simulation can be conducted in a standard conference or meeting room. The only necessity for the location is to ensure the room has enough table space for all the participants to review material and ideally the area should have white boards or other equipment to assist participants in communicating ideas and actions or working through processes over the course of the simulation.

Another step that should be included in preparation of any table-top scenario is to schedule the time and location to conduct the exercise. It is also advisable to establish a strict end time for the exercise and ensure this is adhered to. The ability to limit the amount of time of a table-top scenario is another one of the primary advantages to this type of exercise so you want to ensure you do not run over your allotted time. To adhere to this, some agencies may choose to designate an individual that acts as a timekeeper to ensure the exercise ends at the agreed-upon time—this strict observance to the start and end time will ensure the exercise does not drag on and will be more likely to motivate all of the involved participants to conduct future table-top scenarios or other similar exercises.

Another consideration necessary in the preparation for a table-top scenario is obtaining and organizing all necessary materials. These materials include an agenda, exercise objectives, assumptions, copies of the emergency response plan, and appropriate checklists. The exercise director should develop this documentation prior to the exercise and hand this material out at the start. This material should help to prompt players with the correct response actions, which will create a more productive learning environment for the exercise.

The last consideration in preparation for a table-top exercise is to ensure all appropriate personnel are invited and able to attend. It is unlikely that there can be too many personnel who are participating in a table-top exercise—the major consideration is to ensure that a key member is not absent, as this could limit the benefit of conducting the exercise. It may also be advisable to consider inviting some outside agencies who may be pertinent to the specific type of emergency or who would be required to assist with your organization's response. In the case of a table-top scenario, the more personnel involved, the more likely there will be cross talk and feedback, which will lead to better training and identification of any areas that need improvement.

Conducting the Exercise

Now that we have accomplished the necessary planning steps that are unique to preparing for a table-top scenario, the next step is to actually conduct the exercise. At the start of the meeting, some areas to cover prior to initiation of the scenario should include:

- Review of the exercise agenda, objectives, and assumptions
- Discussion of ground rules along with participant roles and responsibilities
- Reminder of the schedule for the exercise; this is the opportunity to emphasize the start and end times for the simulation
- Distribution of a copy of the exercise scenario
- Ensure an individual is available with the primary responsibility of taking notes and keeping time over the course of the event

Once these preparatory steps have been accomplished, the exercise director should begin by providing input in accordance with the exercise MSEL to the group or applicable participants. In large-scale exercises, the exercise director or other controllers will normally provide only injects to an affected player in one area of the exercise location without any prompting to assist in the response actions of the organization; however, owing to the desire to provide education and training throughout table-top scenarios, the director can choose to act as a mediator to ensure all the participants consider their appropriate response actions—particularly if major actions are missed. These items should still be recorded as an area of improvement but it will ensure a smoother flow over the course of the situation and table-top exercise. Last, the exercise director—in the role as mediator—should also work to promote communication throughout the entire group, as the primary purpose of the simulation is to train everyone on appropriate response actions.

Postexercise Actions

The last step involved in a table-top scenario is to conduct the postexercise actions in accordance with the exercise planning process. Because one of the advantages of a table-top scenario is the firm time limits, it is critical to ensure your schedule allows for these actions and that there is enough time allotted at the end of the meeting—particularly because this step is the most important in the process, as it identifies any lessons learned and areas for improvement within the organization's emergency response plans. These steps should also allow for discussion from all the exercise participants on the following areas:

- Evaluation of the group's response actions to the simulated emergency
- Identification of any equipment items not identified within the current plans but found to be necessary for the organization to accomplish the required response

- Identification of procedural areas for improvement to incorporate into the emergency response plan
- Discussion of the lessons learned as a result of the simulation

Although much of the training and learning will naturally be accomplished over the course of the exercise scenario, a good portion of this education, which includes the areas for improvement, lessons learned, and identification of any long-term improvements necessary to your organization's emergency response plan, is best highlighted at the conclusion of the exercise.

Full-Scale Exercises

A full-scale exercise is the most involved and complex type of exercise that any organization can conduct with regard to its emergency response program. Whereas emergency drills or a table-top exercise can be accomplished with relatively short preparation time and few personnel, significant planning and coordination, not only with your own employees but also with other affected agencies, will be required prior to conducting an actual exercise. To provide some perspective on the amount of planning necessary for these types of endeavors, full-scale exercises at the state and federal level can take months to plan and the actual exercise may last for several days. Fortunately most business organizations do not need to conduct exercises of this magnitude to improve their emergency response plans, so it will be unnecessary to devote the same amount of planning and preparation that these federal agencies require, nor is it necessary to conduct exercises for such long periods of time.

Although full-scale exercises will take more effort than the smaller-scale exercises we have previously discussed, the added benefits in terms of employee training and identifying areas for improvement within your own emergency response plans and procedures make these events well worth the exertion. The extra time and resources necessary to conduct a full-scale exercise will yield a vastly higher level of education and training for all participants because many people learn more from actually doing a task than sitting through a formal presentation. These types of exercises will also provide greater clarity to identify areas for improvement owing to the added realism of the scenario and the higher level of stress found in full-scale exercises, which will come closer to the actual event than any other type of exercise. Ultimately, all of these benefits will result in a higher level of experience gained by your entire staff.

As with any other type of exercise, preparation for a full-scale exercise should include the standard steps we have already discussed. As is expected with any task that is on a larger scale than other similar efforts, however, a full-scale exercise will require some additional preparation steps compared to either an emergency drill or a table-top scenario. Many of these tasks are necessary to provide the added realism inherent in a large-scale exercise. We will cover these additional items as they apply to the exercise preparation, conduct of the exercise, and postexercise actions.

Exercise Preparation

One of the most significant differences in preparing a full-scale exercise compared to the other types of exercises is the additional effort required to develop the necessary detail in the scenario and ultimately in the MSEL document. As discussed earlier, the MSEL is the document that identifies the timing of exercise inputs, summarizes events, details any injects that are to be provided to players, and lists the expected actions necessary for the exercise to progress. Owing to the scope of a full-scale exercise it can be easy to overlook some task, so it is best that the MSEL is developed over several iterations. This will ensure that any and all injects the exercise players would be likely to experience over the course of the emergency situation are not forgotten and closely match what would occur during an actual incident. As such, careful attention should be made when developing this document to ensure all functional areas are involved so that all work areas experience realistic problems related to the scenario. This attention and involvement of all functional areas within your organization will help to ensure that actions in response to an initial inject are thought through and that the appropriate response actions are included and accounted for within the overall situation. We have already provided a sample MSEL for a full-scale exercise in Table 9.2; however, it should be noted that this example is fairly brief. In some cases, MSELs for a full-scale exercise can include dozens or even hundreds of inputs. As such, the expected outcome of any input should be tailored to match your company's responses based on your business structure and as directed within your emergency response plan.

In addition to ensuring the MSEL includes all the necessary events for the planned scenario, the next preparation step that is unique to a full-scale exercise is to determine an appropriate location where you can conduct the exercise. Although most organizations will typically conduct a full-scale exercise within the confines of their own facility and property—and of course there are many advantages to conducting the exercise in your own work areas—there may be instances in which it would be safer or cheaper to conduct the exercise elsewhere. For example, if your organization is located with several other agencies or in a high-rise building, there may be certain types of scenarios in which the necessary response to the emergency could result in disruption to the other companies or personal injury based upon the characteristics of your particular building. If this is the case, you may consider looking at other locations to conduct the full-scale exercise to ensure a less disruptive or safer environment. Another instance in which to consider an alternate location for the exercise could be that responding forces could cause damage to your facility through their standard actions—for example, most law enforcement special tactics units would normally wish to conduct dynamic entry methods to respond to your exercise scenario. These dynamic entry procedures will normally involve breaking down of doors, windows, or walls as they move into the facility. This end result may not be a desired outcome, however, if you have just opened a new facility and if you failed to conduct adequate coordination with these local police units prior to the exercise (so that they believe they can conduct these dynamic entry methods). Instead, you may be able to work with these law enforcement agencies and find a suitable abandoned or derelict building that can be used to provide a venue that allows for more realistic training for all participants. Regardless of where you choose to conduct a full-scale exercise—whether in your own facility or an alternate location—the venue must be large enough to provide the necessary space for your employees' response actions and other agencies. It should also allow for any additional actions that can accommodate the maximum amount of reality possible. Any of these potential issues should be weighed and accounted for when deciding whether to conduct an exercise at your own facility or an alternate location.

Although we have discussed the need to obtain and task the necessary personnel and equipment for exercises, this effort takes on much greater significance during a full-scale exercise. We have already discussed the various roles and responsibilities of the various personnel necessary to conduct an exercise. To conduct a full-scale exercise, it will be necessary to ensure personnel are available to fulfill all these necessary roles and responsibilities. This must include all the players, simulators, controllers, evaluators, and actors needed to provide realism for the event. In addition to personnel, there will probably be more equipment requirements to conduct a full-scale exercise as opposed to an emergency drill or table-top scenario. I would like to note that the only equipment that you should consider procuring for the exercise, prior to the actual event, should relate to simulators, controllers, evaluators, and actors. This will help the exercise accomplish a couple of different things. First, limiting the amount of equipment to the exercise personnel, will limit the amount of items that would need to be procured and save money. This equipment could include communication devices, special uniforms or other identification, or other equipment necessary for the control and running of the exercise scenario. Should your exercise require the use of a simulation cell, some additional communication equipment may be necessary for this section also. Actors may also require some additional equipment, such as makeup or moulage gear (equipment that helps simulate severe injuries or trauma). Second, limiting the purchase of equipment to the exercise controllers, rather than personnel within your own organization, will better test your current procedures and provide a truer picture of what areas need to be looked at and improved. There should not be any special equipment purchases for your own employees—personnel who will act as players during the exercise. This is because the exercise should test the organization's response actions to an emergency based upon the equipment that is available at all times within your company. I have seen organizations temporarily procure equipment to assist in their emergency response to a full-scale exercise (e.g., walkie-talkies, security alarms, etc.) and after the exercise return all this equipment. Although these items may have made the response to the exercise more successful, it would not have provided you with an accurate assessment of your emergency response plan nor would it give a valid assessment of your organization's capability to respond to a real-world incident.

It will also be necessary to notify certain agencies that you are planning to conduct a full-scale exercise. Whereas we have discussed this issue previously, it takes on more importance with the larger full-scale exercise than the other types of scenarios. This notification can include local law enforcement, fire department, or even the media—which agencies should be notified will depend on your business, its visibility within the community, and the type of scenario you plan to conduct. Unfortunately, only you and your organization can make the best determination of who to notify. To illustrate the need for this task, consider a school that is planning to conduct an active-shooter exercise. If they accomplish this exercise with no prior notice to the media and the community, imagine the backlash when a young third-grader goes home and tells his parents that his school had armed police storming into the building to get a man with a gun! It is hoped that your employees can provide a more objective perspective of your exercise scenario than the third-grader, in this example, but any notification after the exercise has already occurred will be much more difficult to explain. Unfortunately, this has actually occurred in many areas and the negative backlash did not help the school in the eyes of its community. This issue can be easily solved, though, by ensuring your organization makes the appropriate coordination prior to any type of exercise. This coordination serves not only to provide this notification but also to afford an opportunity to invite certain agencies that would probably respond and assist in the event of the planned scenario. Again, the agencies and methods your organization should use in this notification process will strictly depend on your particular business environment but it is not an item that can be overlooked.

Conducting the Exercise

To successfully conduct a full-scale exercise, there are several additional considerations that should be taken into account compared with the other types of scenarios. These considerations include an adequate number of exercise evaluators, appropriate communications and other equipment solely dedicated to the evaluation team, and a process to ensure that all evaluators attend internal meetings and discussions prior to the hot-wash that they will conduct with all the exercise participants.

Without a sufficient number of individuals who have the experience and expertise in their respective job area to evaluate the exercise, it will be impossible to provide an objective assessment of the exercise. If there is not an adequate number of evaluators, they will not be able to see all the duty sections that are taking action and accomplishing tasks over the course of the emergency situation and some particular functional areas would not be assessed. This defeats the purpose of conducting the exercise because you must ensure your procedures reach across the entire organization and all work areas. In addition to ensuring there are enough evaluators, you must also be certain that these individuals have the necessary expertise in their respective functional area to truly assess the performance of a particular individual or duty section. This functional expertise and experience should include the duties a particular work area is responsible for, but the evaluator must also be familiar with your organization's appropriate emergency response actions for that particular duty section. Ideally, this level of expertise and experience should be equivalent to that of a functional area's manager or director—the greater an evaluator's job knowledge the better the assessment, so it is important to note that the assignment of an exercise evaluator should not be given to an intern or entry-level employee. A last task that the evaluation team must perform is the control and running of the exercise. This also requires that there are an adequate number of controllers and evaluators to ascertain that the players understand the exercise injects and take the appropriate action. We have already covered these tasks, during our discussion on the preparation of a full-scale exercise earlier in this chapter, but it is still worth noting that a sufficient number personnel must be allocated to provide this role in the exercise. Although the numbers of evaluators and simulation personnel necessary to accomplish a full-scale exercise may sound overwhelming, it is normally sufficient to have one evaluator for each primary functional area, one individual to act as the control and simulation cell, and one exercise director. Another good rule of thumb is that the ratio of players to evaluators can be as high as around 100 to 1. Thus, it is typically possible to conduct an exercise with about a dozen personnel acting as controllers, evaluators, and simulators for most full-scale exercises.

Another item for consideration in conducting full-scale exercises is to ensure that secrecy is maintained prior to the event. We have already discussed the need to ensure that the exercise scenario and detailed MSEL are not known by any players; however, this secrecy should also apply to the equipment that must be procured for the exercise controllers and evaluators. The evaluation team should be provided the necessary equipment to accomplish their duties without the knowledge of other exercise participants. This equipment should include some method of secure communications so that they can coordinate between other evaluators and notify one another of issues or concerns without the knowledge of other exercise participants. The exercise evaluation team should also have a separate location and work area where they can conduct any meetings and discussion prior to the exercise hot-wash to be conducted with all participants. If the exercise evaluators are from outside your own organization, it may also be necessary to furnish them with standard office equipment, such as computers and printers, for them to develop the final exercise report.

In the event the exercise evaluators are from within your own organization it is a good idea to use a standard process and guidelines when conducting the evaluation—particularly if many of these personnel have never evaluated an exercise before. Adhering to a certain set of guidelines not only helps to ensure consistency among all the evaluators but should also minimize any individual beliefs or idiosyncrasies a particular evaluator may have that could diverge from your organization's established procedures. This is an important item—exercise evaluators are not supposed to follow their own ideas of what is the appropriate response, but instead, they are supposed to follow only the formal procedures in their evaluation. The following is a good start on the guidelines that evaluators should follow:

- Meetings should be conducted prior to the exercise with all evaluators, controllers, and simulators to ensure everyone understands the scenario, appropriate actions, and evaluator guidelines.
- Clearly define each evaluator's role and responsibility.
- Each evaluator should be responsible for monitoring workplace safety and should understand that he or she is to stop a player's actions if unsafe.
- Evaluators must always be professional. They should never degrade any exercise participant or his or her actions—any corrections should be accomplished using a positive training and learning environment.
- Evaluators must conduct their evaluation in accordance with the company's regulations, plans, and procedures. It is never acceptable for an evaluator to assess an action based on what she or he thinks should be done with no other basis.
- All evaluators should attend a separate meeting prior to any exercise hot-wash with all participants. This meeting should cover each functional area's evaluations to ensure they are appropriate and meet only the necessary requirements.

By following these guidelines, evaluators will be much more successful in obtaining buy-in regarding their assessment, and the training based on your organization's exercise will be much more productive.

Postexercise Actions

As with the other types of exercises, it is important to properly carry out the actions necessary once the exercise has been completed. These tasks help to make corrections to the emergency response process and identify as many areas for improvement as possible. These actions match that of any other type of exercise and should include an evaluation of the participants' response to the emergency, identification of necessary equipment (both for the actual response and for the evaluators), lessons learned to improve the process for the next exercise, and identification of areas of improvement within the emergency response plan. Owing to the extra information that will be obtained from all of these areas compared with smaller-scale exercises, a formal exercise report is a necessity for any full-scale exercise. This report should be developed by the team that oversaw and managed the entire exercise process. The report should also include all relevant information from the exercise such as the overall scenario and any necessary background that may help a reader to better understand the report and its results. Even after the report has been written and finalized, senior management should track action items based on any identified areas for improvement or recommendations. This will ensure your organization makes the best possible use of the exercise and considers all possible improvements or changes to your current procedures. It will also help that the organization does not lose visibility on these issues based on the level of effort necessary to conduct the full-scale exercise.

Once the report and other postexercise actions have been completed, it would be wise to consider when you should plan to accomplish your next exercise. As we have discussed throughout this section, exercises provide one of the most useful tools not only to identify and correct problems within your emergency response plan but also to accomplish training for your employees so they will better internalize their actions in the event of an actual emergency. Although it may seem that the last thing many organizations would want to do immediately after the effort of accomplishing one exercise is think about when to conduct the next event, it would be best to establish a date for the next scenario (even if it is a smaller-scale effort) while the event is fresh in everyone's mind. Once this date has been established, the organization can then move on to normal business.

When planning your next exercise, it is recommended that your organization think about the following frequency with which to conduct emergency response exercises:

- Augmenting emergency drills with some additional exercise inputs should be conducted a minimum of once a year.
- An additional table-top exercise should be conducted once per year.
- Owing to the significant amount in the effort and planning to conduct a full-scale exercise, it is recommended that these be conducted only once every two to three years.

By conducting, planning, and scheduling exercises on a periodic basis, you will ensure your emergency response program maintains its ability to meet any threats and vulnerabilities your organization may face, both at present and in the future.

Summary of Emergency Response Exercises

Over the course of this chapter, we have looked at the advantages of conducting exercises and how they assist in your overall emergency response program and its training. In this discussion, we covered the areas to consider when planning an exercise and the process of planning and conducting these exercises, along with the various types of exercises that can be accomplished. One of the primary considerations in planning any type of exercise is to ensure knowledgeable personnel are tasked to prepare and conduct these simulations. These personnel should be dedicated solely to the evaluation and control of the exercise scenario and have no role in the actual response actions within your organization.

Next, we covered the exercise planning process, which included the following steps:

- Organize and designate an Exercise Management Team.
- Determine the goal of the exercise.
- Review the emergency response actions required by your organization's plans.
- Develop the exercise scenario and consolidate this information into an MSEL.
- Conduct prior coordination with any applicable emergency response agencies.
- Conduct the exercise.
- Conduct an exercise hot-wash.
- Complete an exercise report.

This process should be utilized regardless of the type of exercise or the scale of the simulation. A significant part of this planning process is to ensure there are adequate numbers of personnel to fulfill the various roles in some of the larger scale exercises. In addition to these roles, we also went into specifics on the method to develop a detailed exercise scenario and Master Scenario Events List, or MSEL, as these items will drive the overall exercise and help to determine its success or failure.

The last area we covered was the various types of exercises that can be accomplished. These exercises can range from a simple emergency drill, such as a fire drill; to a table-top exercise; and finally to a full-scale exercise involving actors, evaluators, exercise controllers, and players. No matter what type of exercise you may choose to conduct within your organization, any of these simulations not only will provide you with a valuable training tool but will also highlight areas that need improvement within your current emergency response plan and procedures.

Responding to Emergency Incidents

Within this chapter, we look at specific types of emergencies that pose concerns for many organizations along with the standardized and accepted response actions that are typically taken in the event that an organization experiences any of these types of incidents. We also discuss the use of checklists for each of these emergencies and how these lists can improve your organization's ability to respond. These checklists not only provide a guide for both your Crisis Management Team and your employees, but also help to remind everyone of the major actions that must be taken to effectively respond to a particular emergency situation.

Various Types of Emergencies and their Accepted Response

There are many different types of emergencies and incidents that can occur to a business. As we previously discussed in the introductory section of this book, it is helpful (and in most cases necessary) for your organization to develop a Risk Assessment Matrix. This document helps senior management to determine the likelihood of these various situations occurring, which ultimately helps your company to prioritize and develop your organization's mitigation strategies. Whereas money and time will limit the number of mitigation measures you can implement to minimize or even prevent these emergency incidents from happening, your emergency response plans and procedures can be implemented with little cost and will enable you to develop response actions for all the potential incidents that could occur to your organization—not just the ones that are the most likely to happen. These plans and procedures will further help to minimize any potential loss or damage that could have an impact on your organization owing to these incidents. As we look at many of the various types of emergencies, this concept—that of implementing plans and procedures first and then looking to augment these practices with equipment to assist in security—is a very effective method to mitigate against these types of incidents.

The following is a fairly comprehensive list of situations that most organizations could encounter and that your emergency response plans and procedures should address. You should develop specific procedures for all of these incidents to ensure you have provided mitigation against all possible situations and detailed your organization's response actions before the incident actually occurs.

- Natural disasters (i.e., floods, tornadoes, hurricanes, and earthquakes)
- Major equipment breakdowns
- Financial loss, which would include embezzlement, fraud, and theft

Emergency Preparedness for Business Professionals.

- Chemical or biological incidents
- Criminal and terrorist acts, which would include active shooters, unauthorized visitors, hostage situations, and other types of workplace violence incidents
- Vandalism
- Fire/arson
- Sabotage
- Travel security
- Loss of key personnel
- Labor disputes

We will provide an explanation for each of these types of emergencies over the next several sections and provide the standardized and recommended response actions that have been accepted as effective and efficient during response.

Natural Disasters

Storms and severe weather incidents account for the emergencies that are included within the natural disaster area (Figure 10.1). These situations include:

- Tornadoes
- Hurricanes
- Earthquakes
- Flooding
- Snowstorms

The response actions for many of the severe weather emergencies that we will cover are basically the same because these types of disasters will normally affect your

Figure 10.1 Natural disasters.

organization in similar ways. The effects of these storms and severe weather incidents will typically result in damage or destruction to your facility and possible injuries to your employees. Many of these natural disasters may also result in interruptions to utility service—another consideration that should always be factored into your procedures when developing plans to respond to any of these types of emergencies.

As stated, the response actions for many types of severe weather are similar and will include the following:

1. Notify staff of the severe weather alert and advise them of actions to be taken (e.g., release, evacuation, shelter in place, etc.).
2. In some cases, local authorities may dictate an evacuation—if this occurs, your organization must ensure you provide your employees adequate time to leave the facility and depart the area if necessary.
3. If the decision is made to shelter in place, personnel should move to interior rooms, basements, or hardened shelter if available. We have previously discussed the preparatory actions an organization must take in the event of a shelter in place. These include the identification of specific shelter areas, providing procedures, and storing equipment that would assist in sealing off areas as needed.
4. In many severe weather events, some additional precautions involving shelter in place are necessary because the vast majority of injuries are caused from breaking glass, so personnel should ensure they are sheltering in areas with no exterior windows. DO NOT use gyms or other large rooms as shelter during any type of severe weather until the storm has passed.
5. Depending on the specific type of response action necessary—either evacuation or shelter in place—supervisors must account for all their employees and report any missing personnel to your organization's designated point of contact to track accountability. In the event of an evacuation, this should occur after personnel have had time to depart the area and arrive at their destination. In shelter-in-place operations, supervisors should conduct this accountability over the course of the incident.

Now that we have looked at the general response actions for severe weather, we will look at individual types of incidents within this area and discuss specific actions for hurricanes, earthquakes, blizzards, and flooding.

There are some specific actions for hurricanes that should be considered. The standard response action for a hurricane is to evacuate and release all employees because of the typical amount of lead time that precedes this type of storm. Prior to releasing your employees, the facility and maintenance personnel should attempt to secure all windows with plywood to minimize damage. It is also advisable that all employees secure the company's critical resources prior to their actual evacuation. These critical resources may include equipment, money, proprietary documentation, or other information and data based on your specific type of business. Your organization's response actions should ensure that these items are protected in locations that will be safe from the hurricane.

If your company is located in an area where earthquakes can occur, there are some specific response actions that should be taken during this type of natural incident. Once the shaking starts, the individual actions your employees should take are to immediately drop, cover, and hold their knees to their chest until the earthquake stops. If indoors, personnel should be instructed to remain indoors. Furthermore, they should move away from windows, shelves, heavy objects, or furniture that may fall, and take cover under desks, tables, counters, and open doorways. In hallways, stairways, or other areas where cover is unavailable, your procedures should instruct your personnel to move to an interior wall and turn away from any windows and remain alongside the wall where they are taking shelter. The greatest danger from earthquake is injury from falling debris. If your personnel are outside of the facility at the onset of an earthquake, they should remain outside and move away from the path of falling walls, power poles, trees, wire fences, and rolling rocks. During the earthquake, any individuals outside building should be instructed to lie down or crouch low to the ground. A final consideration for an organization's procedures is that at the onset of an earthquake maintenance staff should conduct checks of utilities, systems, and appliances and, if necessary, shut off main valves as long as these actions are possible to accomplish in a safe manner. As is the case with any type of emergency, once the earthquake is over supervisors must account for their teams and report any missing personnel to your organization's designated point of contact to track accountability. An additional action at the conclusion of an earthquake is for your company's maintenance staff to determine if any hazardous material has spilled or leaked and, if so, isolate and seal off the area and notify the appropriate agency of the spill.

If your organization has the potential to experience flooding, there are some preparedness and response actions that should be considered for this type of severe weather incident. In preparing for this type of event, the facility and maintenance experts should investigate the range and extent of flooding that could occur around the area where your facility is located. This analysis and study should include the timing and direction of the route any flood waters may take. In many cases, the source of flooding may not be immediately obvious, so it is beneficial to check local drainage and small water run-offs along with obtaining information on previous flooding in and around your property. If weather conditions warrant the potential for flooding, the following actions can be taken to reduce the impact and minimize damage. Placing plywood across openings, blocking ventilation openings, and creating sandbag walls will assist in the protection of areas where water can enter your facility and cause damage. Another action can include moving any critical organizational resources to upper floors or removing them from the facility altogether to protect your business.

In the event your region can experience severe snow and blizzards, there are some added precautions that should be taken in addition to the other common actions related to severe weather. Prior to a major snowstorm, your organization's Crisis Management Team should consider evacuation and release of your employees. This action could preclude the need to house employees in your own facility in the event that travel becomes impossible. Ensure your employees are aware of the situation and, if necessary, that they have adequate food and water in their homes. At the conclusion of the storm, the facility and maintenance personnel should have plans in place to clear the parking lots and entryways into the facility to be able to resume normal business operations for both employees and customers.

As we have seen with the various types of severe weather that can occur, many of the response actions are similar. During shelter-in-place situations, employees should take appropriate cover from the storm by moving to interior areas that will provide protection from the potential damage caused by breaking glass. If evacuation and release are warranted—or directed by local authorities—the Crisis Management Team must ensure they provide adequate time for employees not only to leave the facility but also to evacuate the area if necessary. For this reason, it is important that this team make their decision as early as possible in the process to ensure the safety of all employees. Protection of information and other resources vital to your business operations should also be considered and ensured. In all response actions for any type of severe weather (as is the case with any other type of response), it is critical that your organization have a process to account for all your personnel.

Major Equipment Breakdowns

Even with expert installation and regular maintenance, equipment does break down (Figure 10.2). Depending on the nature of your organization and industry, this mechanical or electrical failure can potentially shut down your business. This situation may not only lead to lost productivity but could result in losses of revenue or even customers. For this reason, it is wise to plan and prepare for this specific type of emergency incident to minimize the possibility of these consequences.

Although there are some response actions to address this type of situation, the primary considerations within any emergency response plan are the precautionary measures that should be taken before any critical equipment actually fails. One such effort is to build in redundant systems that can augment, or even temporarily replace, a piece of broken equipment. A good example of this is the use of generators in the event of a lengthy power outage. Another consideration to prepare for this eventuality is equipment breakdown insurance. There are many insurance companies that provide this service and, depending on your organization, this may be a more cost-effective option than the purchase of redundant systems. A final consideration is to develop work flows and processes that can enable your organization to continue its operations even with the temporary failure of a key piece of equipment. In this manner, your organization can use these alternative processes until repair of the affected equipment can be accomplished.

Figure 10.2 Equipment damage and breakdowns.

Figure 10.3 Robbery, theft, and other financial loss incidents.

Financial Loss Incidents

A significant amount of theft and financial loss occurs that is due to an organization's own employees (Figure 10.3). A 2013 study of U.S. retail businesses showed that the number of employees who were apprehended for theft has increased by 5.5% from 2011.[1] We will look at some response actions to these types of incidents; however, the best method to combat theft is to develop proactive measures that stop, or at least deter, theft in the preparedness phase of emergency response.

Preventative Measures to Combat Financial Loss

One of the best methods to combat many types of financial loss incident is to ensure your organization has processes that help rapidly identify when and if theft occurs. If there is no process that helps to highlight that these incidents are occurring, it will be impossible to catch any perpetrators. There are several different measures and processes that can be implemented to assist your organization in minimizing the potential for theft and other types of financial loss.

1. One measure that can be implemented prior to any type of theft is to use security alarms and video surveillance to protect the company's critical resources, which will normally include any funds you have stored on the premises and any other high-dollar items. Unfortunately, it may be impractical and cost-prohibitive to install these physical security systems to protect all the valuables within your company, as this may lead to alarms throughout the entire facility; thus, there is a need to come up with other methods that will enable the business to identify theft.
2. Another measure that requires minimal cost is to keep up-to-date inventories and logs that track not only your critical resources but all your high-dollar equipment. These records, if frequently maintained and checked, will help to quickly determine if unauthorized access has occurred and if any equipment has become missing, lost, or stolen. Not only will these inventories assist you in identifying possible theft, they may provide deterrence to employees or other perpetrators because there is a means to rapidly identify the loss. Last, the available information from an accurate inventory will assist law enforcement in their investigation of any theft and provide you with an accurate accounting of any missing items for insurance claims and replacement. By developing and maintaining accurate inventories and

logs of your valuables, your organization will have the means to identify any theft or loss and potentially deter these types of incidents.

3. Conducting comprehensive background investigations of all potential employees prior to hiring provides another mitigation measure that can minimize the possibility of theft against your organization. The purpose of the employment background investigation is to identify individuals who may be a risk in regard to employee theft, lawsuits, or losses to the company and prevent these actions before they even occur. The background investigation should look for inconsistencies between an applicant's statements made in his or her application or interview, which could indicate issues with the potential employee's character and integrity. Additionally, a background investigation should include a check of any local security incidences and police files to determine if the individual has any derogatory information that could lead to potential problems. By conducting a complete background investigation prior to hiring an individual, your organization can identify personnel who may pose concerns even before they are working for the business and help to identify employees with good character traits to help minimize the chance of theft or other incidents.

4. A final method to help prevent financial loss and theft is to develop checks and balances within your processes that deal with handling funds. A system of checks and balances, which may also be termed separation of duties, is typically accomplished by having at least two, and in some cases more, employees carrying out similar or sequential tasks so that several individuals are involved in the process and can identify any discrepancies in accounting for funds or other valuables. When this process is first introduced into some organizations there may be some significant discomfort—sometimes this may originate from trusted employees, but in most cases, the people most put out are employees who have not had to undergo any type of check and balance process to review their actions in the past. However, there are several good reasons that every organization should implement this practice, which can be discussed with any employees who may feel this way. First, any individual can make a simple error or accomplish their task incorrectly with the best of intentions; and it is unlikely that even the most conscientious of workers can catch all their own errors. By implementing a check and balance system to separate these duties, a second individual who is verifying the task will provide the organization with assurance that the processes are being done accurately and correctly. The second reason is to ensure that employees are not taking advantage of their authority and responsibilities. An example would be having only one employee responsible for spending, maintaining, and tracking all funds within the organization. In a situation like this, in which there is no separation of duties, this one employee would be easily able to embezzle funds from the company because there is no other individual who checks, or is even aware of, the status of these funds. By dividing tasks involved in procuring, tracking, storing, and spending money, it becomes more difficult for one individual to misuse or steal those funds and makes it easier to identify concerns in the process.

Response Actions for Financial Loss Incidents

Now that we have covered the various preventative measures that can combat financial loss incidents, we look at the primary response action that can be taken in the event that an organization experiences theft. This action must involve a process to investigate employees suspected of violating company rules and regulations—specifically those involved in the possible theft or embezzlement of company funds. In the event your organization must conduct any type of investigation, it is necessary to ensure it meets all the necessary requirements—both from a legal basis and from any employee or union agreements—that it must follow. For this reason, it is best to follow specific steps prior to and throughout the conduct of an investigation to mitigate the possibility of an inaccurate or unsubstantiated investigation. These steps include:

- Designation of qualified investigators within your organization
- Ensuring that investigators follow established methods to collect, handle, and store evidence
- Training and following proper interview techniques with any eyewitnesses, supervisors, and suspects
- Completing investigation reports in the proper format to ensure full documentation of the results of the incident

Finding and designating one individual within your organization, or a small cadre of individuals, with the experience and training to conduct a thorough investigation is a necessary first step that should be taken to accomplish proper and thorough employee investigations. Unfortunately, many organizations will wait to designate an individual to conduct an investigation after an incident has already occurred. This practice is not a good idea because the selected employee may not have any training or qualifications to conduct an investigation and because of the last-minute notice, she or he will not be prepared to make a thorough investigation of the incident in question. Instead, by designating specific individuals to accomplish investigations within your organization prior to their occurrence, you will make sure these individuals are trained and have developed resources that will assist in the investigation. All of this will lessen any potential issues that could occur owing to an inadequate or improper investigation.

During an investigation, it is necessary to follow proper procedures when collecting, handling, and storing any evidence relevant to the issues at hand. The basic rules for collecting and handling evidence must follow the same chain of custody that is required and used in a court of law because it is never known at the outset of an investigation if actual criminal action has occurred. As an investigation progresses, it may become evident that an actual crime was committed and for this reason, all evidence must be properly collected to ensure there is no break in the accounting and possession of any item of evidence from the time it is collected at the scene until the evidence could be used in court, because it will be too late after a piece of evidence is improperly obtained or stored. The purpose of maintaining the proper chain of custody for any evidence collected is to be able to show that the evidence is in the same condition as found at the crime scene and has not been tampered with. By designating certain employees to act as investigators within your organization, you will ensure these personnel are aware of these evidence handling procedures over the course of the investigation.

One of the primary methods that information is obtained and an incident is resolved is through interviews. In order that an investigator is able to obtain as much information as possible over the course of his or her investigation, it is necessary to conduct these interviews with eyewitnesses in an effective manner. Basic information a trained investigator will work to obtain includes background information on the specific incident, additional witnesses and potential suspects, information to verify others' statements, and evidence to assist with the case. These interviewing techniques require training and practice, which is another reason it is wise to designate specific individuals to conduct these investigations.

Once the investigator has completed her or his investigation, it is necessary to fully document the findings. This is done by filling out a comprehensive investigation report.

This report is meant to provide a professional, accurate, detailed, and easy-to-understand account of the events that took place based on the information obtained over the course of the investigation, on interviews, and on the investigator's personal observations. This information is ultimately compiled into an investigation report, which should always include the five W's and one H: Who, What, Where, When, Why, and How. The report should concentrate on the facts and report in chronological order the correct sequence of events as they occurred based on the information obtained during the course of the investigation. This report will typically be the primary document used by senior management and during any additional proceedings against the alleged perpetrator.

In the event that many of the preventative measures we discussed earlier did not deter an individual from committing theft or other type of financial loss incident, having a process to conduct a thorough investigation will be the primary response action by an organization to identify the individual and deter similar acts in the future.

Chemical or Biological Incidents

Should your organization handle hazardous materials, be involved in food-processing efforts, or have food-handling services within your facility, there are various types of incidents that involve chemical or biological hazards that could affect your business. These events can be caused by hazardous material spills or food-borne contaminants (Figure 10.4). As we discuss these chemical or biological emergencies, we also include medical health issues that can also create problems for an organization in how it must respond to these situations. We will look at each of these incidents and what response actions are best suited to deal with them over the next several sections.

Hazardous Material Emergencies

A hazardous material is any substance in a quantity or form that could pose a reasonable risk to individual or community health, the environment, or property. Hazardous materials risks include incidents involving substances such as toxic chemicals, fuels,

Figure 10.4 Chemical and hazardous materials incidents.

nuclear wastes and associated products, and other radiological, biological, or chemical agents. If your company routinely works with hazardous materials or dangerous chemicals such as these, there are many regulations and requirements that must be met, which, when adhered to, will assist in the mitigation of these incidents. These mitigation actions include specific storage requirements for these items along with the installation and use of specific safety equipment (e.g., cleaning and rinsing areas, goggles, and protective clothing) for organizations that use or store hazardous materials. Additional considerations that should be included in your organization's emergency response procedures that will help to mitigate damage or injury include the following:

- Upon any type of hazardous material incident, immediately notify your organization's point of contact and 9-1-1, describing the condition and type of hazardous material (if known).
- Your executive management team, or the responding emergency personnel, should determine if evacuation is appropriate given the circumstances, such as the amount of spillage, location, and threat to personnel.
- Your maintenance staff should determine as much information as possible regarding the hazardous material (e.g., type of material, location, amount, etc.) and provide this information to responding personnel.

Unfortunately, even with these safeguards and procedures in place, it can still be possible for an accident to occur owing to mishandling or some type of overt act involving these materials. In the event of such a situation, the primary threat during any type of hazardous material incident is created by the toxic fumes released from the material; therefore it is important to keep everyone safe by creating distance from the location of the spill and containing the spread of the gases released by the dangerous chemicals. To establish this safe distance, the best response action is to conduct an evacuation of any personnel that are not contaminated. For those individuals who have been contaminated, it is necessary to order them to shelter in place, seal off the area to limit the spread of the material, and work to accomplish decontamination of any affected individuals. As discussed earlier, sealing the area involves closing all vents, fireplace dampers, and as many interior doors as possible. Maintenance personnel should turn off any ventilation systems within the facility or set the system to 100% recirculation to ensure that no outside air is drawn into the building's interior. Further actions for all personnel include sealing all gaps along doorways, windows, and ventilation ducts using plastic sheeting, duct tape, or wet towels. Personnel should remain in the designated shelter location and avoid eating or drinking any food or water that may be contaminated. Depending on the amount of hazardous material your organization handles, the process of sealing areas may require equipment within your facility such as specially designed ventilation systems. Even if these types of systems are not required, it is still wise to prepare for these eventualities by ensuring rooms have the necessary supplies such as plastic sheeting and duct tape to provide some ability to seal off work areas that are at risk to these hazards.

For any personnel who have been exposed, it is necessary to perform decontamination procedures. Normally this will be directed and overseen by public health officials; however, if these agencies are not available, the best method of decontamination is to remove all clothing and store these items in a sealed container, then shower with water. Ideally, the water from these decontamination showers should be drained into storage containers because the water will probably contain any contaminants from the affected individuals.

After a hazardous materials incident, the following guidelines should be followed and documented into your emergency response procedures. Return only when authorities say the building is safe and free from contamination. Upon return to the facility, personnel should open windows and vents and turn on the ventilation systems to circulate fresh air throughout the building. Work with local authorities on the correct procedures to clean up any affected areas. Finally, employees must be aware that they must report any lingering smells, vapors, or other hazards to your local emergency services agencies.

Food-Borne Threats

Each year an estimated 76 million Americans—about one in four—become infected by what they eat.[2] Approximately 325,000 individuals are hospitalized and more than 5000 die, which equates to about 14 affected individuals each day.[3] The true magnitude of food-borne illnesses is likely to be much higher than even these official estimates because most affected people do not seek medical attention for many of the symptoms that follow these types of incidents, such as abdominal cramps, vomiting, and diarrhea. If your organization encompasses food handling or processing, or has a cafeteria or other service that provides food for your employees and visitors, you will need to address the possibility of a food-borne incident such as food contamination or food poisoning.

The best mitigation measure against this type of incident is to ensure your food-handling staff actively enforces proper food storage and handling procedures. With this in mind, it is important that these procedures ensure that all food preparation and food deliveries are accomplished in a controlled and consistent process among all your facilities. These procedures must include requirements that food handlers wash their hands thoroughly with soap and warm water before handling any foods. Another requirement is for all meat, poultry, and eggs to be fully cooked before being served to ensure any bacteria are killed and keeping food hot until purchased or served. Another good practice is to avoid cross-contaminating foods by washing hands, utensils, and cutting boards after contact with raw meats or poultry before these items touch another food. Bacteria can quickly grow at room temperature, so refrigerate any leftovers if they are not going to be eaten within four hours. A last mitigation measure is to clean all fruits and vegetables in running tap water to remove any visible dirt and grime, and remove and discard the outermost leaves from lettuce or cabbage because bacteria can grow on the surface of fruits or vegetables.

In the event of a possible food-borne incident, the following actions, which should be contained in your emergency response procedures, should be taken:

- Personnel at the affected location must immediately inform their supervisor and any local health services agencies.
- Your executive management team should close the affected food service facility and make proper notifications to all employees.

By following both the mitigation methods and the response actions in the event of a food-borne incident, your organization will be as prepared as it can be to ensure you can stop these types of incidents.

Medical Health Outbreak

A medical health or disease outbreak happens when an illness or disease occurs in numbers greater than expected in a community or region, or during a particular season. Any type of outbreak can create severe problems for any organization because of the large number of employees that come in contact with one another on a daily basis through the normal course of doing business. In most cases, it is unlikely that you will be able to identify a severe outbreak of illness within your own organization before local authorities, so it is typical that any determination and notification of a potential medical health epidemic will be initiated by the appropriate local health organization. In the event your business receives such a notification, the primary response your organization will need to consider is whether to close your facility until the medical issues are resolved. In any case, your organization should provide a method that ensures continuous coordination with the health department in your area throughout the emergency to make any further determinations regarding continued closure and when it is safe to open the facility to your employees again.

Criminal and Terrorist Acts

The next type of emergency situation we will look at involves the various types of criminal and terrorist acts that can occur against an organization. Over the past 20 to 30 years, there has been an exceptional rise in the number of serious acts that have occurred within the United States. These acts include workplace violence incidents, which can be as minor as an argument among co-workers but can escalate all the way toward the other end of the spectrum, in that they involve an active-shooter situation in an organization and its employees. Another type of incident we cover within this section includes terrorist incidents, which could include a vehicle-borne attack or the use of bombs against a location or facility; these types of incidents should also be considered within your organizational emergency response plans. The last major type of incident we look at within this section includes other criminal acts, such as gang activity, felonies occurring on your property (including even those not involving your own employees), or vandalism. We will look at each individual type of incident along with any specific mitigation measures and response actions to provide your organization the best methods available so that you can resume normal business operations.

Workplace Violence

Workplace violence is violence or the threat of violence against your organization's employees (Figure 10.5). It can occur at or outside the workplace and can range from threats and verbal abuse to physical assaults and homicide. Deaths caused by workplace violence constitute one of the leading causes of job-related deaths and, within

Figure 10.5 Workplace violence.

the United States, approximately 2 million workers each year are victims of some form of workplace violence.[4]

To mitigate against many of the possible workplace violence issues, there are several measures that can be included in your organization's emergency response procedures to help protect your employees.[5]

- Provide safety education for employees so they know what conduct is acceptable and conversely what conduct is not acceptable. This education should also discuss any instructions and guidance regarding what to do if they witness or are subjected to workplace violence and how to protect themselves from workplace violence.
- Install physical security measures that will help to ensure the safety of personnel throughout the workplace. Where appropriate to your organization's type of business it is helpful to install video surveillance, extra lighting, and alarm systems that help monitor personnel to deter any potential violence. Some additional measures can also include equipment or procedures that minimize access into work areas by outsiders through the use of identification badges, electronic keys, and guards.
- Provide drop safes in cash handling areas to limit the amount of cash on hand and ensure your organization's cash-handling procedures maintain the minimum amount of cash on-site—particularly during evening and late night hours.
- Provide any staff that routinely performs tasks outside the facility with cellular phones and hand-held alarms or noise devices. Require these individuals to prepare a daily work schedule and ensure their supervisor maintains contact with them throughout the work day and that the supervisor is informed of an individual's location throughout the day. If these personnel use company vehicles, ensure these cars and trucks are properly maintained and in good and safe working condition. An additional consideration for company vehicles may be to install GPS tracking equipment to ensure an individual can receive assistance if necessary.
- Instruct employees not to enter any location or area where they feel unsafe. If necessary, consider introducing a "buddy system" or provide an escort service or police assistance in potentially dangerous situations or at night.

We will look at specific incidents that can be included in the broad area of workplace violence along with their associated response actions as we move into the following sections, but your emergency response plans should provide some overall actions that should be accomplished in the event of any type of workplace violence incident.[6]

- Employees should be encouraged to report and log all incidents, along with any threats, of workplace violence.
- Provide prompt medical evaluation and treatment after any type of workplace violence incident.
- Immediately report violent incidents that may occur within your organization to local law enforcement.
- Ensure a process is in place to inform victims of their legal right to prosecute perpetrators of workplace violence.
- Discuss circumstances of a workplace violence incident throughout the organization and encourage employees to share information about ways to avoid similar situations in the future.
- Offer stress management sessions and posttrauma counseling services to assist workers in recovery after any occurrence of workplace violence.
- Thoroughly investigate all violent incidents and threats, monitor trends in violent incidents within the organization by type and circumstance, and institute corrective actions.
- Discuss any changes in your organization's workplace violence program during regular employee meetings.

By using these general actions as the foundation for your response to the specific types of workplace violence incidents an organization may experience, you will be better able to assist your employees and minimize the impact of many types of emergency incidents. With the foundation of these basic types of response actions, we now look at specific types of workplace violence incidents along with their recommended response actions.

Violent or Uncooperative Visitors

Any business organization can experience violent or uncooperative visitors. Employees who experience a bitter divorce, have child custody issues, or suffer abuse can be the victim of situations that require immediate action to remove an unwanted individual before he or she becomes an even larger issue. To deter this type of incident from even occurring, it is important that your organization have some type of process that identifies visitors as they enter the facility and prior to entering work areas. Having this process in place, it will be much more possible to identify potentially disruptive visitors and possibly calm the individual before he or she comes in contact with the person he or she wishes to confront—having the ability to control entry to any nonemployees can significantly discourage this incident from happening. In the event that there is a lack of entry control into the facility, or even with adequate access control procedures in place the violent visitor is able to bypass these controls, it is important to take the following response actions before these situations can escalate into a more severe incident.

- Remain calm and professional with the disruptive individual. In the event your organization has entry control methods in place, it will be up to the employees who monitor the access control system, such as security guards or receptionists, to deal with this type of situation before the person can move farther into the facility and determine what actions should be taken. If there are minimal processes to control and deny entry to unauthorized personnel, it may be up to all employees since anyone could potentially come into contact with the visitor and deal with him or her before the situation becomes more violent. Regardless of who comes into contact with the individual, it is extremely wise to conduct training for your employees that provides them with information on what actions to take in the event they are the person who initially comes into contact with the visitor.

- If the individual is not armed and it is safe to do so, the first employee that comes into contact with the individual should attempt to talk with the visitor to detain him or her from reaching the person he or she wishes to confront.
- Determine the potential threat that the individual may pose. If it is possible and safe to do so, employees should work to continue talking and communicating with the visitor. As this communication continues, other employees should be aware that they should discreetly report the disruptive visitor to the appropriate official or local law enforcement as necessary. Disruptive individuals can pose three types of threats that increase in severity:
  - Level I threat: An individual who has the means, ability, and intent to carry out an issued threat. These persons should be immediately reported to local law enforcement and company executives.
  - Level II threat: An individual who may have the means, ability, and intent to carry out an issued threat. These individuals should also be immediately reported to local law enforcement and company executives.
  - Level III threat: An individual who does not have the means, ability, and intent to carry out an issued threat should be reported to company executives. Your executive leadership can make a determination whether to notify local law enforcement.
- If the individual can be directed to the facility exit and toward the exterior of the building, this should be accomplished. Once they are separated from other employees and work areas, the employee in contact with the individual should continue to talk with the visitor until law enforcement arrives.
- Employees should be aware that they should attempt to obtain information on the disruptive visitor such as documentation of the offender's name and description for further reporting. This information should be passed on to any security guards or receptionists that are made aware of the situation so they may immediately report other attempted entries.
- If the individual leaves the building before this information can be obtained and reported within your organization, security guards or receptionists should still notify law enforcement and company executives in the event of future instances involving the same individual.

Hostage Situations

The next type of workplace violence incident we will look at involves hostage situations (Figure 10.6). Hostage situations can occur at any location, including businesses. Employees experiencing bitter divorce or child custody fights can be the subject of this type of incident. Many of these types of incidents may start as an unauthorized visitor situation but can rapidly degrade into an incident involving hostages. With this in mind, prior to an actual hostage situation many of the response actions for a disruptive visitor should be followed. In the event that the incident escalates into one involving hostages, there are some additional items that should be covered within an organization's emergency response plans.

Specific considerations for hostage situation planning include:

- Immediately contact law enforcement and await their arrival. No attempt should be made to contact the perpetrator by the organization unless communication is initiated by the perpetrator or becomes absolutely necessary.
- Evacuate all employees and visitors who are in areas not directly affected by the situation and who can be safely removed from the facility.
- Building intercoms should not be used to notify employees of the hostage situation, as this may only heighten tensions with the perpetrator.

Figure 10.6 Hostage situations.

- Isolate the perpetrator and the affected area, if possible, from other innocent bystanders or potential victims. This can be done through evacuation or, if this is not possible, by sheltering employees in place to limit their exposure to the situation.
- Secure the perimeter of the area surrounding the hostages. It is important to prevent anyone else from entering the high-risk zone and adding to the number of hostages by ensuring people are not allowed to move into the affected area.
- Your organization's emergency response plans should include training and education to provide guidance for employees who have been taken hostage or become involved in this type of situation. These individuals should be instructed to consider attempting to talk with the perpetrator to develop a relationship and humanize the situation; however, it is vital that everyone understands they must avoid any heroics.
- If your facility has video surveillance or audio capability, you should monitor the affected room or area with any available cameras or intercoms.

Active-Shooter Scenarios

Active-shooter scenarios are unfortunately becoming more and more commonplace within our society (Figure 10.7). Schools, shopping centers, government facilities, houses of worship, and businesses have all experienced this extremely violent act. Ensuring your own organization's emergency response plans provide actions that should be taken in the event this type of situation occurs is critical to providing your employees with the proper ways to respond.

The response actions in the event of an active-shooter incident include the following:

- In the event of notification of an active shooter or upon hearing gunshots, each individual employee should make a determination as to whether evacuation is safe for him- or herself and other co-workers. If the area is safe and an exit route is available that is clear from any perpetrators, they should immediately evacuate the building. Once they are clear from the building and in a safe area, they should notify police by calling 9-1-1.
- If evacuation is not possible or it is unsafe because of the proximity of the intruder(s), employees should initiate a lockdown in the nearest room. As discussed earlier, the goal of a lockdown is to separate themselves from the intruder, whether the perpetrator's location is in an interior hallway or outside the facility. Personnel should be instructed that any intruder should not be given the opportunity to enter the facility, if he or she is outside, or if the

Figure 10.7 Active-shooter situations.

intruder is already inside, that his or her ability to move freely from room to room and have easy access to employees and visitors should be minimized as much as possible.

- Upon notification of a lockdown, personnel should move to the nearest room that has the capability of being secured and immediately lock the door to this room.
- If an intruder is inside the facility, personnel should move away from doors and attempt to reduce noise and ensure no one is visible from outside the room. Room lights should be turned off and, if possible, the door should be barricaded with furniture. If the intruder is inside the facility, it is also recommended to keep any blinds on windows to the outside open, to either evacuate through the windows or provide visual communication to any potential first responders that are outside.
- If the threat is located outside the facility, personnel should move alongside the interior walls below any windows so that they are out of sight from the exterior. Employees should also be instructed to close window and door blinds and attempt to reduce noise and ensure no one is visible from outside the room.
- As police enter the room to clear the facility, employees should remain on the floor and show their hands. DO NOT attempt to get up or request assistance as police enter a room. Police will notify personnel when they are free to move once they have secured the area.

Terrorism Threats

The next type of emergency incidents we will cover involves threats occurring as a result of acts of terrorism (Figure 10.8). Although some of the incidents we discussed in the workplace violence area could also be considered terrorist acts—such as some hostage situations or active-shooter incidents—these types of incidents can normally be caused by as few as one disgruntled individual because of issues he or she may have with society, the work environment, or certain personnel. The incidents we cover as possible terrorist threats are situations that will normally involve several individuals working as part of an organization with the knowledge and resources required to carry out these incidents.

Figure 10.8 Terrorism threats.

One of the mitigation measures that can be effective at minimizing the potential for these acts is an active safety and security program within your organization. This program should be supported by your senior management team. We have previously discussed the positive effects on your organization's security posture of having an active program, in conjunction with physical security measures at your facility and well-known procedures for your employee's response and reaction to potential threats. These effects can result in a significant deterrence of any terrorist act against your company owing to a high level of security awareness, which will be achieved as a result of an active safety and security program. Security awareness helps to promote the ability of your employees to identify and report suspicious situations before they actually result in an actual emergency incident. For this reason, it is critical that all employees are trained to achieve a measure of security awareness.

Even with a high degree of security awareness among your employees, it is still necessary to plan for response against various types of terrorist incidents. These types of situations can include vehicle-borne explosives, bombs and bomb threats, and suspicious packages delivered to your organization. As with all types of emergency incidents, training your personnel on the proper response actions is one of the first items to always consider. We will look at each of these individual terrorism situations to cover the specific actions that will further assist in your organization's response.

Vehicle-Borne Explosives

Vehicle-borne explosives have been a potential form of attack used by both individuals and terrorist organizations (Figure 10.9). This type of terrorist act can be carried out by a small number of individuals, as was demonstrated by Timothy McVeigh in 1995 with his bombing of Oklahoma City's U.S. Federal Building. Larger terrorist organizations have long used vehicle-borne explosives and continue to do so today, with some specific examples including the bombing of the U.S. Embassy in Beirut in 1983 and bombings of the U.S. Embassies in Kenya and Tanzania in 1998. With the wide range of terrorists who have used this method of attack, your organization should ensure there are plans and procedures in place to mitigate and effectively respond in the event of this type of situation.

Figure 10.9 Vehicle-borne explosives.

Because a potential attacker can place a great deal of explosives into a car or truck and ram the vehicle into the building, the primary mitigation measure to defend against these types of attacks is to establish stand-off distance from your building so that vehicles cannot approach directly up to, or ram themselves into, the facility. We briefly discussed several physical security measures in the chapter in which we discussed mitigation. These measures, which include walls and barriers that limit access to a building to only pedestrians, can be used to maximize this stand-off distance by blocking access to vehicles. During our discussion, we covered the use of landscaping, such as berms and ditches, which can be an attractive method to limit space along any entrance routes solely to pedestrians. We also looked at physical security barriers that can also be used to limit vehicle access, including barriers, walls, and fencing. Even with the placement of many of these measures, it is still necessary to plan for your personnel's response in the event that this type of incident actually occurs.

- If employees see a suspicious vehicle parked in close proximity to your facility's entrance, they should immediately report it.
- The vehicle's owners should be found and asked to move the vehicle. If the owner(s) cannot be located or the vehicle cannot be moved, a search of the vehicle should be conducted.
- If the search reveals indications of an explosive device, personnel should immediately be evacuated from the facility and a cordon around the vehicle should be established out to a distance of at least 500 feet (about two football fields). All people should be clear of this area.
- Employees should be aware that they should not approach the vehicle and instead should await law enforcement personnel and explosive detection experts.

In the event that a vehicle crashes into your facility but no explosion occurs, the following actions should be taken:

- Assume the vehicle contains explosives.
- Personnel must immediately evacuate the building and no one should approach the vehicle. Again, the evacuation should ensure that all personnel move a minimum of 500 feet away from the vehicle and building.

Figure 10.10 Bombs and suspicious devices.

- In the event of an explosion, move all survivors away from the building a minimum of 500 feet. Do not approach the building or the area containing the initial explosion, as a practice of many terrorist organizations that conduct these types of attacks is to place secondary explosive devices near the initial explosive device to create further damage and injuries.
- Await law enforcement personnel and explosive detection experts.

Bombs/Bomb Threats/Suspicious Devices

Bomb and suspicious devices pose another type of terrorist threat that can be experienced by an organization (Figure 10.10). As with several of the other incidents we have looked at, there are some mitigation measures that can assist in preparing and planning for these events prior to their occurrence. Having caller ID on your company phones can assist with bomb threats, in terms of helping to possibly identify the perpetrator, but also to determine the validity of the threat. Another action is to ensure your staff regularly conducts checks of their respective work areas and report if they find anything out of the ordinary or items that do not belong.

Bomb threats and suspicious devices not only pose a threat of causing damage and injury within your organization, but also have a unique aspect that many of the other types of terrorist threats do not possess—simply the threat of such an incident can create significant disruptions to your business operations. This potential for disruption to operations from bomb threats is highlighted within the public education sector. Because bomb threats can take significant time away from the classroom and make teaching students extremely difficult, it is unfortunate that many of these threats are initiated by the students themselves. During one school year, one school district in Maryland reported 150 bomb threats, and the South Carolina Department of Education listed "disturbing schools," which included bomb threats, hoaxes, and false fire alarms, among its top 10 crimes, second only to simple assaults.[7] With time in any business being at a premium, it is imperative to have procedures to help an organization properly react to bomb threats and be better able to determine when evacuation is warranted and when the threat is an obvious hoax. There are several indicators regarding bomb threats that will help your organization maintain efficiency and effectiveness in your company's operations. For this reason, it is important to develop criteria and educate your employees on these areas to help determine the validity of a threat. With this in mind, prior to discussing the appropriate response actions for bomb threats and suspicious devices, we will first look at methods to help determine if a bomb threat is valid and should be taken seriously; after this discussion, we look at methods to ensure your personnel know how to properly react.

When considering the validity of any bomb threat, safety is always the paramount consideration, so when in doubt, you should implement procedures based upon the assumption that the bomb threat is valid. Some additional considerations are the number of bomb threats your organization receives. In the case of some schools, this may be a common occurrence; however, if this rarely (if ever) occurs to your facility, the best action is to conduct an evacuation and respond on the assumption that a real threat does exist. Some additional items to consider when determining if the bomb threat is valid is the seriousness of the threat and in general the specificity of the actual threat. Some items that indicate the specificity of an actual threat and ultimately help to indicate if a bomb threat is valid include[8]:

- Specific time and place included within the threat
- Description of the bomb used—the more detail in this description, the greater the likelihood that the threat is real
- Specific targets mentioned or indicated should be taken more seriously
- Motive or reason given or implied in the threat also shows that the threat should be taken seriously

It is important that each bomb threat should be treated as a separate event and if your organization receives few to none of these types of threats, it is advisable to simply treat the threat as real and immediately proceed with the response actions covered in the next paragraphs. If, however, you receive a significant number of these threats, your executive management team may wish to make the determination to conduct an evacuation based on these criteria to help assess the seriousness of the threat.

When your organization chooses to act upon a bomb threat, the following actions should be taken:

- If the bomb threat is received by phone, the staff member should not hang up the phone. Instead, she or he should notify another employee or the organization's appropriate point of contact to call 9-1-1.
- The employee who receives the bomb threat should take notes on any information, including the caller's voice, tone, and mannerisms (see Table 10.1 for a sample bomb threat notification).
- After receipt of a bomb threat the organization's staff should conduct a check of their work areas to see if they can identify if any suspicious items are present. If they do find an item, they DO NOT touch or move the item, but notify their supervisor or security point of contact immediately.
- Your executive management team should determine if evacuation is appropriate based on receipt of a valid threat and reasonable suspicion that a bomb is present, and if evacuation is decided upon, follow your organization's standard procedures. For any type of a valid bomb threat, the evacuation should move personnel a minimum of 500 feet away from the facility to protect them from the affects of the explosion.

Table 10.1 **Sample Bomb Threat Notification**

BOMB THREAT NOTIFICATION

| Date: | | Time: | |
| Time Caller Hung Up: | | Phone Number Where Call was Received: | |

Ask Caller:

| Where is the bomb located? (Building, Floor, Room, etc.) |
| When will it go off? |
| What does it look like? |
| What kind of bomb is it? |
| What will make it explode? |
| Did you place the bomb?   Yes   No |
| Why? |
| What is your name? |

Exact Words of Threat:

Information About Caller:

| Where is the caller located? (Background and level of noise) |
| Estimated Age: Is voice familiar? If so, who does it sound like? |
| Other points: |

	Caller's Voice			Background Sounds		Threat Language
Accent	Disguised	Normal		Animal Noises	Motor	Incoherent
Angry	Distinct	Ragged		House Noises	Clear	Message Read
Calm	Excited	Rapid		Kitchen Noises	Static	Taped
Clearing Throat	Female	Raspy		Street Noises	Office Machinery	Irrational
Coughing	Laughter	Slow		Booth	Factory Machinery	Profane
Cracking Voice	Lisp	Slurred		PA System	Local	Well-Spoken
Crying	Loud	Soft		Conversation	Long Distance	
Deep	Male	Stutter		Music		
Deep Breathing	Nasal					

Once the evacuation has been accomplished, personnel should await the arrival of law enforcement and explosive ordinance personnel to assess the situation. Only upon notification from law enforcement that the area has been declared safe should you can move your personnel back into the facility.

Suspicious Packages

The delivery of suspicious packages can also be a potential method to disrupt or attack a business. Your organization should conduct training of employees—particularly any personnel who work in areas that receive mail. This training should include how to identify a suspicious package and what to do if they receive a package that appears out of the ordinary. Some telltale signs of a suspicious package include the following:

- No return address
- Excessive postage
- Stains
- Strange odor
- Strange sounds
- Unexpected delivery or unique delivery method (e.g., package arrives by means other than UPS, FedEx, or the U.S. Postal Service)
- Poor handwriting
- Misspelled words
- Incorrect or vague job titles
- Foreign postage
- Restrictive notes regarding delivery (e.g., "Must be personally delivered to the CEO")

For suspicious packages received through the mail, there are some actions to consider that will mitigate some of the risks of this type of incident:

- Provide training for personnel with an emphasis on recognizing indications of the various hazards that can be transported through the mail, including bombs and biological and chemical threats, and ensure employees understand the appropriate response. These indications were discussed in the previous paragraph and can include exposed wires, bulky contents, unusual smell of the package, or the presence of gas or particles on the exterior packaging.
- Develop appropriate mail-handling procedures. A further action would be to consider funneling all mail deliveries through a central location or one individual so that this person can better benefit from the training to identify suspicious packages and react accordingly.
- Ensure it is difficult to deliver items directly to employees. Also, ensure that visitors are unable to gain access to much of the facility by limiting building access and funneling visitor traffic through a reception area.

There are a variety of terrorist acts that could have an impact on an organization and your emergency response plans should incorporate both the mitigation measures and the response actions for these potential situations. Within this section, we have covered measures and actions involving vehicle-borne bombs, bomb threats, and suspicious packages. Next, we will look at incidents involving other criminal activities.

Other Criminal Activities

There are several different types of criminal activities that should also be included in any organizational emergency response plan. These incidents include gang activity, felonies occurring on your property, and vandalism. The potential for these events can vary based on your facility and its location; however, regardless of the risk for these incidents, your emergency response plans should detail the necessary response actions.

Gang Activity

The level of gang activity that effects your organization will depend upon the area in which your business operates and the prevalence of gangs in your location (Figure 10.11). If you are unsure what the level of this activity is or what the potential of gang incidents within your area might be, it is advisable to check with your local law enforcement

Figure 10.11 Gang activity.

agency and determine how viable this threat may be. If it is determined gangs are a problem within your organization's area, the success of gang reduction strategies relies on the establishment of effective partner networks with local agencies—this is not only true for your own organization but is a standard response across communities and cities. To ensure this collaboration with the appropriate agencies occurs, there are some primary mitigation measures and considerations to reduce the potential of gang activity.

- Communicate through the local community, your employees, and their families that your facility should be declared neutral ground and in the event that any gang activity occurs, this will result in an immediate response.
- Coordinate with law enforcement and other criminal justice agencies to assist with gang activity education and training among your organization's staff. Training should include information such as gang identification, intervention, and prevention techniques.
- If necessary, institute anti-gang education and prevention programs.

In the event that an incident involving gangs occurs at your facility, the following steps should be taken in response:

- Contact law enforcement.
- If there is active violence outside your facility or on your property, initiate shelter-in-place actions. Ensure all exterior doors are locked to attempt to isolate any activity to the exterior of the building.
- If possible, personnel should move to the interior portions of the building. They should take shelter behind brick walls and under furniture to protect themselves from any bullets, shrapnel from bullet impacts, or breaking glass caused by the situation.
- Await arrival of law enforcement personnel and do not move until given an "all clear" from the responding agencies.

Homicide and Other Felony Criminal Activity

In addition to gang activity there is the potential for your organization to experience significant crimes either within your facility or against your employees. In today's society it is unfortunate that no organization is immune to this type of violent criminal

Figure 10.12 Vandalism.

activity so it is wise to ensure your business is prepared to respond to these situations. Primary considerations that should be included as part of your organization's emergency response procedures for these types of incidents include:

- Contact law enforcement.
- Secure the perimeter of the crime scene as quickly as possible. Not only will this avoid contamination of the crime scene and assist law enforcement in performing their investigation (and ultimately limit the time of the investigation, which would create disruptions within your facility and business operations), but it will also prevent your staff from entering the high-risk zone and minimize the impact on them, as they could come into contact with any violence or graphic images.
- Ensure that no one is allowed into the crime scene after the perimeter has been secured until police take control of the area. This may need to be accomplished by placing personnel along any access points to ensure no curiosity seekers enter the area.
- Compile a list of potential witnesses, friends, and other interested parties and ensure this is made available to law enforcement investigators as quickly as possible. It may be necessary to segregate these personnel from one another to ensure the integrity of the investigation. Again, these actions will assist law enforcement to speed up the process so that you can resume normal business operations.
- Be prepared to provide counseling services for any affected employees who either were victims of the crime or came into contact with the aftermath of the incident.

Although many standard security measures will help to mitigate against possible felony crimes occurring within your building, once an incident occurs the response actions listed above will help law enforcement conduct and complete their investigation, because your primary goal should be to ensure you can resume your normal business as quickly as possible.

Vandalism

Although we have discussed some serious criminal activities in the past couple of sections, the most likely criminal activity that most organizations experience is vandalism against their property or facility (Figure 10.12). Unfortunately, preventing vandalism can be a complex issue because there are so many causes, which can make it difficult to combat the source of the problem. Disgruntled employees, unhappy neighbors, unruly teenagers, or gang activity can all result in minor damage or defacement to your property and facility. The best way to prevent property vandalism and implement mitigation measures is to find out how and why it is occurring and then develop a strategy tailored to the situation. When working to find appropriate mitigation measures with which to combat vandalism, coordination with local law enforcement is critical. These agencies not only will help identify groups that could be the cause of the vandalism, but also can provide their standard level of response and will typically conduct an on-site investigation. In some areas, it is typical for law enforcement to request only that they be notified and provided pictures of the vandalism, whereas in other locations the local police will personally respond to examine the damage or graffiti in order to accomplish an on-site investigation. Depending on your location and the level of crime in your area, it is helpful to know if law enforcement may choose to respond to each and every vandalism incident or if they are unable to respond simply because the level of crime in that respective area is too high to warrant a personalized response to vandalism. As mentioned earlier, it may be common in these instances for law enforcement to request only notification of the incident via email or a hard-copy report that contains the necessary information regarding the vandalism and possibly request photos of an individual incident. Regardless of what the law enforcement response is within your area, it is important that your organization's emergency response procedures cover this process to properly tailor your own mitigation measures and response actions.

Now that we have provided a baseline regarding your local law enforcement's response to incidents involving vandalism, let's look at measures that can help deter these events. The primary mitigation measure used to combat vandalism is to provide for strong physical security measures in and around your facility. If it is difficult to even approach your facility, let alone spend time to accomplish an act of vandalism, because of boundaries that delineate and deter people from entering your property's perimeter, it will be more difficult for individuals to remain outside the building in order to deface the property. Another mitigation measure against acts of vandalism is the placement of cameras located in areas that have been susceptible to these types of incidents. Not only will these cameras provide a visual record of any activity, which will assist in the apprehension of the perpetrators, but their presence will also provide a level of deterrence to individuals considering such action. A last mitigation measure that can help to minimize acts of vandalism is to place alarms in areas that have experienced a high level of these types of acts. These alarms will alert security or law enforcement personnel to any unwanted activity and assist in deterring potential vandals from taking action against your facility.

Now that we have covered mitigation actions against vandalism, we will look at how to respond to these incidents. As stated earlier, many of the specific response actions for your organization in the event of vandalism will depend on the response and process of your local law enforcement agency. Regardless of your local police response, however, there are some standardized tasks that should be considered when developing your own internal response procedures. The first of these tasks is to ensure that the individual act of vandalism is fully documented. This should include the date and time (if known) the vandalism occurred, along with the time the damage or graffiti was actually discovered. This information should also include the specific location where the defacement occurred (i.e., building 3, ground floor on southeast corner, etc.) along with a brief description of the vandalism. Finally, this information should include pictures of the damage to be included in the documentation. The second task involved in these standardized response actions is to ensure your organization reports the incident in the manner that is prescribed by your local law enforcement. As discussed before, this could be by simply reporting the incident and providing the documentation directly to a police officer or sending the information to the appropriate agency within your local police department in lieu of an actual on-site investigation. The last standardized task that should be considered as part of your own response actions involves analyzing the scope of the problem and if your business should take action to implement some of the mitigation measures discussed before. If your building and property experience infrequent acts of vandalism, it is probably not necessary to consider security measures such as improved perimeter boundaries or cameras; however, if these incidents have become a significant problem it may be wise to consider allocating additional resources to attempt to combat the possibility of further occurrences.

Fire and Arson

Virtually any organization can experience a fire at its facility and, as a result, most organizations already have much of the mitigation measures and response actions covered for their company (Figure 10.13). The primary mitigation measure against any type of fire is the presence of a working alarm system. Whereas there are a variety of fire alarms on the market, some type of system is normally required to be in place for structures containing commercial enterprises. The standard response action for any organization in the event of a fire is evacuation from the facility. As discussed in Chapter 5 it is prudent for a business to have procedures for both short- and long-distance evacuations and this can particularly apply to incidents involving fire because the circumstances of some fires may require one type of evacuation or the other based on the severity of the incident or hazardous material contamination due to burning or damage.

Figure 10.13 Fire and arson.

Because it is extremely difficult to determine if arson was the cause of a fire until a full investigation is conducted by an expert, the best action for any organization to take in the aftermath of a fire is to ensure the entire area is off limits until it has been cleared by fire department officials. Within your own organizational emergency response plans, it may be necessary to emphasize this to your employees, as many personnel may desire to reenter the facility as soon as the fire appears to be extinguished to get valuables or personal items or to attempt to secure critical resources belonging to the company located within their own work areas. Because arson will not be able to be identified until after a full investigation and also to ensure the safety of employees, your organization's emergency response plans should ensure that personnel are directed to stay out of the area until it has been cleared by fire department personnel.

Sabotage

Sabotage can take on several different forms in many business organizations and these incidents should be considered in any organization's emergency response plans. Over the next several paragraphs we will look at two different types—sabotage involving proprietary information or clients, conducted by employees departing the company, and sabotage of critical equipment by individuals.

The first instance involves employees departing your organization who steal proprietary information or take clients as they move on to their new endeavor. Before this occurs, there are some mitigation measures that should be considered that may stop these incidents from occurring. One such measure is to include statements within your company's initial hiring agreement and a nondisclosure agreement that should be completed during an employee's departure. These statements should discuss and cover this eventuality and emphatically state that this type of behavior is not allowed. A second mitigation measure is to provide checks and balances so that access to much of this information can be gained only with multiple employees, where these limitations are practical. Admittedly, this second measure could result in various inefficiencies within your business operations because many different work functions require access to customer information, so your organization will need to balance the risks of losing this information against the required efficiencies necessary to accomplish your normal business operations. A final measure to take against potential sabotage and theft of your clients is to ensure that each customer has more than one point of contact within your organization with whom he or she interacts and works. Not only will this ensure your customers and clients are happy and satisfied based on service provided by multiple individuals, but this process will also provide some redundancy. This method will also help develop a relationship between your customers and your overall organization, rather than one specific employee. By considering these various mitigation measures and implementing the ones that are most effective for your particular business, you will help to minimize the potential of any poaching of your organization's customers that you have worked so hard to obtain.

In the event that sabotage involving proprietary information or poaching of clients does occur, there are some response actions your organization should take. The first response is to consider legal action against any former employees who have committed the sabotage. Although this may be the first reaction of many managers, there can be several disadvantages to consider prior to taking this course of action.[9] For one thing, any type of legal action will probably be expensive. The second disadvantage is that the time involved in any type of legal case would create distractions and make it difficult for the organization to accomplish the urgent task of further protecting and rebuilding your business as a result of the sabotage. The last disadvantage is that a protracted court battle would keep the wound of the incident open and have the potential to alienate some of your remaining customers. A better option that alleviates many of these disadvantages is to consider another response action. Instead of trying to punish the saboteur, you could consider using that energy, time, and money to overcome the damage and work within your organization to solidify the business. Using the time and effort to win back any customers that have been stolen, rather than spending this effort on legal action, may be more productive in the long term for your organization. This action will be easier to accomplish if you had implemented the mitigation measures discussed earlier—specifically that these customers have worked with several different individuals within your organization so that these clients feel loyalty to your overall business rather than one person.

The second type of sabotage we will look at involves damage to or hindering operations of your organization's critical equipment. To minimize the possibility of this occurrence, implementing the mitigation measures that work effectively against theft, which we have already covered, will also provide protection and deterrence against sabotage. These measures include physical security systems such as barriers, safes, alarms, and cameras that can help to protect and monitor your critical systems and equipment. In the event that an incident occurs, the primary response action against this type of damage is to repair the critical piece of equipment as quickly as possible. If there are no current security measures protecting the asset, another action would be to consider adding such systems to provide redundancy to preclude such damage in the future.

Travel Safety

If your employees must travel frequently to accomplish your organization's business objectives, it is wise to provide training for safe traveling and include many of the considerations we will cover within your emergency response plans (Figure 10.14). The following are some basic tips to ensure safe travel, within the United States, but particularly when traveling abroad, to better protect your employees while they are away from home and your business.[10]

The first consideration is to be aware of your surroundings and ensure that your clothing does not call attention to you—particularly to identify you as an American. When moving in unfamiliar areas, ensure you get in the habit of looking behind you occasionally to see if there are any suspicious individuals there and especially when you get up to leave somewhere. Travel can be very distracting and it is likely that you will be carrying more than you would be at home, so it can become very possible to leave a jacket or journal at that Parisian café table where you were people watching. To preclude this from happening, keep tabs on your possessions as you move and leave a location. It is also advisable to attempt to blend in as much as possible based on your clothing—particularly

Figure 10.14 Travel safety.

if you are traveling to a foreign country. Many nations are not friendly toward the United States so it would probably be wise to leave that "Born in the USA" T-shirt at home.

The next consideration to include in any training or procedures is the idea of separating your sources of money and maintaining a low profile with regard to your wealth. Although many people will keep all their bank cards or forms of identification in one location within their wallet or purse at home, it is better not to use this practice when traveling. Instead, keep any bank or credit cards along with any identification you will not need that day in a hotel room safe or other location not on your person, and take only one credit card and the actual amount of money you may need that day. Doing this ensures that if your valuables are lost or stolen, you will have a source of money and identification available—in addition, it will minimize the amount of items you must replace. Additionally, it is wise to keep your wallet in your front pocket or the inside pocket of a jacket, especially a pocket that can be buttoned up and secured. Depending on the area of travel, it may be wise to even use a money belt that hangs inside your shirt or around your waist. Last, with regard to money when traveling, it is best to avoid any displays of extravagance. If traveling, especially when traveling to many foreign destinations, it is likely that most Americans will be richer than the locals; however, it is still unwise to wear jewelry or expensive clothing or carry a $2000 camera around your neck, as any of these items will simply highlight your wealth and make you a target for thieves. In the event that you are mugged, the best course of action is to hand over your wallet, watch, and other valuables that the thief asks for. This should not be a problem if you have insurance and you have left all your irreplaceable valuables at home or in your hotel safe—it is simply safer to hand the items over and walk away uninjured.

The next consideration we will discuss involves your identification and travel documentations. Scan all your travel documents and email them to yourself. In the past, it was traditional to photocopy your passport and visas, travel insurance, and other important documents and keep them in a separate part of your luggage; however, in today's digital society another method to accomplish this is to have electronic copies of these documents. Duplicating your critical documents in this manner will ensure that this paperwork will not go missing even if your bags do.

Another consideration regarding travel safety is to be wary of people you don't know during your movement. Although it is hard to get to know the locals at a destination if you don't trust them, there should be limits to how much you should trust them when it comes to your personal safety. For example, upon your arrival at a foreign airport it is unwise to be led by a local national and placed into a taxi that they have provided or recommended. Instead, move with other travelers and attempt to maintain a low profile when you are departing the airport for your hotel. If you blindly follow someone, you may end up in a risky area of town, spending more money than you ever intended, or consuming food or drink—especially if they are not consuming it themselves—that could put you in danger. Another good idea is to do some research on common scams at your planned destination to further protect you from these types of situations.

The next consideration is to take precautions prior to your departure. This can include purchasing travel insurance or getting appropriate vaccinations based on your destination. If you are planning to do any specialized or adventurous activities while traveling (for example, scuba diving, bungee jumping, or parasailing), it is wise to check out the fine print and verify the certifications of any instructors. In addition, it is a good idea to verify the operator's qualifications and safety record before embarking on these exciting adventures.

A last consideration to include in training regarding travel safety is that you should not leave your bags and other belongings unattended in public spaces. This not only applies to physically leaving your bags even for short periods of time, but also includes when you are sitting down in public places. People leave their bags at their feet or hanging from the back of chairs all the time when they are at cafés or restaurants. It is a better idea to keep them on your lap, wrap the strap around your leg, or place the bag in a position that does not allow someone to make a quick snatch of the item.

Loss of Key Personnel

Another incident that occurs to many organizations that should be considered within emergency response procedures is the loss of key personnel within the company. It is a normal part of business that your organization will experience the loss of key personnel over time. This could be caused by an employee's departure for other opportunities, retirement, or an incident that resulted in their injury or death. Regardless of the situation that created this loss, the response actions for any organization are going to be the same and involve following your organization's standardized human resources processes used to locate and hire new personnel. A key factor during this hiring process is to ensure you follow all the necessary actions—no matter how critical this position within your company may be. If the position was extremely vital and there was little notice before the departure of the previous employee, many organizations may feel a need to rush the hiring process; however, it would be unwise to hurry through the process to get a body into the position as this will create more problems later on if you do so. A specific consideration in this process is that the organization carry out a thorough background investigation to identify potential problems with an individual

Figure 10.15 Labor disputes, strikes, and protests.

before she or he begins work. When working to fill any vacancies, it is best to follow your normal hiring process—this way it is much more likely that potential problems will be identified before they can significantly affect your organization.

Labor Disputes

The primary type of labor dispute we will cover involves protest activities (Figure 10.15). Although these types of activities are normally associated with unionized labor, it is possible for any organization to be subject to protestors either from inside or from outside the organization. For this reason, it is important that all organizations have plans in place in the event this type of incident occurs.

Fortunately, most protest activities will be preannounced with the time and place known and well advertised. In this eventuality, response actions should include coordination between your executive management team and local law enforcement personnel a few days prior to the event. This coordination is meant to advise the police of the upcoming protest and obtain assistance if available. Depending on the nature of the protest, law enforcement may decide to locate some officers at your facility during the start of the event to monitor the situation. There are some actions that you can take in addition to contacting local law enforcement (and implement even if there is no notice of the protest):

- Communicate with your employees to ensure that they understand that interaction between your staff and the protestors should be avoided. If it is inevitable that your employees will come into contact with the protestors—for example if the protestors are located directly outside the entry and exit to the facility—your personnel should be instructed to treat all protestors courteously and professionally.
- Employees should be instructed to carry on with their normal activities and use a low-key approach with protestors. If there are alternate entrances and exits into the facility that can be used to avoid the protestors and their activity, these should be used to further minimize contact.
- Consider positioning an employee to watch the entrance located nearest the protestors. This individual should monitor the protest and notify higher authorities or law enforcement if the group becomes violent or attempts to gain entry into the facility.
- In the event the protest has the potential to, or becomes, violent, your staff should immediately secure the facility and notify law enforcement.

Emergency Response Checklists

Now that we have covered the standard response actions to several different types of emergency incidents, we will look at emergency response checklists. These documents provide one of the best tools to enable your organization to rapidly react to an emergency. These checklists are short (normally one page long) documents that provide everyone some basic actions to take in the event of a specific emergency. Although these documents will not provide specific actions for each eventuality that could occur over the course of a specific type of situation, they will provide an organization with the assistance to remind everyone of the initial tasks that need to be done and help guide the Crisis Management Team and other employees toward the basic response actions for that particular incident.

Emergency response checklists should be developed prior to an incident and they should be included as part of any organization's emergency response plans. These checklists are designed to provide key personnel with necessary actions in the event of an emergency particularly during the initial moments of the event, because the complexity of an emergency situation will typically overwhelm even the best leaders and managers no matter how highly trained they or their team may be. To assist in the response to these complex and volatile events, these checklists will provide personnel with a tool that helps remind them of the overall actions they need to take so they can move on and concentrate on the other decisions and tasks that will be necessary to the specific emergency as it progresses.

A complete list of emergency response checklists for all the major types of incidents that could occur to most organizations is contained in Appendix B. Whereas each individual checklist will require additional revision based on the hierarchy within your own organization and key individuals that would be required to accomplish certain actions within these documents, these templates should provide you with a good starting point to include in your organization's emergency response plans and tailor for use within your company. Checklists such as the ones in this appendix can greatly assist with your organization's response and ensure the organization can move on to the necessary actions throughout an emergency. This guidance and assistance can pay dividends by ensuring major actions are accomplished during the initial phases of an incident as you work to minimize further loss or damage to your business operations.

Summary of Responding to Emergency Incidents

Over the course of this chapter we looked at certain types of emergency incidents that can occur to an organization. Although the probability that some of these incidents may be small for your particular organization, we provided mitigation measures along with standard and accepted response actions to each to provide you with a baseline of what actions your particular organization's response should include. We looked at various types of natural disasters, situations that involve major equipment breakdown, incidents involving financial loss, chemical or biological incidents, criminal and terrorist acts, vandalism, fire and arson, sabotage, travel safety, loss of key personnel, and labor disputes. After we discussed these incidents, along with various mitigation measures and standard response actions for each, we briefly touched upon emergency response checklists and their usefulness in helping organizations, individuals, and a Crisis Management Team in their response to an actual emergency incident. Templates for these checklists to assist with a variety of incidents are included in Appendix B of this book.

End Notes

1. Chad Brooks, *Employee Theft On the Rise and Expected to Get Worse* (Business News Daily, June 19, 2013), Retrieved from Web on December 10, 2013, www.BusinessNewsDaily.com.
2. The National Academies, *What You Need to Know About Infectious Disease: Food Borne Pathogens*, Retrieved from Web on September 16, 2014, needtoknow.nas.edu.
3. The National Academies, *What You Need to Know About Infectious Disease: Food Borne Pathogens*.
4. United States Department of Labor, *Workplace Violence Fact Sheet* (Occupational Safety & Health Administration), Retrieved from Web on September 16, 2014, www.osha.gov.
5. United States Department of Labor, *Workplace Violence Fact Sheet*.
6. United States Department of Labor, *Workplace Violence Fact Sheet*.
7. Graeme R. Newman, *Bomb Threats in Schools* (2002).
8. Graeme R. Newman, *Bomb Threats in Schools* (2002).
9. Norm Brodsky, *How to Handle Employee Sabotage* (Inc, May 1, 2012), Retrieved from Web on September 19, 2014, www.inc.com.
10. Mark Broadhead, *Top Tips for Safe Travel* (Lonely Planet, January 30, 2013), Retrieved from Web on September 18, 2014, www.lonelyplanet.com.

Emergency Response Case Studies

11

Now that we have covered the primary considerations along with many of the standardized response actions to various types of emergencies that should be included in an organizational emergency response program; we will attempt to reinforce these concepts through a review of specific emergency incidents and the actual response actions taken by the affected organizations and a look at some lessons learned from these actual events. To help you better understand what impact the specific response actions had on the organization—in both positive and negative respects—we will initially cover the background of the particular incident and then discuss the lessons learned and how these actions relate to the emergency response concepts we have covered thus far, in order to provide you with ideas that you can apply to your own organization's plans and procedures. We will first look at the Columbine High School shooting.

Columbine High School Active-Shooter Incident

On 20 April 1999, in the small, suburban town of Littleton, Colorado, south of Denver, two high school seniors, Dylan Klebold and Eric Harris, enacted an all-out assault on Columbine High School during the middle of what had started as a normal school day. The boys' plan was to kill hundreds of their fellow students, and as they carried out this plan the two boys walked the hallways throughout the school with guns, knives, and a multitude of bombs. When the day was done, they had carried out their plan, which resulted in 12 students, one teacher, and the two murderers dead, along with 21 more students injured (Figure 11.1).[1]

According to journals, notes, and videos that Klebold and Harris left to be discovered after their attack, Klebold had been thinking of committing suicide as early as 1997 and both boys had begun thinking about staging a large massacre as early as April 1998—a full year before the actual event. These issues and plans appear to coincide with the point in time that the two had begun to run into trouble with the law. In late January 1998, Klebold and Harris were arrested for breaking into a van. As part of their plea agreement and because they were first-time offenders, the two began a juvenile diversion program in April, which allowed them to purge the event from their record if they could successfully complete the program. For almost a year, the two attended workshops, spoke to counselors, and worked on volunteer projects as part of their program. Based on discussions with counselors and others they were able to convince everyone that they were sincerely sorry about the break-in; however,

Figure 11.1 Columbine high school
students react to shooting.

in actuality their time in the program resulted only in bitterness in Klebold and Harris
and they began to make plans for what they considered revenge through a large-scale
massacre at their high school.[2] Added to their run-in with the law was the fact that the
two young men were angry. Not only were they angry at athletes, or popular students
that made fun of them, or Christians, or blacks, as some people have reported in the
aftermath of this incident; but it appears that they basically hated everyone except
for a small handful of people.[3] Although many people may have similar feelings, it
is unfortunate that both Klebold and Harris were serious about acting on this hate,
and as early as spring of 1998, they wrote about killing and retaliation in each other's
yearbooks. One image that was particularly telling of this desire to act on their hatred
was an image that had been drawn of a man standing with a gun, surrounded by dead
bodies, with the caption, "The only reason your [sic] still alive is because someone has
decided to let you live."[4]

As a result of their run-ins with the law and their hatred, Klebold and Harris began
to work out a plan to carry out their revenge. They developed a plan to attack their
high school using both bombs and automatic weapons. To begin preparation for their
plan, the two did research using the Internet to find recipes for pipe bombs and other
explosives. In addition to these explosives, they amassed an arsenal over the next
several months and they eventually were able to stock a variety of guns, knives, and
99 explosive devices. Their desire was to kill as many people as possible during their
attack on the school, so they focused on the cafeteria during meal times. The two stud-
ied the influx of students in the cafeteria, noting that there would be over 500 students
after 11:15 a.m., when the first lunch period began. As a result, their plan was to start
by planting large explosives in the cafeteria—the bombs would be timed to explode at
11:17, and at that point the attackers would begin to shoot any survivors as they came
running out of the exits from the school lunch room.[5]

The attack started at 11:10 a.m. on Tuesday, 20 April 1999, as Dylan Klebold and
Eric Harris arrived at Columbine High School to carry out their plan. They drove
separately to the high school and parked in spots in the junior and senior parking lots,
which enabled the two to flank their target and enclose the school cafeteria to attain
maximum casualties as students would flee the building. Around 11:14, the boys carried two 20-lb propane bombs (with timers set for 11:17) hidden in duffel bags and
placed them near tables in the cafeteria. No one noticed them placing the bags, as the

bags containing the bombs blended in with the hundreds of other school bags that students normally brought with them during their lunch period. The boys then went back outside to wait for the explosion. Fortunately, the bombs failed to explode—it is believed that if the bombs had exploded, it is probable that all 488 students in the cafeteria would have been killed. The boys waited a few extra minutes for the cafeteria bombs to explode, but still nothing happened and so they realized something must have gone wrong with the timers. Although their original plan had failed, the boys decided to enter into the school anyway and begin to attack students using their other bombs and weapons.[6]

Klebold and Harris entered the school wearing black trench coats to hide the weapons they were carrying and the utility belts they wore, which were filled with ammunition. They also carried knives and had bags full of bombs. At 11:19, two pipe bombs that the boys had set up in an open field several blocks away exploded (they had timed the explosion so that it would be a distraction for police officers from the main explosions in the cafeteria). At this point in time, Klebold and Harris started firing their first shots at students who were sitting outside the cafeteria. Unfortunately, many of the other students didn't realize what was happening when the explosions and initial gunfire occurred. It was only a few weeks until graduation and, as is tradition among many American schools, seniors often pull a "senior prank" before they leave. As a result of this tradition, many of the students believed that the shootings were just a joke—part of a senior prank—so they didn't immediately flee the area.[7]

Klebold and Harris moved to rooms alongside the cafeteria and continued to fire at several groups of students. Although most students continued to believe the gunfire was part of the senior prank or a movie being filmed, a teacher, William "Dave" Sanders, and two custodians realized that this was not just a senior prank and that there was real danger.[8] They tried to get all the students away from the windows and to lie down on the floor while other students evacuated the room by going up the stairs to the second level of the school. Because of these actions by Mr. Sanders, when the boys returned to the cafeteria, Klebold peered in and the area looked empty so the two attackers decided to move to other areas within the school.

Harris and Klebold walked along a hallway as they began to go through the school, shooting and laughing as they went. Most of the students not at lunch were still attending class and they didn't know what was happening (the incident had been going on for approximately six minutes at this point).[9] Dave Sanders, the teacher who had earlier directed students to safety in the cafeteria and elsewhere, was coming up the stairs and as he rounded a corner he came in sight of Klebold and Harris with their guns raised. He quickly turned around and tried to turn a corner to get to safety when he was shot. Sanders managed to crawl to the corner of the hallway and another teacher dragged Sanders into a classroom away from the attackers, where a group of students were already hiding. The students and the teacher spent the next few hours trying to keep Sanders alive.[10]

At 11:29, Klebold and Harris entered the school library, which was located on the second floor. In the library there were 56 students who had taken refuge.[11] Over the next seven and a half minutes, the two boys moved through the library, shooting, as they killed 10 and injured 12 students.[12] They then moved back outside the library and moved through the halls, looking into various classrooms and making eye contact with some of the students; however, they didn't try very hard to get into any of the rooms. Many of the students stayed huddled and hidden in many of the classrooms with the doors locked; however, there was little attempt to barricade the rooms as many students and teachers thought that locks would not have been much protection if the gunmen had really wanted to get in.[13]

At 11:44, Klebold and Harris headed back downstairs and reentered the cafeteria. Harris shot at one of the duffel bags they had placed earlier, trying to get one of the 20-lb propane bombs that they had placed prior to the start of the incident to explode, but it didn't. Klebold then went over to the explosive device and began fiddling with it but still there was no explosion. Klebold then stepped back and threw a bomb at the propane bomb and when the thrown bomb exploded it started a fire, and the sprinkler system was triggered. The two boys saw that the fire from the bomb had been extinguished so they moved out of the cafeteria again and continued to wander around the school throwing bombs as they headed back upstairs to the library.[14]

When the two moved back into the library, nearly all the uninjured students from their earlier attack had escaped, whereas any remaining people were hidden in cabinets and side rooms from the main area. Klebold and Harris moved to the windows of the library and shot out the windows toward the policemen and paramedics that had gathered outside the school over the 45 min since the start of the attack. Sometime between 12:05 and 12:08, Klebold and Harris went to the south side of the library and shot themselves in the head, ending the Columbine massacre.[15]

One of the major issues that occurred at the conclusion of the incident was that, because no one saw the two gunmen commit suicide, no one was sure it was over until police were able to clear the entire building—even though police were on scene almost immediately. Within five minutes of the first shots fired, a sheriff's deputy who was assigned to work at the school was outside in one of the parking lots and he was soon joined by six other policeman who took positions around the building; however, none of them entered the facility to engage the attackers and instead they decided to wait on the SWAT team to arrive.[16] Unfortunately, SWAT did not arrive until almost an hour after the start of the attack and as a result they did not enter the building until 12:06. Furthermore, it was almost three hours before the team was able to determine the gunmen were dead as they swept the school building.[17] The lengthy period of time that it took to accomplish the building sweep and find out that the two boys were dead caused several injured personnel to wait for rescue and at least one death owing to the inability of medical responders to provide initial care. One injured individual, Patrick Ireland, who had been shot two times in the head when the gunmen had been in the library, managed to escape at 2:38 p.m. out the library window—two stories up. He fell into the waiting arms of the SWAT team while television cameras broadcast the scene across the country—amazingly, Ireland survived the ordeal.[18] Dave Sanders, the teacher who had helped hundreds of students escape and who had been shot around 11:26 a.m., lay dying in the science room he had taken refuge in as SWAT continued to clear the building and determine the status of the gunmen. The students in the room tried to provide first aid, were given instructions over the phone to give emergency aid, and placed signs in the windows to get an emergency crew inside quickly, but no one arrived. It wasn't until 2:47 p.m., when Sanders was taking his last breaths, that SWAT finally reached his room, and he died as a result of his injuries.[19]

Students who had escaped over the course of the attack were transported to a nearby elementary school where they were interviewed by police and then put on a stage for parents to claim; however, the school did not have a system in place to account for all the students and staff. As the day wore on at the elementary school, the parents that remained were those of the victims, but confirmation of those that had been killed did not come until a day later.[20]

Lessons Learned

There were many mistakes that occurred in the attack on Columbine High School, both by the responding law enforcement personnel and by the emergency response actions of the school itself. We will briefly cover some of the major issues from the standpoint of the police; however, our main focus will be on the school itself because these actions encompass what should be the responsibility of any organization that experiences a similar active-shooter incident.

Law Enforcement Lessons Learned

The first major lesson learned for law enforcement was that active-shooter situations happen quickly—they will normally start and end in a matter of minutes. Thus, it is critical that law enforcement accomplish a sweep of the building in an attempt to stop the attackers and find survivors. This resulted in one of the most significant results from Columbine: to change police tactics in response to an active-shooter incident based on the lengthy time it took to clear the building and determine that the shooters were dead. Before this incident, the typical law enforcement response to this type of situation was for patrolmen to respond to the location and establish a perimeter to keep personnel away from the facility; however, these personnel were not to enter the building and instead they were to wait for the specially trained SWAT personnel to arrive and accomplish this mission. Based on the lesson learned from Columbine and other similar incidents, this strategy was found to be flawed because most of these situations normally end within a short time and when the gunmen commit suicide rather than being neutralized by police. Until this point in time, when the shooters are dead, it has been found that the perpetrators will continue killing until they run out of ammunition or cannot locate any more targets. The new tactic regarding law enforcement response to active-shooter incidents is for the first responders to enter a location as soon as they have adequate numbers of personnel for a sweep team and begin a search for the gunmen as quickly as possible. In the governor of Colorado's report on Columbine, it was stated that the primary emphasis of law enforcement training and policy in relation to these types of situations is that the "highest priority of law enforcement officers, after arriving at the scene of a crisis, is to stop any ongoing assault."[21] Unfortunately, previous tactics against active-shooter situations had been to wait until SWAT arrived and they would handle the incident.

The other primary lesson learned by law enforcement is the establishment of an incident command system that ensures designated law enforcement command personnel are trained to take command of an emergency situation at the beginning of a crisis, to control the assembled personnel, and to communicate incident objectives clearly to their subordinates.[22] As covered during our discussion of the event, there were several law enforcement officers in and around the school—in fact, when SWAT finally entered the building there were approximately 75 police located around the school.[23] Unfortunately, there was minimal effort by any one police officer to take charge of this large number of armed personnel and direct them to enter the school to neutralize the gunmen and rescue survivors. Law enforcement has taken strides to ensure personnel know that they should take charge and begin to act as quickly as possible in the event of an active-shooter incident.

Lessons Learned for All Organizations and Businesses

Although there were missteps as a result of the law enforcement response involved with the Columbine incident, there were several more issues based upon the school and the district's response actions with regard to this event. From these failures, however, there are a great deal of lessons that apply not only to schools but to all organizations and businesses with regard to their own emergency response planning. We will cover each of these items over the following paragraphs.

Columbine High School failed to have an emergency response plan tailored to meet security and safety concerns for that facility.[24] As we have discussed several times throughout this book, it is necessary for every organization to have such a plan along with procedures that specify response actions for possible emergency incidents. These incidents should be based on the various risks and threats posed against an organization according to its Risk Assessment Matrix—something that this particular school had failed to ever accomplish.[25] In drawing up these plans for your own organization, you should consult local law enforcement and other rescue agencies, along with all work functions within the company. The lack of any emergency response plan by Columbine High School, or any safety and security plan for that matter, led to a significant lack of security awareness among the students and staff, which would probably have resulted in much earlier detection of the incident. For the many months leading up to the incident, if students had been more aware of security issues, those close to Klebold and Harris may have been able to notify school officials of the numerous writings and videos they had posted before the event. At the time of the incident, having a greater sense of security awareness may have also enabled students or staff to notice when the two boys entered the cafeteria and deposited two large bags—both of which contained the 20-lb bombs and should have appeared suspicious—and then left. Although it is difficult to tell if the incident could have been stopped with an improved sense of security awareness and a comprehensive emergency response plan, it would have definitely minimized the damage by enabling students and staff to better know the response actions that should have been taken.

Directly tied to the first lesson learned, the lack of an emergency response plan, the school had not conducted any type of training and preparedness for such an incident. This specifically includes emergency response exercises, which would have helped to ensure that students and staff knew the proper response actions in the event of an active-shooter incident.[26] This lesson learned led to several other issues that negatively affected the safety of students and staff over the course of the incident. One issue was that there was never any process to notify everyone within the school of the incident and to inform them to take action. This inability to communicate throughout the building resulted in many students continuing to believe the two shooters were just a senior prank well after people started dying, and as a result, several students failed to attempt to move to a room, take cover, or get out of the building. Another issue is that students took shelter in certain locations but failed to barricade themselves into the room to prevent the gunmen from easily entering the location. The situation in the school library provides the most critical example of this issue, as it was extremely easy for the attackers to repeatedly enter this area over the course of the incident. If the school had conducted emergency response exercises and practiced the various types of response actions to include notification and shelter-in-place requirements, it is likely that more personnel would have survived.

The last major lesson learned that we will discuss deals with the failure of Columbine High School to have a process to account for students and staff.[27] As you will recall from our discussion of the incident itself, the school district transported all the students they were able to locate to an elementary school and then had parents claim them. You can imagine the feelings of all the parents of the missing, injured, or dead teenagers as time passed and they were unable to locate their sons or daughters. This is obviously not the way to break this type of news. Had the school system developed a process to account for all students and staff and included these procedures in an emergency response plan, they would have been much more able to work with individual parents who had lost loved ones, rather than compound the shock of this loss through the method that was actually used. A final issue regarding this lesson learned involves the fact that the school failed to provide for any type of counseling or victim advocacy to the parents of students who had died or were injured as a result of the incident.[28] As we have discussed earlier, ensuring accountability of all personnel involved in an emergency incident is one of the most important aspects any organization must worry about. The Columbine incident highlighted the need for this process, as the failure in this particular incident created significant and long-term problems regarding the school district's operations and performance and their relationship with the local community.

Oklahoma City Federal Building Truck Bombing

On the morning of 19 April 1995, an ex-Army soldier and security guard named Timothy McVeigh parked a rented Ryder truck in front of the Alfred P. Murrah Federal Building in downtown Oklahoma City. Inside the vehicle was a bomb weighing approximately 4000 lb[29] and made out of a deadly cocktail of agricultural fertilizer, diesel fuel, and other chemicals.[30] McVeigh got out, locked the door to the truck, and headed toward his getaway car. He ignited one timed fuse and at precisely 9:02 a.m. the bomb exploded (Figure 11.2).[31]

Figure 11.2 Oklahoma city federal building bombing.

Within moments, the affected area looked like a war zone. A third of the building had been reduced to rubble and the powerful explosion had blown off the building's north wall, with many floors flattened like pancakes. Dozens of cars were incinerated and more than 300 nearby buildings were damaged or destroyed as the damage extended throughout Oklahoma City's downtown, covering an estimated 48-square-block area.[32] The strength of the explosion knocked out primary and backup phone lines for the Emergency Medical Services Authority, which provided service for the local ambulances. As a result of the loss of this communication system the 9-1-1 emergency service was the only remaining method of communication.[33] In addition to the damage to the downtown area, the human toll was still more devastating: 168 souls were killed—this figure included 19 children—with more than 650 people injured.[34]

As emergency crews raced from across the country to Oklahoma City to assist with the rescue effort, a massive hunt for the bombing suspects ensued. Two days later, an eyewitness description of the bomber led authorities to charge Timothy McVeigh. Ironically, McVeigh was already in jail, having been stopped for a minor traffic violation and then arrested for unlawfully carrying a handgun several hours after the actual bombing.[35] That same day, Terry Nichols was identified as an associate of McVeigh's and it was determined that he had also assisted in the bombing. Nichols surrendered in a small town in Kansas and both men were found to be members of a radical right-wing survivalist group based in Michigan.[36] A few months after the bombing, Michael Fortier, a friend of McVeigh's from the Army and who knew of McVeigh's plan to bomb the federal building, agreed to testify against McVeigh and Nichols in exchange for a reduced sentence[37] and as a result, McVeigh and Nichols were indicted on charges of murder and unlawful use of explosives.

How did these individuals reach the point at which they were determined to accomplish such an attack against their own country? McVeigh was raised in western New York, and during his formative years, he acquired a penchant for guns and began honing survivalist skills he believed would be necessary in the event of a showdown with the Soviet Union. He graduated from high school in 1986 and enlisted in the Army two years later, where he proved to be a disciplined and meticulous soldier. While in the military, McVeigh befriended fellow soldiers Nichols, a man more than 12 years his senior, and Fortier—both of whom shared many of his survivalist interests.[38]

In early 1991, McVeigh was deployed to fight in the Persian Gulf War and he was decorated with several medals for his military service; however, after failing to qualify for the Special Forces program, McVeigh accepted the Army's offer of an early discharge and left in the fall of 1991.[39] The early discharge was possible because at the time, the American military was downsizing after the collapse of the Soviet Union. With the end of the Cold War, McVeigh shifted his hatred of foreign communist governments to a suspicion of the U.S. federal government, especially after the election of Bill Clinton, who had successfully campaigned for the presidency on a platform that included gun control measures.[40] In addition to Clinton's election, McVeigh, along with his associates, was deeply radicalized by such events as the August 1992 shootout between federal agents and survivalist Randy Weaver at his Idaho cabin, in which Weaver's wife and son were killed, and the 19 April 1993 inferno near Waco, Texas, in which 75 members of a Branch Davidian religious sect died.[41] As a result of his evolving ideology and these events, McVeigh decided to plan an attack on the Murrah Building, which housed regional offices of such federal agencies as the Drug Enforcement Agency, the Secret Service, and, perhaps most important, a division of the Bureau of Alcohol, Tobacco, Firearms and Explosives, the agency that had launched the initial raid on the Branch Davidian compound.[42]

This planning ended on 19 April 1995, the two-year anniversary of the disastrous end to the Waco standoff, when McVeigh parked the rented truck outside the Murrah Building and fled.

Lessons Learned

Rescue personnel who participated in the response to the Oklahoma City bombing identified several lessons learned from this incident, not only based on the attack itself but also as a result of the subsequent response from emergency fire, medical, and rescue personnel from across the nation. Ultimately, these lessons learned can be considered and integrated into any organization's emergency response plans. One of the initial lessons learned from the Oklahoma City bombing is the need to create stand-off distance from vehicle access and a facility's entrance. The farther away you can place vehicles and other items that could carry a large amount of explosives, the less effective these types of devices will be. As we discussed in Chapter 3, when we covered mitigation measures, there are several different physical security items that can assist with creating this stand-off. They include landscaping features such as berms, walls, bollards, and water features, to name a few. Owing to the size of the bomb used in the Oklahoma City bombing, it is unlikely that enough distance could have been created to completely negate the effects of such a large explosion—particularly within a downtown metropolitan area; however, any additional distance would have minimized the effects of the explosion. Fortunately the probability that a similar size bomb would be used against your organization's facility is small; thus, any stand-off distance you can achieve around the entrances and exterior of your own organization's facility will minimize the possibility of a similar event.

The next lesson learned from this incident showed that it is good practice to provide a process for the intake and storage of the massive amount of donated and requested goods that will be received in the event of an emergency. This lesson learned not only applies to the type of incident involving a vehicle-borne explosive but can and should also be applied to plans regarding any type of disaster. In most instances, an organization that experiences a major emergency will receive a massive influx of supplies in a very short time to assist with the recovery effort. Getting equipment needed for the effort will normally not be a problem, but the issue becomes the tracking and storage of what items are available and where they are located so that they can help with the response. In large emergency incidents this can become a significant challenge based on the sheer magnitude of items that will be received. During the Oklahoma City bombing, there was such an enormous amount of goods that were donated, and these items arrived in the area at such a high rate, that it became very, very difficult to verify what items were on scene at any given time and be able to use items when they were needed.[43] Another problem with the inventory control of all these received items was that because of the sheer number of volunteers and the fact that each group used different documentation and tracking methods—and additionally most of this information was accomplished manually—there was no ability to track all of the available equipment that was on-site, nor were the personnel able to get the supplies to the responders when necessary. One example of this is that, in the aftermath of the bombing, one worker commented to a reporter that they needed gloves to assist in working through the rubble. The reporter passed this need on to their viewers and, as a result, truckloads of gloves began arriving over the next few days. The unfortunate thing was that there had been boxes of gloves available when the worker had made these comments—they were simply unaware that these items were on-site and could have been provided.[44] This example shows that the logistics behind the intake and storage of supplies are vital for any rescue effort to fully be a success. Some tasks to help with this can alleviate similar problems within your organization. First, there should be one single computer system keeping track of the entire inventory of these items. This system should incorporate a database that would track the time of arrival and the precise location of each item. Although it will be necessary to have different staging areas, linking them though a computer system will solve the problem of not knowing at which staging area particular supplies are located. The second important task from this lesson learned is that all supplies need to be tracked electronically through one overall inventory manager. It is crucial that each emergency response plan have an inventory management system set up and ready to be put into action if a terrorist attack occurs. This system should track the arrival time and location of each item donated so that rescuers can easily access goods that are needed. Finally, the last task is to develop a priority system to be put into place indicating which items are more important and a higher priority in response activities and, as a result, need to be readily available. Again, it will probably not be necessary to worry about rescue efforts on the scale of the Oklahoma City bombing; however, these logistical efforts will still be necessary to consider in your own organization's plans so that you can better provide the necessary supplies throughout the company in the event of a significant catastrophe.

The last lesson learned that we will discuss involves the need to have alternative communication methods. We have covered this issue during our discussion of internal emergency response planning; however, the Oklahoma City bombing provides a perfect illustration of this requirement. One of the major problems we have seen in many disasters involves telephone communication or, more precisely, the failure of this system, and this particular emergency was no exception. One of the main reasons for this problem was that soon after the explosion, telephone lines became jammed. Add to this problem the fact that cellular phones were also jammed owing to the demands on the system. Last, there were many affected organizations from the incident that did not have a listing of key contact names and cell phone numbers. To resolve these issues, there are some considerations you can ensure are provided for in your own emergency response plans. First, it is necessary that you are prepared to provide some alternative means of communication. We have previously stated having radios or walkie-talkies to provide this—in the Oklahoma City bombing, they solved this issue through the donation of cell phones that operated on a network separate from the standard network in the local area.[45] The second issue, that of failing to have contact lists, is easier to solve by simply having a complete listing of key personnel and several contact methods within your organization's emergency response plans.

These lessons learned—providing stand-off distance around your facility, ensuring a system to track and handle donated supplies, and providing methods to communicate across your organization—can be taken from the events and aftermath of the Oklahoma City bombing and incorporated into your emergency response planning.

Hurricane Katrina

Hurricane Katrina was the most destructive natural disaster in U.S. history when measured in terms of its damage to property. The overall destruction wrought by Hurricane Katrina, which was a large and powerful hurricane that also resulted in catastrophic flooding, vastly exceeded that of any other major disaster, including the Chicago Fire of 1871, the San Francisco Earthquake and Fire of 1906, and Hurricane Andrew in 1992.[46] We first provide an overview of the storm and how it formed before looking at the consequences of the hurricane. Once we have covered this background we then look at some lessons learned from the event that can be applied to your organization.

Hurricane Katrina: Formation of the Storm

The tropical depression that became Hurricane Katrina formed over the Bahamas in August 2005 and meteorologists warned people living within the Gulf Coast states that a major storm was on its way. Over the next several days the storm began to gain strength and forecasters tracked its progress. On 28 August, one day before the storm made landfall, the National Weather Service predicted that after the storm hit, "most of the [Gulf Coast] area will be uninhabitable for weeks ... perhaps longer."[47] By this date, evacuations had begun across the region and the region braced for the impact of the storm.

New Orleans was at particular risk. Although half the city actually lies above sea level, its average elevation is about six feet below sea level; adding to this vulnerability is that the city is completely surrounded by water. These issues magnified the potential for damage from the approaching storm and created severe concerns for the town and its inhabitants. To alleviate some of these concerns based on the city's vulnerabilities, the Army Corps of Engineers had built a system of levees and seawalls over the course of the twentieth century to help keep the city safe from flooding. Unfortunately, although the levees along the Mississippi River were strong and sturdy, those built to hold back Lake Pontchartrain, Lake Borgne, and the waterlogged swamps and marshes to the city's east and west were much less reliable.[48] Even before the storm hit, officials worried that those levees, which in many cases had been jerry-built atop sandy, porous, erodible soil, might not withstand a massive storm surge.[49] Added to this problem, many of the neighborhoods that sat below sea level housed the city's poorest and most vulnerable people and were at greatest risk of damage from any flooding.

As a result of these concerns, the day before Katrina hit, New Orleans Mayor Ray Nagin issued the city's first ever mandatory evacuation order. He also declared that the Superdome, a stadium located on relatively high ground near downtown, would serve as a "shelter of last resort" for people who were unable to leave the city (an estimated 112,000 of New Orleans' nearly 500,000 people did not have access to a car).[50] By nightfall, almost 80% of the city's population had evacuated and some 10,000 people remaining in the area sought shelter in the Superdome, whereas tens of thousands of others chose to wait out the storm at home.[51]

Hurricane Katrina: Storm and Flooding

Early in the morning on 29 August 2005, Hurricane Katrina struck the Gulf Coast of the United States. When the storm made landfall, it had a category 3 rating on the Saffir-Simpson hurricane wind scale and it brought sustained winds of 100–140 miles per hour.[52] Although the storm was powerful, another factor that added to the extreme amount of damage was the massive size of the hurricane—the overall storm stretched some 400 miles across and covered nearly 93,000 square miles of the Gulf Coast—an area roughly the size of Great Britain.[53]

New Orleans, the largest affected city and the area that dominated much of what Americans saw on their televisions, suffered significant damage, both from the initial impact of Katrina and then from the subsequent flooding resulting from the breaches along its 350-mile levee system.[54] By the time Hurricane Katrina struck the city, it had already been raining heavily for hours. When the storm surge (as high as nine meters in some places) arrived, it overwhelmed many of the city's unstable levees and drainage canals. Owing to the heavy rain that had been falling before the storm hit, along with the storm surge, water seeped through the soil underneath some levees and swept others away altogether. As a result of these events and the destruction of the levees, at approximately 9:00 a.m. the day the storm hit, low-lying areas within the city were under so much water that people had to scramble to attics and rooftops for safety. Over an estimated 18-h period, approximately 80% of the city was eventually flooded with 6–20 ft of water, necessitating one of the largest search and rescue operations in the nation's history (Figure 11.3).

Figure 11.3 New Orleans flooded after Katrina.

Hurricane Katrina: The Aftermath

Although the storm itself caused a significant amount of damage, its aftermath was catastrophic. Hundreds of thousands of people in Louisiana, Mississippi, and Alabama were displaced from their homes, and experts estimate that Katrina caused more than $100 billion in damage.[55] In an effort to rescue and care for these displaced persons, many individuals and organizations acted heroically in the aftermath of Hurricane Katrina. The Coast Guard, for instance, rescued some 34,000 people in New Orleans alone. In other cases, many ordinary citizens commandeered boats, offered food and shelter, and did whatever else they could to help their neighbors.[56] Unfortunately, the negative aspects of the disaster highlighted the severe problems in the response and recovery actions, as the government—particularly the federal government—appeared unprepared for the catastrophe.

One of the primary organizations typically used as an example to highlight the government's unpreparedness in its response to Hurricane Katrina was the Federal Emergency Management Agency, or FEMA. FEMA took days to establish operations in New Orleans, and even after they were on the ground the agency did not seem to have a sound plan of action. Officials, including even President George W. Bush, seemed unaware of just how bad things were in New Orleans and elsewhere. Part of this problem was that the systems meant to provide information on magnitude of the storm and its effects failed to perform. This information system was unable to cope with the sheer magnitude of the number of people stranded or missing, how many homes and businesses had been damaged, and how much food, water, and aid was needed. As a result, FEMA and many other relief organizations were unable to determine the major issues and prioritize items needed to respond to the area. Another example was at the local government level; New Orleans city leaders had no real plan for helping the many stranded persons. As a result, many people were unable to obtain shelter, which resulted in degrees of lawlessness and a breakdown in basic law and order. This was shown through one instance in which tens of thousands of people desperate for food, water, and shelter broke into the Ernest N. Morial Convention Center complex and caused a great deal of damage—ironically, after breaking into the facility these individuals did not find any supplies but instead found nothing there but chaos. As a result of these organizational failures, Katrina left in her wake what one reporter called a "total disaster zone" in which people were "getting absolutely desperate."[57]

Added to the failure of many agencies tasked to perform rescue and relief efforts were the significant impacts people experienced as a result of the storm. One major issue that illustrates this was the fact that many citizens had nowhere to go, or did not have the means to leave the city, when the evacuation order was given. Although the Superdome in New Orleans had been designated as a safe haven for these individuals, agencies had been unable to provide enough supplies and thus, with limited food, water, and other necessities, after officials accepted 15,000 refugees from the storm on Monday they locked the doors, although there were many others desiring shelter. For many individuals within New Orleans it was nearly impossible to leave the city. Many poor people had no cars and no other transportation options, so they were trapped in the city, even after the evacuation order had been issued. Some people tried to walk to other areas outside the city, but many of these efforts failed—in one ironic instance, citizens tried to walk over the Crescent City connector bridge to the nearby suburb of Gretna, but police officers with shotguns forced them to turn back.[58] Many of these issues resulted in major changes in the government's plans and methods for responding to major emergencies.

Lessons Learned

As with the Oklahoma City bombing, the scale of the Hurricane Katrina disaster is likely to be well beyond that of your organization; however, there are still some lessons learned that can be gained from this emergency and its aftermath and be applied to your standard emergency response operations.

One of the first lessons learned from this incident is to ensure your organization has an existing emergency response plan and that this plan is revised as your environment changes. Although this is an extremely basic lesson learned, in the case of Hurricane Katrina many organizations at both the state and the federal levels failed to have adequate emergency response plans or, if they did, these plans had not been updated as changes to circumstances occurred. This failure to maintain and properly update these plans resulted in requirements that failed to take into account contingency situations in which some of the state and local governments would be incapable of effective response. During Hurricane Katrina, the plans that were in existence depended upon support at all the different levels of government; however, this assistance was unavailable in many cases. Because these plans had not been properly maintained—and still contained many of these assumptions—affected areas that had planned on this support were placed into extreme situations when many of these response and recovery efforts could not occur. Based upon this lesson learned, it is wise for your organization to ensure that your Crisis Management Team conducts periodic reviews of your internal emergency response plans so that it can update any changes within the organization or local community. This could be as simple as changes in personnel and their associated contact information or it could encompass major changes such as the addition of new resources within your company or major business shifts that could change the organization's overall risks and vulnerabilities. Regardless, the failures from Katrina should highlight the need for an organization to periodically check its own emergency response plans and ensure they are updated with current information and realistic expectations of aid or assistance.

Another lesson learned from Hurricane Katrina is based on the lack of training of many of the personnel tasked to lead the emergency response efforts. This applied to both federal and state agency leadership. In relation to your own organization, this lesson learned should emphasize the need to train your personnel in emergency response. This training should particularly apply to the members of your Crisis Management Team to ensure they are capable of conducting their duties in the high-stress crucible that will be present during any type of emergency.

Yet another lesson learned from Hurricane Katrina was the failure of many governmental agencies to properly utilize the available organizations that had been sent to the region to assist with response and recovery. A good example of this is that many of the state and local governments did not provide leadership and control over the numerous military, law enforcement, and rescue agencies that were sent to help. With the lack of any centralized command and control structure from the government, many of these agencies simply acted on their own. Although these actions helped to provide a small measure of relief to the many areas where these personnel responded, the lack of any oversight or ability to synergize their efforts by local governments resulted in an unorganized and inefficient response. Within your own organization, this lesson learned should highlight the need not only to provide adequate leadership to the response effort but also to coordinate all your response and recovery efforts with the many agencies that will provide assistance, to ensure you do not make any additional work or perform multiple tasks to accomplish the same goal.

As with many of the other incidents we have looked at, communications was an issue and emphasizes another lesson learned. For several days after the initial landfall of Hurricane Katrina, communication was unavailable owing to the failure of the overall system. Added to this issue was the fact that many of the various agencies that responded to the region operated communication systems that did not work with systems used by other responding organizations. As stated in our discussion of communication as part of your preparation efforts, your organization should ensure not only that it provides redundant communications systems to enable your own staff to provide direction but also that you can talk with outside agencies such as law enforcement, emergency medical services, and other rescue personnel.

A final lesson learned from Hurricane Katrina that we will cover and that can be applied within your own organization is the need to have the ability to rapidly access funds for immediate response actions and the initial recovery efforts. During Hurricane Katrina, the bureaucracy of the various government agencies made transfer of many of these funds difficult. Although there was a vast amount of money made available for hurricane relief of the Gulf Coast region, the complexities of transferring these funds made it almost impossible to use them in a timely manner and almost never when these funds were required. As a result of this concern, it is wise for your emergency response plans to ensure you have procedures that will allow for rapid access of any necessary funds to accomplish response efforts during various emergency situations.

We could cover many other lessons learned (the Hurricane Katrina lessons learned report contains 125 separate issues)[59]; however, the issues we have discussed should provide some broad guidelines to help you not make similar mistakes in your own emergency response program.

"Simply Smashing" Embezzlement Case

Sue Tashima worked as a bookkeeper for a small T-shirt company in Oakhurst, California. Shortly after starting work in 2006 at Simply Smashing, Inc., she began to embezzle funds, and over the course the next five years, from 2007 to 2012, she stole $685,000 from Simply Smashing, Inc., along with an additional $360,000 from a Fresno real estate investment business that she moved to after emptying the coffers from the smaller T-shirt company.[60] Tim Fruehe and his wife, Barbara, the owners of Simply Smashing, commented on Ms. Tashima's hiring, saying "We hired her based on her supposed spotless background, 20 years of bookkeeping experience, and her charming personality." Fruehe added that "Sue [Tashima] quickly earned our trust and appeared to be saving us money through her efficiency and skill. Everyone loved her. Like most employees at a small business, she became like family to us—you would never guess she was stealing thousands and thousands of dollars from us."[61]

Based on these perceived qualities, Fruehe quickly promoted her to head the company's accounting department and provided her complete access to the organization's funds—this is when Tashima began to steal from the company coffers. Within a week after taking over the accounting department, Tashima took $6500 through an extra payroll check to herself. Fruehe stated she was able to hide this theft as "She blended that check in with other payroll checks from another department so it would not readily show up on our profit and loss statement."[62]

Based on her success with this initial theft she became bolder, and in 2007 Tashima, who was making only about $25,000 from her part-time job as a bookkeeper, ended the year after her promotion to head of the accounting department by doubling her income with the theft of an additional $25,000 from the company over the last three months of 2007. Owing to her success with these efforts, her thefts became more and more frequent, and over the next four years Tashima stole approximately $5000–$10,000 a month—during the same period in which many businesses across the country were struggling through one of the worst economic downturns in history. Fruehe stated "we were blaming our losses to the recession at the time and never even considered to look at our trusted bookkeeper."[63]

Fruehe said that the resulting embezzlement and its ongoing damage to the company (and the Fruehe's personal financial situation) was like a bad TV movie with a script hard to believe—particularly because Tashima spent much of these stolen funds on a lavish lifestyle while those in the company struggled. "She took three of my employees to Las Vegas to celebrate her birthday in 2009," Fruehe said. "They went to Vegas, had suites at the Venetian Hotel, and partied" with money that none of them knew had come from the Simply Smashing business funds.[64] To allay any possible suspicion from her crimes, Tashima worked hard to befriend her bosses, as she volunteered to babysit the Fruehe's children, bought gifts for a grandson's baby shower, and bought both Tim Fruehe and his bride Barbara a nice gift basket to take on their honeymoon when they were married in 2009. The irony is that while Fruehe's business was losing money as a result of the embezzlement, Tashima lived extremely well. Fruehe stated that "Due to the business losses, we got married at the court house in Mariposa and could only afford to spend one night in Yosemite for our honeymoon. Eight months later she [Tashima] invited us to her $60,000 wedding." Fruehe stated that they now know this wedding was paid for with their own money; however, Tashima was able to move any suspicion from herself and continue perpetrating these thefts by claiming her extravagant lifestyle was not only due to her new husband, who was a wealthy businessman from nearby Fresno, but also based on an early inheritance from her family in Watsonville—both stories that were proven false when the facts finally came out.[65]

By 2010, the company's finances were so bad that Fruehe was forced to liquidate personal assets to keep Simply Smashing in business and ensure his employees could continue working. Unfortunately, the problems (along with the thefts) continued and the company was eventually forced to file for bankruptcy in late 2011. According to Fruehe, "Simply Smashing was just a remnant of its former self, yet still in business ... barely." When it was apparent that Simply Smashing had no more money to steal, Tashima moved on to work as a bookkeeper at another company—and she began to embezzle funds at her new job. Tashima kept up her appearance as a good employee when she had been part of Simply Smashing and maintained her supposed friendship with the Fruehes. In fact, she agreed to stay part-time with Simply Smashing through the end of 2012—although this action was primarily designed to keep the company from hiring a new bookkeeper who might discover what she had been doing.[66]

Finally, in June 2013, Tashima's new employer became aware of theft within their organization and determined that the culprit was their new bookkeeper. The police contacted Fruehe as part of their investigation involving Tashima's alleged theft with her new company and, upon receiving this notification, Fruehe began to review his books—it was then that Tashima's embezzlement over the many years became apparent. Fruehe began to dig deeper as he looked at every bank statement from the company from 2007 through 2012 and found $325,000 in theft, along with forgeries and doctored bank statements. He stated that, during this period, the company was doing about $300,000 a month in sales, so the amounts that Tashima stole ($5000–$10,000 a month) were not easy to spot because she buried these transactions among a multitude of expense and payroll accounts.[67] At Tashima's conviction, Fruehe concluded this tale by stating "I'm telling this story so other small business can be aware of what can happen to them once someone steals your trust."[68]

Lessons Learned

As with any theft or embezzlement incident, the best lesson learned is to ensure that your organization practices proper checks and balances of the company's funds and other resources. No matter how good you think your bookkeeper or other financial managers are, or how much you trust them, it is critical that there is a system in place so that another person conducts routine checks of all financial information and bank statements. An additional lesson learned is for an organization to have a system of reporting any unusual activity in relation to an employee's lifestyle and income. In the instance of the Simply Smashing case study, it may have been quite possible that several employees questioned Tashima's lavish trips, luxurious wedding, and other unusual circumstances as an individual who made a very minimal salary. Unfortunately, there was no system to highlight this information and bring several questionable activities to light until Ms. Tashima was caught. Within your own organization it would be wise to ensure there are available means to communicate similar concerns that could help to identify questionable financial activities by employees.

This is an all too familiar story that has been repeated over and over in many businesses. By implementing just a few theft prevention policies and procedures, or providing some redundancy in their financial processes, many organizations could have been saved from similar losses that ultimately damaged their business. This is why it is advisable that your organization implements emergency response procedures that can not only address but mitigate against these issues before they occur or cause irreparable damage to your business.

Conclusion of Emergency Response Case Studies

Over the course of this chapter, we looked at four major emergency incidents: the Columbine High School shooting, the Oklahoma City truck bombing, Hurricane Katrina, and an embezzlement case involving a small business, Simply Smashing, Inc. These incidents covered a variety of types of emergencies and are meant to provide you with lessons learned to improve your emergency response plans and procedures. By reviewing these actual incidents, we hope that we have emphasized much of the required items that should be included in your planning as you begin to develop your own emergency response plans.

End Notes

1. Rosenberg, Jennifer. "Columbine Massacre." 20th Century History. Retrieved from web on 22 September 2014, history1900s.about.com.
2. Rosenberg, Jennifer. "Columbine Massacre".
3. ibid.
4. As quoted in Cullen, Dave, "Columbine Report Released." *Salon.* 16 May 2000, Retrieved from web on 23 September 2014, www.salon.com.
5. See note 2 above.
6. See note 2 above.
7. See note 2 above.
8. See note 2 above.
9. See note 2 above.
10. See note 2 above.
11. See note 2 above.

12. See note 2 above.
13. See note 2 above.
14. See note 2 above.
15. See note 2 above.
16. Kohn, David. "What Really Happened at Columbine: Did So Many Have to Die?" *60 Minutes*. Retrieved from the web on 23 September 2014, www.cbsnews.com.
17. Kohn, David. "What Really Happened at Columbine: Did So Many Have to Die?".
18. See note 2 above.
19. See note 2 above.
20. See note 2 above.
21. Columbine Review Commission, Honorable William H. Erickson, Chairman. "The Report of Governor Bill Owens' Columbine Review Commission." *State of Colorado*. May 2001, Retrieved from web on 22 September 2014, www.state.co.us.
22. Columbine Review Commission, Honorable William H. Erickson, Chairman. "The Report of Governor Bill Owens' Columbine Review Commission.".
23. See note 17 above.
24. See note 22 above.
25. See note 22 above.
26. See note 22 above.
27. See note 22 above.
28. See note 22 above.
29. United States Department of Justice. "Section G: Oklahoma City Bombing." Retrieved from web on 24 September 2014, www.justice.gov.
30. Federal Bureau of Investigation. "Terror Hits Home: The Oklahoma City Bombing." *Famous Cases & Criminals*, Retrieved from web on 23 September 2014, www.fbi.gov.
31. Federal Bureau of Investigation. "Terror Hits Home: The Oklahoma City Bombing".
32. Larson, R., Metzger M., and Cahn M., "Emergency Response for Homeland Security: Lessons Learned and the Need for Analysis." Create Report. *Center for Risk and Economic Analysis of Terrorism Events* (University of Southern California), Retrieved from web on 23 September 2014, create.usc.edu.
33. Larson, R., Metzger, M., and Cahn M., "Emergency Response for Homeland Security: Lessons Learned and the Need for Analysis".
34. History Channel Web site. "Oklahoma City Bombing." *History*. Retrieved from web on 24 September 2014, www.history.com.
35. History Channel Web site. "Oklahoma City Bombing".
36. ibid.
37. University of Missouri – Kansas City School of Law. "The Oklahoma bombing Conspirators." Retrieved from web on 24 September 2014, law2.umkc.edu.
38. See note 35 above.
39. See note 35 above.
40. See note 35 above.
41. See note 35 above.
42. See note 35 above.
43. See note 33 above.
44. See note 33 above.
45. See note 33 above.
46. Townsend, Frances Fragos. "The Federal Response to Hurricane Katrina: Lessons Learned." Assistant to the President for Homeland Security and Counterterrorism. Retrieved from web on 24 September 2014, library.stmarytx.edu.

47. History Channel Web site. "Hurricane Katrina." *History*. Retrieved from web on 24 September 2014, www.history.com.
48. History Channel Web site. "Hurricane Katrina".
49. ibid.
50. See note 48 above.
51. See note 48 above.
52. See note 48 above.
53. Townsend, Frances Fragos. "The Federal Response to Hurricane Katrina: Lessons Learned".
54. ibid.
55. See note 48 above.
56. See note 48 above.
57. See note 48 above.
58. See note 48 above.
59. See note 53 above.
60. Wilkinson, Brian. "Bookkeeper Pleads Guilty to Embezzlement." *Sierra Star*. 9 April 2014, Retrieved from web on 22 September 2014, www.sierrastar.com.
61. Wilkinson, Brian. "Bookkeeper Pleads Guilty to Embezzlement".
62. ibid.
63. See note 61 above.
64. See note 61 above.
65. See note 61 above.
66. See note 61 above.
67. See note 61 above.
68. See note 61 above.

Legislation Related to Emergency Response

12

This chapter looks at legislation that is applicable to many emergency response requirements. This information is intended to help managers understand the various requirements, regulations, and compliance issues as they relate to an organizational emergency response program. Over the next several paragraphs we look at the requirements that dictate an organization have some form of an emergency response plan and some of the specific items within these plans. One of the primary agencies with such requirements is the Occupational Safety and Health Administration, or OSHA, which requires emergency response plans in certain instances. Another agency is the Federal Emergency Management Agency (FEMA), which has detailed the National Incident Management System (NIMS), which is meant to provide guidance and direction on many of these types of plans and procedures. We look at these various requirements over the next several sections.

Occupational Safety and Health Administration Requirements

Almost every business is required to have an emergency action plan according to OSHA's Code of Federal Regulation (CFR) 1910.38. The only business that is exempt from this requirement is a company that has an in-house fire brigade, in which every employee is trained and equipped to fight fires. Whereas this OSHA requirement deals with the need to provide detailed methods and explanations regarding an organization's evacuation procedures—with particular emphasis on incidents involving fire—there are several additional items that OSHA recommends be addressed as part of these procedures to improve them and make them more comprehensive. Over the next several paragraphs we look at both the actual requirements that are directed by OSHA and the recommendations that they cover to assist an organization in the development of its emergency response plans.

The actual requirements OSHA demands are meant to ensure the safety of employees by making certain they know what actions to take in the event of a fire. To meet this requirement, all businesses must address evacuation procedures within their established emergency response plans. Specific requirements for these plans in accordance with CFR 1910.38 are as follows:

- An emergency action plan must be in writing and kept in the workplace so the document is available to employees for review. In small businesses with 10 or fewer employees, the plan can be communicated orally to all employees.
- It is required that an emergency action plan include the following minimum items:
  - Procedures for reporting a fire or other emergency;
  - Procedures for emergency evacuation, including type of evacuation and exit route assignments;

- Procedures to be followed by employees who must remain to operate and perform specific functions for critical plant operations before they evacuate;
- Procedures that detail how an organization will account for all employees after evacuation;
- Procedures to be followed by employees who are tasked to perform rescue or medical duties;
- The name or job title of every employee who may be contacted by employees who need more information about the plan or an explanation of their duties under the plan.
- It is required that an employer have and maintain an employee alarm system that complies with OSHA requirements detailed in CFR 1910.165.
- An employer is required to designate and train employees on methods to assist in a safe and orderly evacuation of other employees.
- An employer is required to review the emergency action plan with each employee covered by the plan during the following instances:
  - When the plan is initially developed or the employee is assigned to a job;
  - When the employee's responsibilities under the plan change;
  - When the plan is changed.

In addition to the requirements demanded by OSHA there are additional guidance and recommendations provided within CFR 1910.38 to assist an organization in the development of its emergency response plans. It should be noted that even though this guidance is contained in federal requirements, much of this supplemental information is not mandated but only recommended. In addition, much of this supplemental information has already been discussed in this book; however, OSHA has emphasized these specific considerations and it was felt important enough to highlight these items in their guidance and recommendations for an organization to consider as it develops its own emergency response plans. We will thus look at these various considerations over the next several paragraphs to help you as you develop your own emergency response plans.

The first recommendation that OSHA makes is meant to help organizations properly define the various details within their own emergency evacuation plans by asking that these plans properly detail specific procedures and methods to fully explain employee actions so that all personnel can easily understand what they must do in the event of an incident. OSHA emphasizes the need for plans to ensure that employees know exactly what they must do in the event of an evacuation. As discussed earlier, there are both short- and long-distance evacuations that may be necessary and, in line with OSHA's guidance, any plans should provide specific information with regard to assembly areas for both situations. This information should include the distance from the facility and the length of time that the evacuation may last, and your plans should provide a process that enables this information to be communicated to employees. Another aspect to consider within any plan is how to deal with your organization's decision-making process to determine whether release of personnel is more appropriate than evacuation. Although there are instances in which the nature of the emergency is extremely grave and total and immediate evacuation of all employees is necessary, there may be other situations in which a partial evacuation of nonessential employees is necessary, whereas other key people may need to remain in the facility for a short period of time to ensure continued plant operations. In some other cases, only those employees in the immediate area of a fire may be expected to evacuate or move to a safe area, such as when a local application fire suppression system discharge alarm is sounded. In the event that a modified evacuation is necessary—specifically that only a portion of the facility should be evacuated—OSHA recommends that refuge or safe areas should be determined and identified in an emergency response plan. In a building divided into fire zones by fire walls, the refuge area may still be within the same building but in a zone different from where the emergency occurs. It is also possible that an exterior refuge or safe area be designated and this may include parking lots, open fields, or streets. Any evacuation assembly area should be located away from the site of the emergency and provide sufficient space to accommodate the necessary number of people that could evacuate the facility. As with any evacuation, employees should be instructed to move away from the exit doors of the building and to avoid congregating close to the building where they may hamper emergency operations. Whatever type of evacuation the specific situation warrants, your organization's emergency response plans should cover the necessary information based on the specific facility layout or hazards within your own business operation. Other items that OSHA recommends be included within an organization's emergency response plan, to provide better detail and instructions, are floor plans or workplace maps that help to clearly show available emergency escape routes. OSHA also suggests color-coding these routes to further aid employees in determining their route assignments and assist in a safe and rapid evacuation. A last item to consider including in any emergency response plan is to identify what rescue and medical first aid duties are to be performed and by whom from within your own organization. As we discussed earlier in the book, it is not only possible but likely that medical responders could take time to reach injured employees, so it would be helpful to provide guidance on how to assist in immediate first aid measures until these professionals arrive on scene. All employees should be told what actions they are to take in any emergency situation that the employer anticipates may occur in the workplace. Although this first recommendation within OSHA's documents is not rocket science—to make certain your own emergency response plans contain the necessary details and instructions for many areas—it is important that all of your employees are sure that they know what is expected of them to ensure their safety from fire or any other type of emergency incident.

Another area we have previously discussed over the course of this book, but that OSHA highlights within their guidance and recommendations, is the need to conduct emergency response training. Because we have already discussed many of the aspects of this training, we will look at only one specific item brought up by OSHA, which is for organizations to consider designating specific individuals as evacuation wardens—personnel who are meant to assist with the evacuation by ensuring orderly movement and safety of employees as they move from the facility. One consideration in designating individuals in these positions is to ensure that an adequate number of employees are available at all times during working hours to act as evacuation wardens so that employees can be swiftly moved from the danger location to the safe areas. As we mentioned in our earlier discussion of this task, the general rule of thumb is to identify one warden for every 20 employees in the workplace in order to provide adequate guidance and instruction at the time of a fire emergency. The employees selected or who volunteer to serve as wardens should be trained and knowledgeable about the complete workplace and building layout along with alternate escape routes and all of the possible assembly areas people may be required to move to upon exiting the building. All wardens and fellow employees should also be made aware of any handicapped employees, or other people who require additional assistance, so that they can provide help such as using the buddy system. These wardens should be made aware of any hazardous areas that should be avoided during emergencies. A final instruction for these evacuation wardens that should be included within emergency and evacuation plans is that these individuals should be tasked to check rooms and other enclosed spaces in the workplace before they leave the facility to ensure there are no employees who may be trapped or otherwise unable to evacuate the area. By having evacuation wardens designated and trained, your organization can provide for a much more organized and safer process to accomplish any type of evacuation.

OSHA also emphasizes the need to ensure that any emergency response plan addresses a process of accountability for all personnel within the facility. Although OSHA's guidance and recommendations are primarily geared toward evacuations, we have previously discussed the need to accomplish this task in several other chapters within this book for any type of incident. With this in mind, we will not discuss this recommendation in any detail but because it has been included as part of OSHA's guidance we hope to show the importance of having a comprehensive process to accomplish this critical task in the event of an emergency.

Another recommendation that OSHA covers within their requirement documentation is the need to coordinate your organizational emergency plans with other employers within the same building (should you share your facility with other businesses). A building-wide or standardized plan for the entire location is an excellent idea provided that all employers inform their respective employees of their duties and responsibilities under the plan. According to OSHA, this standardized plan need not be kept by each employer in the multiemployer building, provided there is an accessible location within the building where the plan can be reviewed by any affected employees. When multiemployer building-wide plans are not feasible, employers should coordinate their plans with the other employers within the building to ensure that any potential conflicts and confusion resulting from employee actions in the event of an incident are avoided. One last aspect of this recommendation is that, in multistory buildings with more than one employer on a single floor, it is essential for these employers to coordinate their plans with one another to avoid conflicts and confusion.

The next recommendation from OSHA with regard to emergency response plans deals with procedures to ensure the safe containment of hazardous materials. In many facilities that work with hazardous materials, it is necessary to accomplish proper shutdown procedures for certain equipment to preclude any release or spillage of these materials. In these cases, these processes should operate to ensure safety, mitigate significant damage, or minimize the potential of severe consequences if the items were left running without any supervision. These operations could include the monitoring of plant power supplies, water supplies, and other essential services that cannot be shut down for every emergency alarm. Other examples of these essential plant operations include chemical or manufacturing processes that must be shut down in stages or

steps for which certain employees must be present to ensure that safe shutdown procedures are completed. To help mitigate against the possibility that this equipment is not
properly turned off, OSHA recommends that applicable organizations list in detail the
individuals responsible for accomplishing this equipment maintenance to ensure that
no additional incidents occur as a result of the initial situation. Plans should provide
these personnel guidance and procedures so that they know who has been selected to
remain behind and what their responsibilities are to care for essential plant equipment
or operations until either they have fully contained any hazardous materials or their
evacuation becomes absolutely necessary in the interest of safety.

OSHA provides guidance to help minimize the potential of fires in their discussion
regarding maintenance of equipment, which should be included in an organization's
fire prevention plan. Certain equipment is often installed in workplaces to control
heat sources or to detect fuel leaks. An example is a temperature limit switch often
found on deep-fat food fryers found in restaurants. There may be similar switches for
high-temperature dip tanks or flame-failure and flashback-arrester devices on furnaces
and similar heat-producing equipment. If these devices are not properly maintained
or if they become inoperative, a definite fire hazard exists. Within your own plans, it
is necessary to ensure that both employees and supervisors are aware of any specific
types of control devices on their own equipment that is involved with combustible
materials and that these plans provide the means to ensure that these controls are properly maintained and operable through periodic inspection or testing. As part of these
plans, it is advisable to follow the manufacturers' recommendations with regard to the
proper maintenance procedures.

The final recommendation from OSHA that we will look at is termed within their
own guidance as housekeeping issues meant to assist with fire prevention. The OSHA
standard calls for the control of accumulations of flammable and combustible waste
materials—the intent of this standard is to make certain that hazardous accumulations of combustible waste materials are controlled so that a fast-developing fire, rapid
spread of toxic smoke, or explosion will not occur. This does not necessarily mean
that each room storing such material must be cleaned, swept, and emptied every day;
however, employers and employees should be aware of any hazardous properties or
materials in their workplaces, where they may accumulate, and the degree that each
hazard poses. Certainly oil-soaked rags have to be treated different from general paper
trash in office areas, but even large accumulations of waste paper or corrugated boxes,
etc., can pose a significant fire hazard and should thus be avoided. Accumulations of
more hazardous materials that can cause large fires, generate dense smoke, be easily
ignited, or spontaneously combust are definitely the types of situations with which
this recommendation is concerned. Providing your employees with some guidance on
what hazards exist and where they are located and instructions on when and how often
these areas should be cleaned should be included in your emergency response plans.

Over the last several paragraphs, we have looked at guidance from OSHA regarding an organization's emergency response plans. Although much of this guidance
was simple recommendations that should be considered, there were some specific
requirements that must be followed to ensure compliance with federal regulations.
These specific requirements are the need to ensure your facility has adequate fire

prevention measures along with a written emergency response plan that is available to all employees. Following not only these requirements but also the recommendations that OSHA provides will help you ensure your overall plan is comprehensive and will assist in minimizing any possible damage or injury from an emergency incident.

National Incident Management System

The NIMS was developed by FEMA and it is meant to provide a systematic, proactive approach to help guide organizations in working seamlessly in their response to emergency incidents. This system provides a basis for departments and agencies at all levels of government, nongovernmental organizations, and organizations in the private sector, regardless of the type of business, its size, its location, or the complexity of its specific operations, to reduce loss of life, loss of property, and harm to the environment in the event of an emergency incident. It should be noted that the NIMS is not a stand-alone process but instead is an essential part of the overarching National Preparedness System (NPS) for the country. Ultimately, the purpose of NIMS is to provide a template to help improve any organization's management of incidents as they develop the four emergency response planning factors—mitigation, preparedness, response, and recovery.

Although many of the concepts and recommendations that comprise both NIMS and NPS have been discussed throughout this book, we provide you with an overview of these items here to better enable you in developing your own emergency response plans and also to provide another source of this information to promote understanding of these theories. To accomplish this improved understanding we provide an overview of the NPS, and once we have covered this high-level process, we then look at the individual areas that form the basis of NIMS. Again, much of this information may be repetitive from other portions of this book, but it is hoped that this background will provide you with the ability to better comprehend these theories and actions and integrate them together into the best emergency response planning process you can achieve within your own organization.

National Preparedness System

The NPS provides a systematic process to develop your own organization's emergency response plans and enable you to respond and recover from potential incidents in a more effective and efficient manner. To allow a better understanding of the NPS process, we'll briefly go through the system's recommended actions and then discuss how to integrate these actions into the process we have covered throughout this book to develop an emergency response plan. The NPS process recommends following these actions:

- Identifying and assessing risk
- Estimating capability requirements
- Building and sustaining capabilities

- Planning to deliver capabilities
- Validating capabilities
- Reviewing and updating

We look at each of these specific actions over the next several paragraphs.

Identifying and assessing risk involves the collection of historical and recent data on existing, potential, and perceived threats and hazards. We covered this process and its associated actions when we looked at the development of your own organization's Risk Assessment Matrix. As we discussed earlier, the results of these risk assessment forms the basis for many of the remaining steps—not only within NPS but also within the overall emergency response planning process—as they provide a prioritization of what risks and vulnerabilities need to be addressed immediately and what items could be looked at later as you consider and implement various security measures.

Once you have defined the various risks and vulnerabilities that could occur against your organization, you next should estimate capability requirements according to the NPS process. This means that you should begin to determine the specific capabilities and activities (we have used the term mitigation and security measures throughout this book) to best address those risks. As we have discussed, these mitigation measures could be the purchase or installation of various physical security measures, such as alarm systems, CCTV, or strengthened protective measures for the building, or these measures could simply be development and implementation of improved procedures among your personnel that provide greater protection.

The NPS process next looks at building and sustaining capabilities, which involves a determination to find the best way to use the limited available resources to purchase, build, or implement the possible capabilities or mitigation measures. As we have discussed earlier, your organization should accomplish this through the prioritization of risks and vulnerabilities that could affect your business as contained within your Risk Assessment Matrix—in this manner, you will ensure that the highest probable risks or threats that could result in the greatest consequences should be addressed before working to mitigate against other concerns.

Planning to deliver capabilities is the next action within the process provided by the NPS. This item refers to ensuring your organizational emergency response plans are coordinated with applicable organizations. We discussed the need to ensure your plans are discussed with agencies in your area within several sections of this book. It is important that this coordination should not only include first responder agencies, such as law enforcement, emergency medical services, fire, and other rescue agencies, but also include other entities that could assist with or affect your response and recovery actions. These agencies could include individuals, other businesses, nonprofit organizations, community and faith-based groups, and all levels of government.

The next action that NPS discusses within their process is validating capabilities. This item refers to conducting training, exercises, and simulations throughout your organization to promote better understanding of your own organization's plans and procedures among employees. These areas were covered in great detail within both Chapters 10 and 11. Conducting and participating in these activities will not only help to identify gaps in your plans and capabilities but will also help you to see progress as your organizations moves toward meeting preparedness goals to mitigate against possible emergencies.

The last action within the NPS process is reviewing and updating. As we have covered earlier, it is important to regularly review and update all capabilities, resources, and plans in your organization's emergency response program. This should be made a periodic task for your own Crisis Management Team, so that this function is codified and accomplished, because it can be easy to put off otherwise. Risks and resources available to combat these threats all evolve, and so should your preparedness efforts, to ensure your overall emergency response plans will provide the absolute best protection to your company's critical resources and employees.

National Incident Management System Approach

As mentioned earlier, the purpose of NIMS is to provide a common approach for managing incidents. The process of developing an emergency response plan that we have covered throughout this book will help make sure your organization meets all of the concepts within NIMS. All of these processes provide for a flexible but standardized set of incident management practices with an emphasis on common principles, a consistent approach to operational structures and supporting mechanisms, and an integrated approach to resource management.

In addition to the instructions within the book, there is additional information available on the NIMS Web site, which has been divided into six different subjects: doctrine supporting guides and tools, training, resource management and mutual aid, implementation guidance and reporting, administrative information, and incident command system resources. These areas are shown in Figure 12.1.

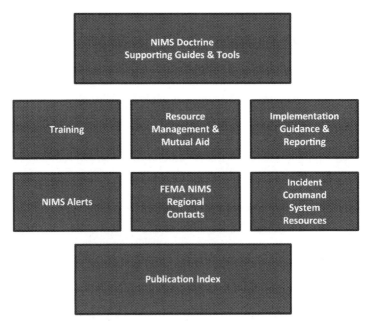

Figure 12.1 National Incident Management System.

Within the doctrine supporting guides and tools area, there are a variety of information and tools provided to assist organizations in understanding and implementing many of the emergency response processes. These tools and aids address specific content and processes that help build and sustain emergency management capabilities. This content includes basic guidance for public information officers, communications and information management standards, and intelligence and investigations guidance.

The training area provides information and offers various online courses to assist in developing detailed instructions with regard to emergency response. These courses include lessons on the Incident Command System, methods to accomplish multiagency coordination, and resource management during emergency situations, to name just a few of the available lessons and information.

Resource management and mutual aid covers information regarding equipment, funding, and other property that can be requested and used in the event of an emergency along with the process and methods to follow to obtain these items. Another piece of information contained within this area includes discussion of the various terms used within NIMS. These terms, listed below, are meant to ensure that organizations across the country can use a consistent process when attempting to obtain these resources and request aid.

- Resource typing is defining and categorizing, by capability, the resources requested, deployed, and used in emergency incidents.
- Qualifying and credentialing personnel ensures that the identity and attributes of individuals or members of teams are validated against an established set of minimum criteria and qualifications for specific job titles.

The National Mutual Aid System within NIMS is built upon the integration of all types of mutual aid, including local, intrastate, regional, interstate, tribal, and international mutual aid, and a method to consolidate these processes into a single system. Each of these levels of aid utilizes the agencies below it to synergize all of the available organizations to create a unified national system meant to provide a better response to significant emergency incidents.

Implementation guidance and reporting provides objectives and metrics to help assess the effectiveness of response for various departments and agencies across the state and federal levels. As part of this information, there are some compliance requirements for local emergency planning committees (at the local government level) that are necessary when preparing for and responding to chemical emergencies. These requirements are designed for governmental agencies; however, it is useful for your organization to be aware of them to increase your knowledge level and ultimately result in improving your own plans and procedures. The required elements for these governmental agencies to include within a community emergency response plan are as follows[1]:

- Identify facilities and transportation routes of extremely hazardous substances.
- Describe emergency response procedures, on- and off-site.
- Designate a community coordinator and facility coordinator(s) to implement the plan.
- Outline emergency notification procedures.
- Describe how to determine the probable affected area and population by releases.

- Describe local emergency equipment and facilities and the persons responsible for them.
- Outline evacuation plans.
- Provide a training program for emergency responders (including schedules).
- Provide methods and schedules for exercising emergency response plans.

The remaining areas deal with administrative information for NIMS. The alerts area details various updates, revisions, and changes to the NIMS system and any process changes that may apply to the overall system. The regional contacts area provides the name, address, telephone number, and email address for various NIMS coordinators across the country and what locations are assigned to their respective region. The Incident Command System resources area provides fact sheets on various aspects involving NIMS. Finally, the publications index area provides links to several documents on NIMS doctrine and supplemental guides providing additional information.

Incidents typically begin and end locally, and they must be managed on a day-to-day basis at the lowest possible geographical, organizational, and jurisdictional level. There are instances, however, in which success depends on the involvement of multiple jurisdictions, levels of government, functional agencies, and/or emergency-responder disciplines. These instances necessitate effective and efficient coordination across this broad spectrum of organizations and activities, which is the purpose of NIMS and ultimately the NPS process. By using NIMS, both private organizations and communities ensure they are part of a comprehensive national approach that improves the effectiveness of emergency management and response personnel across the full spectrum of potential threats and hazards (including natural hazards, terrorist activities, and other human-caused disasters) regardless of their size or complexity.

End Note

1. Federal Emergency Management Agency, "NIMS Compliance Requirements for Local Emergency Planning Committees," *FEMA Fact Sheet*. Retrieved from Web on 24 September 2014, www.fema.gov.

Appendix A

Example—Emergency Response Plan

1. Executive summary
   1.1. Introduction. *An overall introductory section with some basic information on security and emergency response.* Typical verbiage can be as follows: Businesses are not immune to security incidents and crises as seen over the past several years. These incidents can be as minor as vandalism and petty theft; however, they can also include more serious events such as natural disasters; threats against the facility, visitors, and staff; active-shooter scenarios; or environmental hazards. These incidents may result in significant catastrophes which can disrupt business operations or cause harm to individuals. This plan is designed to provide response actions for the organization's staff in order to mitigate against these potential crises, ensure they are prepared, respond in the event they actually occur, and recover from an incident so that the organization regains operational capability.

       1.1.1. *Summary of the local area where your business operates. This brief description should include information regarding the geographic area, major population centers, and the types of typical criminal activity in the area such as minor burglary, vandalism, theft, break-in, or more violent crimes.*

       1.1.2. *Summary of the size of the business (e.g., number of buildings; number of staff; number and frequency of visitors, budget, etc.).*

       1.1.3. Security Risk Assessment. *This section should include some basic information on security risk assessment along with a brief discussion on your organization's specific risk assessment results. It should also provide a specific listing of the business's risks based upon the results of your organization's risk assessment matrix.* Typical verbiage can be: The organizational risk assessment matrix helps identify and prioritize what risks and vulnerabilities could potentially be experienced within the organization. These risks have been consolidated into the overall risk assessment matrix as shown (the actual completed matrix should be included here).

           1.1.3.1. Risks and Vulnerabilities with a High Probability of Occurrence. Include a list of specific risks within the organization that have a high potential of occurring which would result in critical consequences based upon the results of your risk assessment.

           1.1.3.2. Risks and Vulnerabilities with a Moderate Probability of Occurrence. *Include a list of risks with moderate potential of occurring which would result in serious consequences based upon the results of your risk assessment.*

           1.1.3.3. Risks and Vulnerabilities with a Low Probability of Occurrence. *Include a list of the risks with low potential of occurring. Although it may be unnecessary to take immediate action to mitigate these threats, your plan should include these risks as they could be addressed in the future.*

   1.2. Plan Objectives. *This section should describe the goal of the organization's emergency response plan and how this information should be disseminated within the workforce.*

2. Emergency Response

    2.1. Introduction. *This section of the plan provides tools and checklists that ensure your organization is fully prepared to appropriately respond to an incident.* Typical verbiage can be: There are four primary areas that ensure your organization's ability to appropriately respond to any type of emergency incident. These areas are recognized as the four emergency response planning factors and include mitigations, preparedness, response, and recovery.

    2.2. Mitigation. Typical verbiage can be: Mitigations are efforts taken prior to an incident to lessen its impact. Many of these efforts include the implementation of physical, information, and personnel security measures based upon your organization's risk assessment and available resources.

    These paragraphs should detail some of the various mitigations your organization has implemented.

        2.2.1. Physical Security and Mitigation Measures. *This section of the plan provides specific physical security measures that have been implemented across your organization's safety and security system. Subparagraphs within this section should detail all of the various physical security measures that are currently included within your security system design within each of the following categories.*

            2.2.1.1. Perimeter Security Measures. *This section should specify any natural and artificial barriers that have been used around the perimeter of your property.*

            2.2.1.2. Doors and Windows. *This section should detail any specifications and requirements for exterior doors and windows, along with any additional specifications you may wish for interior doors.*

            2.2.1.3. Exterior and Interior Lighting Requirements. *This section should specify both exterior and interior lighting and how it integrates into your security system.*

            2.2.1.4. Access Control Systems. *This section should detail how your organization accomplishes and limits access control into your facility. You should also discuss what type of access control you use (e.g., receptionist, entry control guard, or automated access control system). This section should also detail other aspects of your organization's access control system to include employee identification cards and the location of any card readers (in the event that your organization utilizes an automated access control system).*

            2.2.1.5. Key Control System. *This section should specify the process within your organization to maintain control over keys and locks within your building.*

            2.2.1.6. Alarm Systems. *This section should cover what type of alarm system is contained within your facility along with the notification process and what response occurs in the event of an alarm.*

            2.2.1.7. Closed-Circuit Television (CCTV). *This section discusses the CCTV systems both outside and inside your facility. This section should also cover any notification, alarms, and response that augment the CCTV cameras in place within the building.*

            2.2.1.8. Safes and Vaults. *This section covers what safes and vaults are necessary to protect your organization's critical resources. This information should include whether safes or vaults are more appropriate and what type of protection (e.g., fire or theft) is the desired objective of these devices.*

2.2.3. Information Security and Mitigation Measures. *This section of the plan provides specific information security measures that have been implemented across your organization's safety and security system. Subparagraphs within this section should detail the various measures as they relate to the three pillars of your organization's information security program (confidentiality, integrity, and availability).*

    2.2.3.1. Confidentiality. *This section details how your information security program ensures confidentiality of data to include specific software, hardware, and procedural methods to assist with this, and the other pillars, within an information security program.*

    2.2.3.2. Integrity. *This section details how your information security program ensures integrity of data.*

    2.2.3.3. Availability. *This section details how your information security program ensures availability of data.*

2.2.4. Personnel Security and Mitigation Measures. *This section of the plan provides specific personnel security measures that have been implemented across your organization's safety and security system. Subparagraphs within this section should detail the three primary steps that help to ensure a comprehensive program, the preemployment screening process, investigations, and methods to mitigate against discriminatory practices in hiring or termination.*

    2.2.4.1. Preemployment Screening Process. *This section covers how your organization conducts the entire screening process for potential employees. Any subparagraphs within this section should detail various aspects of this process to include the organization's application, credit checks, and background investigations.*

    2.2.4.2. Investigations. *This section discusses how your organization will conduct various types of investigations to conduct background checks and issues involving alleged inappropriate behavior. The plan should cover the following specifics.*

        2.2.4.2.1. Designated Investigators. *This section covers who should conduct investigations within your organization, along with any training and other guidance these individuals should follow.*

        2.2.4.2.2. Evidence Handling Procedures. *This section discusses the basic procedures to ensure evidence is handled correctly and appropriately.*

        2.2.4.2.3. Interview Techniques. *This section covers the necessary procedures and techniques in conducting interviews associated with any investigations.*

        2.2.4.2.4. Investigation Reports. *This section specifies the correct format of an investigation report for your organization.*

    2.2.4.3. Discrimination against Hiring and Termination Actions. *This section discusses the various requirements that apply within your particular organization. These areas should include various discriminatory regulations and privacy requirements.*

2.3. Preparedness. *This area covers the various items that assist with preparation of your organization's emergency response program.* Typical verbiage can be: Preparedness provides your organization's staff with tools to prepare and plan for response and recovery in the event of an emergency incident.

2.3.1. Command and Control. *This section delineates the chain of command during an emergency incident. It should also detail the various roles and responsibilities of each individual necessary to accomplish tasks during an emergency. This team should detail your organization's membership of the Crisis Management Team.*

    2.3.1.1. Crisis Management Team. *This section details the various members and responsibilities of your organization's Crisis Management Team. At a minimum, this section should delineate the following items.*

        2.3.1.1.1. Crisis Management Team Membership. *This section discusses the specific roles and what position within your organization fulfills this role. At a minimum, your organization's Crisis Management Team should include the following roles:*

            2.3.1.1.1.1. Incident commander

            2.3.1.1.1.2. Administrative support

            2.3.1.1.1.3. Facility and maintenance

            2.3.1.1.1.4. Information technology or information systems

            2.3.1.1.1.5. Logistical and transportation

            2.3.1.1.1.6. Communications and public affairs

            2.3.1.1.1.7. Human resources

        2.3.1.1.2. Recall of the Crisis Management Team. *This section covers the process to recall the team members. It should also include what equipment is required for each team member.*

        2.3.1.1.3. Crisis Management Team Kits. *This section details the necessary equipment that each member of the Crisis Management Team should prepare and have available in the event of an emergency.*

2.3.2. Communications. *This section should specify the various communication methods necessary in the event of an actual incident. Within this section there should also be telephone numbers of personnel within your organization along with contact information for other agencies that may need to be contacted in the event of any emergency you could experience.*

    2.3.2.1. Notification Procedures. *This section should specify the procedures and methods used to notify the organization and its leadership at the onset of an actual situation. It should also detail the notification procedures to recall the Crisis Management Team.*

    2.3.2.2. Communications Equipment. *This section should detail what equipment will be used in the event of an emergency along with the redundant items to ensure continued communication through an incident. This section should also include a prioritized list of communications methods in the event that various equipment items may fail as a result of the emergency. Lastly, this section should discuss any capabilities and limitations inherent in your organization's current communications system.*

    2.3.2.3. Communication with External Agencies. *This section should discuss how your organization will plan to conduct coordination with outside agencies. This should include all agencies (to include emergency responders, media, and relief agencies) along with points of contact and telephone numbers but also discussion on who is responsible to accomplish this coordination and who within your own organization will ensure this contact list is maintained and updated.*

2.3.2.3.1. Fire Management Operations. *This section should cover any necessary information that should be coordinated with local fire departments. This information should include evacuation plans, building layouts, and fire suppression systems within your facility.*

2.3.3. Collection and Distribution of Resources. *This section identifies available resources necessary to protect personnel and designates where they should be located. There are several different types of resources that should be included.*

2.3.3.1. Inventory Management System. *This section covers your organization's process on how to track and provide any equipment available throughout an emergency situation. This system should not only provide processes for currently available items that the organization possesses but should also discuss methods to track any equipment received through donations as a result of the incident.*

2.3.3.2. Critical Resources. *This section should discuss what equipment and information is designated as critical to your business operations and how you will provide some backup for these items.*

2.3.3.3. Transportation. *This section identifies the point of contact and circumstances where your organization should consider obtaining transportation for your employees.*

2.3.3.4. Medical Care and Supplies. *This section should cover areas within your own facility that are designated as casualty collection points. You should also discuss what type of medical equipment you should procure and store in these areas to assist with basic medical care of any injured in the event that emergency medical responders will not be immediately available.*

2.3.3.5. Emergency Supplies. *This section covers what emergency supplies are available and where they are located in the event of an emergency. These supplies include water, food, and hygiene items.*

2.3.4. Coordination Considerations. *This section discusses the various departments within your own organization and external agencies within the local community and government that should be contacted prior to any emergency incident in order to determine their response actions and what assistance they can provide to your own business.*

2.3.5. Congestion. *This section should identify any areas of congestion and ensure there are work-arounds developed prior to the onset of any type of emergency incident.*

2.4. Response. *This section covers specific actions which your organization should implement in the event of an actual emergency incident. Although there is a brief discussion on command and management during the event, the primary instructions within this section should cover the primary response actions: evacuation and shelter-in-place operations.* Typical verbiage can be: Response includes the activities necessary to address situations as they arise over the course of an actual emergency.

2.4.1. Command and Management of Emergency Operations. *This section should provide instructions and procedures regarding the chain of command during an emergency incident and specifics regarding your organization's Crisis Management Team.*

2.4.1.1. Chain of Command. *This section should specify who will be in overall charge in the event of an emergency. It should include a prioritized* list of leadership in the event that any one individual is unavailable or incapacitated as a result of the incident.

2.4.1.2. Crisis Management Team. *This section should refer to your discussion on the Crisis Management Team that was covered in the Preparedness section of this plan.*

2.4.1.3. Communication with the Media. *This section should detail your organization's procedures regarding contact with the media. This information should discuss which employee is the primary point of contact to conduct this communication and how individual personnel should interact with the media. This instruction should include if employees are authorized to contact the media or if all communications should be coordinated through the media point of contact.*

2.4.2. Evacuation Procedures. *This section should cover the specific instructions on how your organization will conduct an evacuation. This section should discuss how notification will be made across all work areas and where personnel should go in the event of an evacuation.*

2.4.2.1. Fire Management and Facility Evacuation Operations. *This section should include information obtained from your local fire department, designation of specific personnel who would assist with the evacuation.*

2.4.2.2. Crowd Control Operations. *This section discusses issues involving evacuation of the facility. This area is concerned solely with the evacuation of the building itself.*

2.4.2.2.1. Movement Routes. *This section should discuss the designated evacuation routes both inside and outside your facility. It should also provide instructions to ensure interior hallways that are designated as primary routes are kept clear of equipment and are wide enough to accommodate the necessary numbers of personnel.*

2.4.2.2.2. Evacuation Wardens. *This section covers who is designated as an evacuation warden and where these personnel will be stationed.*

2.4.2.3. Traffic Control Operations. *This section deals with evacuation once personnel have exited the facility. It should designate personnel responsible to maintain crowd and traffic control in the event of an evacuation along with movement routes to accomplish the evacuation. These procedures should cover areas both within your company's facility and on the grounds and include any necessary equipment to accomplish these operations. It is very likely that coordination with local law enforcement in the development of this paragraph will be necessary to ensure that your plans do not impede the ability of first responders to access your facility.*

2.4.2.4. Shut Down of Equipment. *This section should detail whether your organization has equipment that should be operated (e.g., fire extinguishers) or shut down to minimize further damage to the facility or personnel. If there is such equipment in your organization, you should detail who should be responsible to shut down or operate the equipment and how to balance the individual safety with the requirement to disable the equipment in order to minimize further damage.*

2.4.2.5. Gathering and Rally Points. *This section covers specific locations where employees should gather in the event of evacuation. These locations should include areas that can be used in the event of both standard evacuations and long-distance evacuations.*

2.4.3. Shelter-In-Place Procedures. *This section should cover the specific instructions on how your organization conducts shelter-in-place operations. These procedures should include instructions on how to accomplish the two types of sheltering methods: sealing areas against hazardous materials and barricading areas against hostile intruders.*

2.4.3.1. Lockdown Procedures. *This section details the specific requirements for employees to follow in the event a lockdown is required. Standard procedures include personnel moving into the closest available room, closing and locking the door, covering any windows (in the event that a perpetrator is inside or outside the building), moving away from exterior windows, and using furniture as protection or to barricade the door.*

2.4.3.2. Sealing Areas against Hazardous Materials. *This section should include what actions should be accomplished by maintenance personnel (e.g., shut down ventilation systems) and actions by individual employees. These latter actions include shutting any vents, sealing vents/doors/ windows using plastic and duct tape, and remaining inside the area to await for the first responders.*

2.4.4. Accountability. *This area must specify your organization's process to accomplish accountability of all employees in the event of any type of emergency incident. This process must account not only for all employees but also for any visitors to your facility at the time of an incident. This information should include the designation of the organization's overall point of contact, how the accountability information is consolidated, responsible personnel to obtain this information within each work section, and the method to report this information to the Crisis Management Team.*

2.4.5. Internal Rescue Operations. *This section identifies teams and processes to accomplish the rescue, care, and safe removal of employees should this become necessary.* Typical verbiage can be: Should emergency response personnel be overwhelmed if the emergency extends beyond your organization, they may be unable to accomplish rescue operations in a timely manner.

2.4.6. Emergency Medical Operations. *This section should provide for the treatment of injured personnel and if necessary assistance with coroner operations in the event of any deaths.*

2.4.7. Staff Care and Shelter Operations. *This section should discuss the process to provide for basic human needs of your organization's staff such as lodging, food, and child care. If your organization has equipment prepositioned within the building in the event of an emergency, this is the section to specify what equipment should be stored and where these kits are located.*

2.4.8. Emergency Response Checklists. *Your organization should develop checklists for some of the significant emergencies that could occur in your area and this section includes the various checklists necessary to assist in response to different types of emergency situations (note: we will include templates for detailed emergency response checklists in Appendix B).* Typical verbiage can be: Checklists help people accomplish all the necessary tasks—even when they may not be thinking clearly—to ensure damage and personal injury are minimized. It is advisable to limit the number of checklists and provide them as a separate booklet to responsible individuals. Some of the areas that should be covered by a checklist include:

2.4.8.1. Active shooter

2.4.8.2. Hostage situation

2.4.8.3. Bomb threat

2.4.8.4. Suspicious package

2.4.8.5. Felony criminal activities

2.4.8.6. Biological/chemical threats

2.5. Recovery. Typical verbiage can be: Recovery occurs after an emergency has occurred and includes necessary actions to return your organization to full, preincident operations.

2.5.1. Damage Assessment. *This area details how initial damage assessment estimates will be accomplished. It should include the responsible individuals to accomplish this task along with the process to collect data and schedule items necessary to obtain information. This area should also include information on where to obtain detailed inventories and surveys of your company's facility so that they can baseline this effort. There should also be separate paragraphs that cover each individual task involved with the damage assessment process.*

2.5.1.1. Initial Situation Overview. *This section covers the process to accomplish this overview to include how this is accomplished and who will conduct the overview within your organization.*

2.5.1.2. Initial Damage Assessment. *This section details how this assessment is accomplished. It should also include any forms or documentation that will assist in this assessment.*

2.5.1.3. Damage Assessment and Needs Analysis. *This section specifies how your organization will identify needs and requirements needed in order to recover the company to its full business capability.*

2.5.1.4. Damage and Loss Assessment. *This section covers how your organization will consolidate the various cost information that is associated with any repairs and construction, along with any costs to replace items that were lost as a result of the emergency.*

2.5.2. Cleanup and Salvage Operations. *This section should cover who oversees cleanup and decontamination along with any tasks and responsibilities associated with this effort. This section should include any safety considerations and personal protective clothing if your organization's emergency response plans require them.*

2.5.2.1. General Precautions. *This section should discuss any necessary safety precautions during cleanup and salvage operations. This section should first direct that an initial safety inspection should be conducted of the damaged work areas prior to any actual cleanup. It should also include the process to contact medical authorities and the reporting procedure in the event that safety concerns are identified.*

2.5.2.1.1. Decontamination of Hazardous Materials. *This section should detail the specific precautions necessary in the event of any hazardous material spill. It should include requirements to warn personnel of known areas that contain these materials, wear of personal protective equipment, and decontamination procedures.*

        2.5.2.2. Electrical Hazards. *This section should discuss how your organization will work with any potential electrical hazards. This should include a process to identify such hazards and the specific personnel who will deal with these issues prior to entry and work in an area.*

        2.5.2.3. Fire Protection. *This section should cover any fire protection considerations during cleanup and salvage operations.*

    2.5.3. Facility Management and Plant Operations. *This section covers any temporary purchase or construction necessary to either maintain or relocate your organization in order to maintain operations during the course of the emergency (should this be necessary or even possible).*

    2.5.4. Customer and Client Information. *This area focuses on the responsible individuals or office that maintains all customer and client information. This section should also include procedures to provide the public and your customers with accurate information regarding any changes in service hours, location, or procedures.*

    2.5.5. Mutual Aid and Agreement Activities. *This section determines what assistance, outside agencies can provide and attempts to obtain support from these agencies.*

    2.5.6. Business Restoration. *This section covers the processes necessary to permanently bring your business back on line after an emergency situation has occurred. Much of this section will be particular to your location and type of business.*

    2.5.7. After Action Review. *This section should discuss your organization's process to conduct an after action review of the emergency situation. This review should cover your response actions, feedback, areas of improvement, and any necessary changes to your current plans and procedures based upon the lessons learned from that particular incident.*

3. Business Continuity Plan

    3.1. Introduction. *This section of the plan provides the areas to include in your organization's Business Continuity Plan.* Typical verbiage can be: Business Continuity Planning is a proactive process that ensures critical services or products within your organization can continue to be delivered during an emergency incident which causes disruption. This process identifies your organization's critical resources that are necessary with the continuity of your business operations. These resources include personnel information, equipment, financial allocations, legal counsel, and infrastructure protection.

    3.2. Business Impact Analysis. *This section identifies the organization's mandate and defines critical services or products; ranks the order of priority of services or products to ensure their continuous delivery or rapid recovery; and identifies internal and external impacts of potential disruptions.*

    3.3. Recovery Plan for Critical Business Functions and Processes. *This section covers the method to identify the organization's critical services and products and determines the priority of these resources according to the maximum tolerable downtime for that particular service.*

    3.4. Formal Business Continuity Plan. *This section uses the information from the Business Impact Analysis and the recovery plan for the critical business functions and processes to formulate and develop the organization's Business Continuity Plan.*

    3.5. Business Continuity Training. *This section discusses the various methods to train your organization in its Business Continuity Plan.*

4. Emergency Response Training

    4.1. Introduction. *This section of the plan provides the methods to accomplish emergency response training through both formal training and the conduct of exercises and simulations.* Typical verbiage can be: Emergency response cannot be effectively implemented if they are solely words on paper and there has been no process to help your employees understand their roles and responsibilities and internalize these methods. For this reason, an overall training program to help educate your employees and emphasize these concepts is critical to your overall emergency response program.

    4.2. Initial Emergency Response Training. *This section identifies how your organization accomplishes this training. It is recommended that this training is done through a formal classroom presentation since this will set the tone for your organization and will promote the concept that emergency response and the ability to protect your employees is an important part of doing business within your company. This training also provides new employees with the necessary information regarding their responsibilities and actions when an emergency incident occurs before they can review the emergency response plan.*

    4.3. Recurring Emergency Response Training. *This section should specify the methods and processes to accomplish this recurring training. This area should include the frequency that this training is conducted and how this will be accomplished.*

    4.4. Emergency Response Exercises. *This section should cover your organization's process to plan and conduct exercises and simulations. There should be separate sections on the following areas.*

        4.4.1. Exercise Management Team. *This section should discuss the membership along with the roles and responsibilities of this group.*

        4.4.2. Types of Exercises. *This section discusses the various types of exercises that your organization can conduct.*

            4.4.2.1. Emergency Drills. *This section should detail what types of emergencies and events are accomplished through an emergency drill.*

            4.4.2.2. Table-Top Scenarios. *This section should detail what types of emergencies and events are accomplished through a table-top scenario.*

            4.4.2.3. Full-Scale Exercises. *This section should detail what types of emergencies and events are accomplished through full-scale exercises.*

        4.4.3. Frequency of Exercises. *This section should specify how often your organization will conduct an exercise or simulation and what type of exercise should be accomplished.*

Appendix B

Emergency Response Checklists

1. Active Shooter Emergency Response Checklist
2. Hostage Situation Emergency Response Checklist
3. Bomb Threat Emergency Response Checklist
4. Suspicious Package Emergency Response Checklist
5. Felony Crime Incident Emergency Response Checklist
6. Biological/Chemical Threat Emergency Response Checklist

Active Shooter Emergency Response Checklist

Action	Responsible Agent
Accomplish building-wide notification over public address system and intercoms (if available)	Crisis Management Team
Notify Law Enforcement via 911	Applicable staff member
Provide information on assailant(s)—location, number, race/gender, clothing description, physical features, type of weapons, backpack, identity	
Notify company senior management (per company instructions)	Applicable staff member
Initiate evacuation with staff in unaffected areas (if possible)	Crisis management team leader
Coordinate with incident commander as requested	Crisis management team leader
Personnel outside the building immediately evacuate the area	Applicable staff member
Personnel inside the building should evacuate (if possible). If not, they should proceed to the nearest safe room	Applicable staff member
Personnel remaining in building accomplish shelter-in-place. They should lock safe room/classroom and barricade door	Applicable staff member
Block visibility into safe room	Applicable staff member
Pull drapes and blinds (if intruder is outside facility)	
Place paper over interior room window (if intruder is inside facility)	
Turn off lights and silence cell phones	Applicable staff member

Continued

—Cont'd

Action	Responsible Agent
Do not unlock or open room until notified by law enforcement	Applicable staff member
Determine personnel accountability in respective room and report to designed organizational point of contact	Supervisors and/or team leaders
At conclusion of incident, report total accountability to organizational point of contact. List shall include: • Total personnel • Separate list of injured personnel • Separate list of casualties	Supervisors and/or team leaders
Provide grief counseling services for staff as necessary	Crisis Management Team

Hostage Situation Emergency Response Checklist

Action	Responsible Agent
Initiate building-wide notification through runners (do not use intercom for notifications)	Person with access to building intercom
Notify Law Enforcement via 911 • Provide information on assailant(s)—location, number, race/gender, clothing description, physical features, type of weapons, backpack, identity • Provide information on number of hostages and location (if available)	Applicable staff member
Notify organization senior management	Applicable staff member
Establish perimeter around the affected classroom/area	Crisis Management Team
Attempt to monitor affected classroom/area using building intercom—*do not attempt to contact perpetrator*	Crisis Management Team
Lock and secure all exterior building doors	Building maintenance
Evacuate nonaffected staff	Crisis Management Team
Coordinate with incident commander as requested and attempt to meet any law enforcement negotiators at a predesignated entrance	Crisis management team leader
Staff within the incident perimeter should: • Lock and barricade door • Pull drapes and blinds • Place paper over interior room window (if applicable) • Turn off lights and silence cell phones	Applicable staff member
Do not unlock or open rooms within the incident perimeter until notified by law enforcement	Applicable staff member
Determine personnel accountability in respective room and report to designed organizational point of contact	Supervisors and/or team leaders

—Cont'd

Action	Responsible Agent
At conclusion of incident, report total accountability to organizational point of contact. List shall include: • Total personnel • Separate list of injured personnel • Separate list of casualties	Supervisors and/or team leaders
Provide grief counseling services for staff as necessary	Crisis Management Team

Bomb Threat Emergency Response Checklist

Action	Responsibility
If bomb threat is received by phone:	
Remain calm and professional with individual. *Do not hang up*, even if the caller does	Call recipient
Note the date, time, caller's phone number (if caller ID is available), time caller hung up, and phone number where call was received	Call recipient
Notify a coworker to contact law enforcement and district administration	Call recipient
Complete the Bomb Threat Checklist. Write down as much detail as possible and attempt to restate caller's exact words	Call recipient
Immediately upon termination of the call, *do not hang up* and await further instructions	Call recipient
If bomb threat is received by handwritten note:	
Notify senior management (per company instructions or directives)	Note recipient
Handle note as minimally as possible	Note recipient
If bomb threat is received by e-mail:	
Notify senior management (per company instructions or directives)	E-mail recipient
Handle note as minimally as possible	E-mail recipient
Determination to evacuate:	
Senior manager shall determine if evacuation is appropriate based upon receipt of a valid threat and if there is reasonable suspicion that a bomb is present. If so, notify staff via public address system	Crisis Management Team
Notify Law Enforcement via 911 and request bomb squad/detector support if evacuation occurs	Secretary
Prior to leaving, staff should conduct a visual inspection—*do not move anything in their area*—and notify officials of any suspicious items	All staff
Do not use two-way radios or cell phones within 500 feet of the building as radio signals have the potential to detonate a bomb	All staff

Continued

—Cont'd

Action	Responsibility
At conclusion of incident, report total accountability to organizational point of contact. List shall include: • Total personnel • Separate list of injured personnel • Separate list of casualties	Supervisors and/or team leaders

Suspicious Package Emergency Response Checklist

Action	Responsibility
Notify Law Enforcement via 911 • Attempt to provide specific and detailed information regarding the description of item and its exact location	Applicable staff member
Announce evacuation over public address system and include the following: • Turn off all cell phones and do not use • Do not touch or handle any suspicious items • Location for evacuation (if different from standard evacuation area)	Crisis Management Team
Evacuate the building	Crisis Management Team
Preidentified staff members monitor exits during evacuation and lock doors when complete	Building maintenance
Notify executive management (per company instructions)	Applicable staff member
Coordinate with incident commander as requested and ensure evacuation is outside safe distance (normally 500 feet)	Crisis management team leader
Conduct a sweep of building to verify everyone has evacuated (dependent upon time and circumstances)	Designated staff
Determine personnel accountability and report to company designee	Supervisors and/or team leaders
At conclusion of incident, report total accountability to organizational point of contact. List shall include: • Total personnel • Separate list of injured personnel • Separate list of casualties	Supervisors and/or team leaders

Felony Crime Incident Emergency Response Checklist

Action	Responsible Agent
Notify Law Enforcement via 911	Applicable staff member
Notify senior management (per company instructions or directives)	Applicable staff member
Secure a perimeter around the crime scene and *do not allow any* personnel in or out of the area	Crisis Management Team
Secure and lock all alternate entrances and ensure personnel do not leave the facility until released by law enforcement	Crisis Management Team
Determine personnel accountability and report to company designee	Supervisors and/or team leaders
Await arrival of law enforcement to take control of crime scene	Crisis Management Team
When available, report total accountability to organizational point of contact. List shall include: • Total personnel • Separate list of injured personnel • Separate list of casualties	Supervisors and/or team leaders
Provide grief counseling services for staff as necessary	Crisis Management Team

Biological/Chemical Threat Emergency Response Checklist

Action	Responsible Agent
If threat is received through mail:	
Handle note as minimally as possible, leave mail on a desk, and note the possible contamination area (e.g., where the item has been while in the facility)	Applicable staff member
Notify senior management (per company instructions or directives)	Applicable staff member
Initiate building evacuation and await response—avoid contamination area	Crisis management team leader
Notify Law Enforcement and Fire Department via 911	Applicable staff member
Seal affected area and accomplish required maintenance actions to shutdown ventilation systems in order to minimize potentially contaminated areas	Crisis Management Team
Determine personnel accountability and report to company designee	Supervisors and/or team leaders
If threat occurs through spillage or equipment damage:	
Notify senior management (per company instructions or directives)	Applicable staff member

Continued

—Cont'd

Action	Responsible Agent
Initiate building evacuation and await response—avoid contamination area	Crisis management team leader
Notify Law Enforcement and Fire Department via 911	Applicable staff member
Seal affected area and accomplish required maintenance actions to shut down ventilation systems in order to minimize potentially contaminated areas	Crisis management team
Determine personnel accountability and report to company designee	Supervisors and/or team leaders
If exposure has occurred to individuals:	
Contaminated personnel should immediately look for a hose or other water source and wash away all possible contamination	Affected individuals
Initiate decontamination areas and accomplish proper decontamination	Crisis Management Team
Seek medical attention	Affected individuals
Provide grief counseling services for staff as necessary	Crisis Management Team

Bibliography

Kean, J.M., ed., 9/11 Commission Chairman, (July 22, 2004). "The 9/11 Commission Report." Retrieved from web on 4 December 2013, www.9-11commission.gov.

Apgar, C., (2013). "Secure Data Transmission Methods," *Search Security*. Retrieved from web in November 2013, www.searchsecurity.techtarget.com.

A&E Television Networks, (November 27, 2013). "9/11 Attacks," *History Network*. Retrieved from web in November 2013, www.history.com.

Baker, P.R., and Benny, D.J., (2012), *The Complete Guide to Physical Security*. Boca Raton, Florida: CRC.

Broadhead, M., (January 30, 2013). "Top Tips for Safe Travel," *Lonely Planet*. Retrieved from web on 18 September 2014, www.lonelyplanet.com.

Brodsky, N., (May 1, 2012). "How to Handle Employee Sabotage," *Inc*. Retrieved from web on 19 September 2014, www.inc.com.

Brooks, C., (June 19, 2013). "Employee Theft on the Rise and Expected to Get Worse," *Business News Daily*. Retrieved from web on 10 December 2013, www.BusinessNewsDaily.com.

Coleman, K., (August 27, 2008). "The Key to Data Security: Separation of Duties," *Computerworld Magazine*. Retrieved from web in November 2013, www.computerworld.com.

Honorable Erickson, W.H., Chairman, (May 2001). Columbine Review Commission. "The Report of Governor Bill Owens' Columbine Review Commission," *State of Colorado*. Retrieved from web on 22 September 2014, www.state.co.us.

Cornell University Law School. "29 CFR 1910.38 – Emergency Action Plans." Retrieved from web on 24 September 2014, www.law.cornell.edu.

Cullen, D., (May 16, 2000). "Columbine Report Released," *Salon*. Retrieved from web on 23 September 2014, www.salon.com.

DeMichele, M., Ph.D., and Adam Matz, M.S. "Responding to Gang Violence," *APPA Grant at Work for Community Corrections White Paper*. United States Department of Justice. Retrieved from web on 18 September 2014, www.appa-net.org.

Department of Homeland Security Lessons Learned, (2013). "Exercise Controller and Evaluator Handbook," *Department of Homeland Security HSEEP-DD07*. Retrieved from web on 29 January 2014, www.llis.dhs.gov.

Di Salvo, D., (August 2, 2012). "10 Smart Things I've Learned from People Who Never Went to College," *Forbes*. Retrieved from web on 10 September 2014, www.forbes.com.

Emazzanti Technologies. "Selecting a Backup Solution for Your Critical Information." Retrieved from web on 2 September 2014, www.emazzanti.net.

Emergency Management Australia, (1998). "Evacuation Planning," *Emergency Management Australia Manual 11*. Retrieved from web on 28 August 2014, www.em.gov.au.

Federal Emergency Management Agency, (2012). "Business Continuity Plan," *Department of Homeland Security*. Retrieved from web in November 2013, www.ready.gov.

Federal Emergency Management Agency. "FEMA Exercise Training Manual," *Department of Homeland Security*. Retrieved from web on 30 August 2014, www.training.fema.gov.

Federal Emergency Management Agency, (August 2004). "Food and Water in an Emergency," *Department of Homeland Security*. Retrieved from web on 5 September 2014, www.fema.gov.

Federal Emergency Management Agency. "National Incident Management System," *Department of Homeland Security*. Retrieved from web on 24 September 2014, www.fema.gov.

Federal Emergency Management Agency. "NIMS Compliance Requirements for Local Emergency Planning Committees," *FEMA Fact Sheet.* Retrieved from web on 24 September 2014, www.fema.gov.

Federal Emergency Management Agency, (2007). "Site and Urban Design for Security," *Department of Homeland Security.* Retrieved from web in November 2013, www.fema.gov.

Federal Emergency Management Agency. "Unit 4 – Damage Assessment," *State Disaster Management Course – IS 208.a.* Retrieved from web on 6 September 2014, www.training.fema.gov.

Federal Bureau of Investigation. "Terror Hits Home: The Oklahoma City Bombing," *Famous Cases & Criminals.* Retrieved from web on 23 September 2014, www.fbi.gov.

"Fundamental Security Concepts," (2013). *Cryptome.* Retrieved from web in November 2013, www.cryptome.org.

Gardner, R.A., (April 1981). "Crime Prevention through Environmental Design," *Crimewise.* Retrieved from web on 19 January 2014, www.crimewise.com.

Gates, M., (September 3, 2013). "Pre-employment Screening and Social Media," *Security Management Magazine.* Retrieved from web in November 2013, www.securitymanagement.com.

Gelbstein, Ph.D.,ed., (2011). "Data Integrity—Information Security's Poor Relation," *ISACA Journal, Volume 6.* Retrieved from web in November 2013, www.isaca.org.

Graduate School Online Reference Document, (2013). Security Terms and Definitions. Retrieved from web in November 2013, www.graduateschool.edu.

Government of Vermont. "Development of a Master Scenario Event List (MSEL)." Presentation. Retrieved from the web on 19 September 2014, hsu.vermont.gov.

Harrison, J., Ph.D., and Andress, E., PhD. "Preparing an Emergency Food Supply, Long Term Food Storage," *The University of Georgia, College of Agricultural and Environmental Sciences &Family and Consumer Services.* Retrieved from web on 5 September 2014, www.caes.uga.edu.

Harvard Information Security & Privacy, (2013). "Protecting Confidential Information on Networks," *Harvard University.* Retrieved from web in November 2013, www.security.harvard.edu.

History Channel Website. "Hurricane Katrina," *History.* Retrieved from web on 24 September 2014, www.history.com.

History Channel Website. "Oklahoma City Bombing," *History.* Retrieved from web on 24 September 2014, www.history.com.

Hoelzer, D., (April 26, 2010). "Teach Your Boss to Speak Security: Separation of Duties," *Forbes Magazine.* Retrieved from web on 10 December 2013, www.forbes.com.

International Organization for Standardization and International Electrotechnical Commission, (2005). "Information Technology – Security Techniques – Code of Practice for Information Security Management," *International Standard ISO/IEC 17799:2005(E), ISO and IEC.* Retrieved from web in November 2013, www.iso.org.

Information Systems Audit and Control Association, (2013). "Control Objectives for Information and Related Technology DS 11 – Manage Information," *ISACA.* Retrieved from web in November 2013, www.isaca.org.

Internal Revenue Service. "Disaster Relief: Providing Assistance through Charitable Organizations." Retrieved from web on 9 September 2014, www.irs.gov.

Kohn, D. "What Really Happened at Columbine: Did So Many Have to Die?" *60 Minutes.* Retrieved from the web on 23 September 2014, www.cbsnews.com.

Knabb, R., Ph.D. "Take Action," *The Weather Channel.* Retrieved from the web on 14 September 2014, www.weather.com.

Larson, R., Metzger, M., and Cahn, M. "Emergency Response for Homeland Security: Lessons Learned and the Need for Analysis." Create Report. Center for Risk and Economic Analysis of Terrorism Events, University of Southern California. Retrieved from web on 23 September 2014, create.usc.edu.

Manufacturing Technology Committee – Risk Management Working Group. "Hazard & Operability Analysis (HAZOP)," *Product Quality Research Institute*. Retrieved from web on 17 February 2014, www.oshrisk.org.

Management Study Guide. "Crisis Management Team." Retrieved from web on 10 September 2014, www.managementstudyguide.com.

Marshall, J., PhD., (2011). "An Introduction to Fault Tree Analysis (FTA),"*University of Warwick*. Presentation. Retrieved from the web on 17 February 2014, www2.warwick.ac.uk.

McConnell, K.D. "How to Develop Good Security Policies and Tips on Assessment and Enforcement," *SANS Institute*. Retrieved from web on 18 February 2014, www.giac.org.

Miller, R. "Hurricane Katrina: Communications & Infrastructure Impacts," *National Defense University*. Retrieved from web on 12 September 2014, www.carlisle.army.mil.

Missouri Department of Public Safety State Emergency Management Agency. "Hazardous Materials Incident." Retrieved from web on 16 September 2014, sema.dps.mo.gov.

Muuss, J.P., and Rabern, D., (2006), *The Complete Guide for CPP Examination Preparation*. CRC Press.

National Institute for Chemical Studies, (November 1999). "Shelter in Place at Your Office: A General Guide for Preparing a Shelter in Place Plan in the Workplace." Retrieved from web on 4 September 2014, www.nicsinfo.org.

National Travel Association, (April 2013). "Crisis Management Plan Structure." Retrieved from web on 12 September 2014, www.ntaonline.com.

Naval Civil Engineering Laboratory, (1993). "Design Guidelines for Security Fencing, Gates, Barriers, and Guard Facilities," *Military Handbook 1013/10*. Retrieved from web in October 2013, www.concentricu.com.

Newman, G.R., (2002). "Bomb Threats in Schools," *United States Department of Justice Community Oriented Policing Services Policy #32*. Retrieved from web in November 2013, www.cops.usdoj.gov.

Nucleus Research, (March 2004). "Indirect Benefits: The Invisible Return on Investment Drivers," *Nucleus Research*. Retrieved from web on 17 January 2014, www.NucleusResearch.com.

Occupational Safety and Health Administration Office of Communications. "OSHA Evacuation Plans and Procedures," *OSHA*. Retrieved from web on 3 September 2014, www.osha.gov.

Occupational Safety and Health Administration Office of Communications. "OSHA Employer Responsibilities," *OSHA*. Retrieved from web on 20 January 2014, www.osha.gov.

Occupational Safety and Health Administration Office of Communications. "Regulations (Standards – 29 CFR)," *OSHA*. Retrieved from web on 24 September 2014, www.osha.gov.

Office of the Deputy Under Secretary of Defense for Installations and Environment, (2005). "Unified Facilities Criteria (UFC), Security Engineering: Entry Control Facilities/Access Control Points," *Department of Defense*.

Oklahoma Department of Civil Emergency Management. "After Action Report: Alfred P. Murrah Federal Building Bombing." Retrieved from web on 23 September 2014, www.ok.gov.

Product Quality Research Institute. "Hazard & Operability Analysis (HAZOP)," *Manufacturing Technology Committee – Risk Management Working Group*. Retrieved from web on 17 February 2014, www.oshrisk.org.

Public Safety Canada. "A Guide to Business Continuity Planning." Government of Canada. Retrieved from web on 21 September 2014, www.publicsafety.gc.ca.

Purdue University Campus Emergency Preparedness and Planning Office, (July 14, 2010). "Exercise Plan: Full Scale Active Shooter Exercise." Purdue University. Retrieved from web on 20 September 2014, rems.ed.gov.

Rosenberg, J. "Columbine Massacre," *20thCentury History*. Retrieved from web on 22 September 2014, history1900s.about.com.

SafetyInfo, (2013). "Emergency Management Planning Guide: Emergency Management Program Considerations." Safety Information. Retrieved from web in November 2013, http://www.safetyinfo.com.

Smith, J. "Business Continuity Planning (BCP) & Disaster Recovery Planning (DRP)," *Purdue University Presentation, Information Technology at Purdue*. Retrieved from web on 10 September 2014, www.purdue.edu.

The National Academies. "What You Need to Know about Infectious Disease: Food Borne Pathogens." Retrieved from web on 16 September 2014, needtoknow.nas.edu.

Tipton, H.F., and Krause, M., (2003). "Information Security Management Handbook," (fifth ed.) Boca Raton, FL: Auerbach.

Townsend, F.F. "The Federal Response to Hurricane Katrina: Lessons Learned." Assistant to the President for Homeland Security and Counterterrorism. Retrieved from web on 24 September 2014, library.stmarytx.edu.

United Kingdom Environment Agency. "Flooding – Minimising the Risk: Flood Plan Guidance for Communities and Groups." Retrieved from web on 14 September 2014, www.gov.uk.

United Kingdom Health Protection Agency, (2012). "United Kingdom Recovery Handbook for Chemical Incidents." Retrieved from web on 8 September 2014, www.gov.uk.

United States Department of Homeland Security, *Ready.gov website*. Retrieved from web on 2 September 2014, www.ready.gov.

United States Department of Justice. "Section G: Oklahoma City Bombing." Retrieved from web on 24 September 2014, www.justice.gov.

United States Department of Labor. "Fact Sheet on Natural Disaster Recovery: Cleanup Hazard," *Occupational Safety & Health Administration*. Retrieved from web on 8 September 2014, www.osha.gov.

United States Department of Labor. "Tornado Preparedness and Response," *Occupational Safety & Health Administration*. Retrieved from web on 14 September 2014, www.osha.gov.

United States Department of Labor. "Workplace Violence Fact Sheet," *Occupational Safety & Health Administration*. Retrieved from web on 16 September 2014, www.osha.gov.

United States Small Business Administration. "Disaster Assistance," *Emergency Preparedness*. Retrieved from web on 9 September 2014, www.sba.gov.

University of Missouri – Kansas City School of Law. "The Oklahoma Bombing Conspirators." Retrieved from web on 24 September 2014, law2.umkc.edu.

Ventisys Technology, (2010). "The Three Information Security Pillars." Ventisystems Technology. Retrieved from web in November 2013, www.theventiblog.com.

WebMD. "What Are Epidemics, Pandemics, and Outbreaks." Retrieved from web on 16 September 2014, www.webmd.com.

Wilkinson, B., (April 9, 2014). "Bookkeeper Pleads Guilty to Embezzlement," *Sierra Star*. Retrieved from web on 22 September 2014, www.sierrastar.com.

Index

Printed in the United States
By Bookmasters